KIERKEGAARD AND KANT

D1595367

SUNY Series in Philosophy
George R. Lucas, Jr., editor

KIERKEGAARD AND KANT

The Hidden Debt

RONALD M. GREEN

State University
of New York
Press

Published by
State University of New York Press, Albany

Printed in the United States of America

For information, address State University of New York
Press, State University Plaza, Albany, NY 12246

Library of Congress Cataloging-in-Publication Data

Green, Ronald Michael.
    Kierkegaard and Kant : the hidden debt / Ronald M. Green.
        p.   cm.
    Includes index.
    ISBN 0-7914-1107-9 (alk. paper) : $49.50. — ISBN 0-7914-1108-7
(pbk. : alk paper) : $16.95
        1. Kierkegaard, Søren, 1813–1855. 2. Kant, Immanuel, 1724–1804.
    I. Title.
    B4377.G715   1992
    198'.9—dc20
                                                            91–30775
                                                            CIP

10 9 8 7 6 5 4 3 2

For three good friends

Andrew G. Bromberg
Sandra W. Curtis
Gordon D. Marino

CONTENTS

ACKNOWLEDGMENTS

It is customary for an author, when mentioning those who have provided help in the preparation of a book, to add the caution that none of these people are responsible for the positions the author defends. This caution is particularly appropriate for a book like this, which challenges many conventional views of Kierkegaard's intellectual formation.

I owe a debt of thanks to Ms. Julia Watkin of the Kierkegaard Library at the University of Copenhagen. Her assistance made my time in Copenhagen productive and pleasant. At different stages in the preparation of the manuscript, Bruce H. Kirmmse, Mark C. Taylor, Stephen N. Dunning and my own colleague at Dartmouth, Fred Berthold, provided very helpful critical readings. During some despairing moments, Richard Crouter helped buoy my morale about the importance of this study.

Seemingly undaunted by a plethora of foreign languages, Susan Forn did a wonderful job copyediting the manuscript. A Senior Faculty Grant from Dartmouth College funded the time abroad needed to start this work. My daughter, Julie, helped greatly by preparing the index.

A very special word of thanks is due Gordon Marino. Our evening conversations in Copenhagen are among the special memories of writing this book. Out of the wealth of his knowledge of Kierkegaard, Gordon also provided some of the clues that stimulated my research.

Portions of Chapters 4 and 5 initially appeared as "The Leap of Faith: Kierkegaard's Debt to Kant," in *Philosophy and Theology* (1989), and "Deciphering *Fear and Trembling*'s Secret Message," *Religious Studies* (1986).

Above all, I want to thank my wife, Mary Jean, for her encouragement and support. When I first started work on this book we were living in Blois, France, where Mary Jean was responsible for a Dartmouth language study program. During this period, Mary Jean had to put up with my frequent research trips to Denmark. On my return, I would often ignore the beautiful Loire region and for days bury myself in the notes on my laptop computer. Fortunately, Mary Jean proved far more supportive than the wife of Nicolaus Notabene, the pseudonymous author of Kierkegaard's *Prefaces,* who, knowing how distracted an author can be, forbade her husband ever to write an entire book.

INTRODUCTION

Despite its scholarly apparatus, this book is really a detective story. It had its beginning several years ago when I received a letter from Robert Perkins, editor of the *International Kierkegaard Commentary* series, asking me to contribute an article to a planned volume on Kierkegaard's *The Concept of Anxiety*. Perkins was familiar with my previous work on Kant's philosophy of religion and was interested in having someone with my background examine Kierkegaard's discussions of ethics and religion in *The Concept of Anxiety*.

Curiosity moved me to accept the invitation. Although I had read most of Kierkegaard's pseudonymous works as an undergraduate, my interests since then had taken me into ethical theory and I had not carefully reread Kierkegaard in years. Furthermore, I had long accepted the common view that Kierkegaard was opposed to German rationalist philosophers, particularly Hegel but also, by implication, Kant. This view seemed to be supported by my cursory reading of *Fear and Trembling*, which I took to be a criticism of Kant's conception of autonomy in ethics. Perkins's invitation, therefore, was an opportunity for me to see whether Kierkegaard's treatment of ethics in *The Concept of Anxiety* fit in with this familiar view that Kierkegaard was hostile to Kant's thought.

To my astonishment, as I carefully examined Kierkegaard's discussion of ethics and sin in the opening pages of *The Concept of Anxiety*, I had an experience of déjà vu. Before me were a series of remarkable parallels between Kierkegaard's discussion and Kant's treatment of ethics and sin in the first book of his most important work on the philosophy of religion, *Religion within the Limits of Reason Alone*. Not only was Kierkegaard's discussion organized like Kant's, but at many points it almost seemed as though, without acknowledgement, Kierkegaard had lifted words, phrases, or ideas from Kant. I subsequently mentioned this in my article for the *Commentary* volume.[1] Although I was unable then to document whether Kierkegaard had worked closely with the *Religion*, I noted that our understanding of some of the more interesting and opaque statements in the opening sections of *The Concept of Anxiety* was enhanced by examining them in relation to Kant's position in the *Religion*.

My work on this *Commentary* article left me with many questions, none of which the available secondary literature on Kierkegaard readily answered. To what extent, I wondered, was Kierkegaard familiar with Kant's writings? Had he read the *Religion*, *The Conflict of the Faculties*, or any of the other works in which Kant presents his developed philosophy of religion? If so, what was his attitude toward Kant? Did he appreciate Kant's efforts to move from ethics to a facsimile of biblical religion, or did he fundamentally reject Kant's enterprise? Several months later, my interest in these questions was further stimulated while preparing a graduate seminar on divine command ethics I was to offer as a visitor at Stanford University, when I had occasion to reread *Fear and Trembling* with great care. Again, to my surprise, I found not just the familiar aspects of that book that could be interpreted as opposed to Kant's or Hegel's ethics, but also many important points in the text where Kierkegaard seemed actively to be wrestling with some of Kant's most penetrating insights in the *Religion* and *The Conflict of the Faculties*.

By this time, the question of the degree of Kierkegaard's familiarity with Kant had come to absorb me, and the "detective story" that lies behind this book began in earnest. I asked myself, was I being excessive, seeing Kant's influence everywhere, even in the writings of an outspoken critic of "speculative rationalism"? Or was some deep but unacknowledged debt really to be found here? Many parallels I saw had to do with ideas at the heart of Kant's philosophy of religion. Only someone who had taken pains to comprehend the most difficult reaches of Kant's thought could appreciate these ideas. Yet there were few citations to Kant in Kierkegaard's published writings. Was there any reason to think that Kierkegaard had put this much effort into the study of Kant's work? If so, why did he fail to acknowledge his debt?

For a further period, teaching and administrative duties prevented me from actively pursuing answers to these questions, and the information I gathered from the research I could do hardly satisfied my curiosity. The standard biographies of Kierkegaard said little or nothing about Kierkegaard's relationship to Kant. Lowrie's voluminous biography is an example.[2] Its 636 pages and index contain not one reference to Kant. Otherwise excellent secondary studies of Kierkegaard's thought, such as those by Reidar Thomte, James Collins, Hermann Diem, Gregor Malantschuk, Niels Thulstrup, Stephen Crites, John Elrod, or Mark C. Taylor, provided only a little more help.[3] For these writers, "the philosopher" in Kierkegaard's life is usually Hegel, and if they mention Kant it is usually only to indicate Kierkegaard's rejection of Kantian "ethics" in *Fear and Trembling*. Some commentators, such as George Stack, in his study *Kierkegaard's Existential Ethics*,[4] note that *ethics* for Kierkegaard virtually meant Kantian ethics, and in this respect they acknowledge an important link between the two thinkers. But this is usually taken to be the limit of Kierkegaard's involvement with Kantian thought. Kant's philosophy of religion is barely mentioned, and even on the ethical plane, Kierkegaard is viewed as ultimately rejecting the kind of ethical rationalism and autonomy Kant defended. Thulstrup, perhaps the most informed student of Kierkegaard's intellectual formation, sums up the state of scholarly opinion on this matter when he observes, in a review of Kierkegaard's knowledge of the philosophical and theological tradition, that despite some parallels between the two thinkers, "Kierkegaard showed no overwhelming interest in Kant."[5]

While pursuing these preliminary inquiries, two sources of information at first struck me as promising, but they, too, soon proved to be of little help. The first was a series of studies over the past twenty years seeking to reevaluate the relationship between Kant and Kierkegaard and asking whether we can properly conclude that Kierkegaard's opposition to Hegel extended to Kant. Articles by Jerry Gill, John Glenn, Robert Perkins, R. Z. Friedman, and Peter J. Mehl fit into this category, as do monographs or doctoral dissertations by Jeremy Walker, Alastair Hannay, William Peck, and C. Stephen Evans.[6] Also worth noting is the effort by German-speaking theologians and philosophers over half a century ago to assimilate the publication in German of Kierkegaard's deeply Kantian *Purity of Heart* to their previous—and largely negative—understanding of the relationship between Kierkegaard and Kant.[7] Each of these writers sketches some broad parallels between Kant and Kierkegaard on ethical or religious matters, and each in various ways presents Kierkegaard's thought as a movement "back to Kant" in reaction to Hegelian speculation. Although these studies confirmed my hunch regarding Kierkegaard's debt to Kant, none helped answer my questions concerning how familiar Kierkegaard was with Kant's writings. All confine themselves to identifying one or another broad conceptual parallel, none seeks to trace the exact extent of Kierkegaard's debt to Kant, and none tries to determine whether Kierkegaard actually studied Kant closely. Peck typifies these writers' approach when, at the beginning of his dissertation, he confesses "I do not know whether Kierkegaard ever read Kant closely, or indeed whether he ever read him at all."[8]

Only a little more helpful were the seventeen explicit references to Kant found in the works published by Kierkegaard during his lifetime or the thirty-one entries mentioning Kant (excluding references in reading or lecture notes) found in Kierkegaard's posthumously published *Papers*.[9] Together, these strongly suggest that Kierkegaard was familiar with Kant's conception of 'radical evil', a doctrine presented only in the *Religion*. They also betray a student's knowledge of the main lines of Kant's epistemology. Noteworthy, as well, is the tone of these references and entries. Whereas most of Kierkegaard's references to Hegel and the Hegelians are bitingly sarcastic and hostile, mentions of Kant, even where they seem critical of an aspect of his thought, show respect and admiration. He is invariably "honest" (*ærlige*) Kant, the thinker who strove to remain within his self-identified bounds of knowledge and who avoided the wild speculative excesses of many of his later Idealist followers. There are also several explicit appreciations of Kant's wit and sense of humor.

We'll eventually see that these isolated references furnish important clues to Kierkegaard's general relationship to Kant. By themselves, however, they told me little about the extent or depth of Kierkegaard's knowledge of Kant. Had I stopped here, I might have concluded my inquiry with something like the observation made by Howard and Edna Hong, the editors of the English translation of the *Journals and Papers*, who, in a long preliminary footnote to the series of topical entries on Kant, focus on

Kierkegaard's essential disagreements with Kant.[10] Thus, after mentioning Kierkegaard's appreciation of Kant's "sobriety," the Hongs emphasize a point that dominates the *Journal* entries: Kierkegaard's discomfort with Kant's unwillingness to move beyond his transcendental skepticism to affirm a possible knowledge of ultimate reality (*das Ding an sich*). In these brief remarks the Hongs confirm, with some precision, the standard assessment of Kierkegaard's relation to Kant. For Kierkegaard, Kant remains a thinker unwilling to step beyond the sphere of human reason and experience into the domain of religious faith. Characteristically neglected in these comments are those broad aspects of Kant's thinking that Kierkegaard clearly takes over but that he never specifically credits to Kant in the published or posthumous writings.

Although these preliminary investigations did not answer my questions in any way, they suggested to me that a deeper mystery was to be found here than I had initially suspected. By now I had accumulated considerable circumstantial and some direct evidence that Kierkegaard was familiar with key features of Kant's epistemology and philosophy of religion. Yet I also noted that Kant is rarely, if ever, mentioned by Kierkegaard in connection with these important topics, just as he is seldom cited whenever Kierkegaard makes positive use of any aspect of his thought. This suggested to me an effort on Kierkegaard's part, whether deliberate or unconscious, to obscure the degree of his indebtedness to the German thinker.

This possibility, combined with some further items of information gleaned from my preliminary inquiries, now suggested the direction for future research. Various accounts of Kierkegaard's studies and reading, including the Auctioneer's Sales Record (*Auktionsprotokol*) of the books in his library at the time of his death, furnish an idea of writings by Kant that Kierkegaard might have studied.[11] Since Kierkegaard's debt to Kant might be largely unacknowledged, I was now obliged to reread the entire corpus of Kierkegaard's work side by side with those Kantian texts he could be presumed to have read. Beyond the *Religion* and the two major Kant texts Kierkegaard certainly owned (the *Critique of Pure Reason* and the *Critique of Judgment*), a principal focus of this research would be on the many

shorter treatises and essays on ethics and religion gathered in a
three-volume edition of Kant's *vermischte Schriften*, edited by
Johann Heinrich Tieftrunk and published in 1799 in Halle, Ger-
many.[12] Apart from a few important additional facts concerning
Kierkegaard's study of Kant gleaned from further research, this
comparative reading of both thinkers' writings was the principal
means available to me of answering my questions concerning the
extent of Kierkegaard's knowledge of Kant.

The chapters in this book are my answers to the question of
Kierkegaard's relationship to Kant, the results of the "detective
work" on which I had inadvertently embarked. Based largely on a
close comparative reading of the corpus of both thinkers' writings, but supplemented whenever possible by whatever remains in
the historical record, they furnish a remarkable picture of major,
and largely unacknowledged, intellectual borrowing. Overall, I
believe I can support the claim that Kierkegaard is indebted to
Kant for not only some of the most important elements of his
intellectual and religious position but also for many smaller ideas,
terms, and illustrations that are familiar to Kierkegaard's readers.
It would not be correct to say that Kierkegaard plagiarizes Kant
(although several important but unacknowledged textual borrowings reveal substantial terminological parallelism). Kierkegaard
brings to the Kantian position his own unique contribution as a
religious and literary figure, and on some central matters he either
disagrees with or "goes beyond" Kant. But even when he does so,
Kierkegaard is in dialogue with Kant and is deeply influenced by
Kant's posing of the issues. In summary, this research suggests
that Kierkegaard is not only one of Kant's best nineteenth century
readers but also the genuine heir to the legacy of Kant's developed
religious and ethical thought.

The chapters ahead seek to substantiate these claims. The
first chapter examines the historical record itself. Here I explore
the grounds we have for believing that Kierkegaard was familiar
with Kantian philosophy, and I give particular attention to identifying with some precision the works by Kant we might suppose
him to have read carefully.

Chapter 2 is a necessary prelude to the detailed comparison
of positions I begin in Chapters 3 and 4. A primer of sorts, it
presents a rapid survey of Kant's work on epistemology, ethics,

and philosophy of religion. A reader familiar with Kant's thought might be tempted to skip this chapter, although the few original contributions I make there to our understanding of Kant's positions, contributions that have some value in clarifying Kierkegaard's debt to Kant, recommend at least a skimming of this discussion by even the knowledgeable reader.

In Chapter 3 I get down to business. Here, under the heading "Points of Contact," I gather together and topically arrange matters on which Kant's and Kierkegaard's writings display substantial parallels. Since on many of these matters Kierkegaard also displays differences with Kant or a tendency to be shaped by other thinkers, I claim here not so much an exclusive debt to Kant as an active involvement with Kant as a major figure in Kierkegaard's intellectual environment. In contrast, the fourth chapter, "Deep Engagements," focuses on themes or issues for which Kierkegaard's contribution, even when he disagrees with Kant's conclusions, is hard to imagine apart from his reliance on Kant's thinking. Principal among these debts is Kierkegaard's understanding of the ideality of ethics, the inescapability of sin, and the need for ethics to complete its fractured project by a volitional "leap" of faith. In many ways, this chapter is the core of this book: a record of the extraordinary encounter of one great mind with another.

The effort in these chapters to document and develop the extent of Kierkegaard's borrowing from Kant has more than historical importance. Since so much of Kierkegaard's thinking is based on a foundation laid by Kant, an understanding of these lines of relationship greatly assists our understanding of Kierkegaard himself. The fifth chapter illustrates this by showing how altered our understanding of Kierkegaard's important work, *Fear and Trembling*, is when we read it against a background of Kierkegaard's involvement with Kant's philosophy of religion. Although this book has usually been read simply as a repudiation of Kant's ethics, the understanding that it is in dialogue, point by point, with Kant's *Religion within the Limits of Reason Alone* and *The Conflict of the Faculties* shows it to be basically unconcerned with normative ethical issues and instead oriented toward critiquing and extending Kant's own suggestive forays into the logic of sin, repentance, and grace. Directly provoked by

Kant, I argue, Kierkegaard uses the figure of Abraham to establish his position concerning the role of historical faith in human moral salvation.

Finally, in view of the substantial evidence that Kierkegaard drew deeply on Kant's writings, it becomes important to ask why the record of this indebtedness is so obscure. In the conclusion I advance the view that Kierkegaard deliberately went out of his way to erase the lines connecting him to Kant. *The debt to Kant is hidden*, I argue, *because Kierkegaard wanted it to be*. I review the evidence for this claim and I also engage in some speculation about the motives that might have prompted Kierkegaard to undertake this process of concealment.

In some ways my effort in this book is the kind of work that Kierkegaard condemned. A study of the sort undertaken by those particular objects of his scorn, "assistant professors," it represents an objective, dispassionate scholarly analysis instead of the "single reader's" personal engagement with his thought as an occasion for existential decision.[13] Be this as it may, and apart from the fact that I am no longer an "assistant professor," I believe Kierkegaard would appreciate this study. His writings display a love of irony, of mystery and riddle, of messages concealing messages, "like the boxes in a Chinese puzzle."[14] If I am right, Kierkegaard's debt to Kant is one of these hidden messages, indeed, one of the more important in Kierkegaard's authorship. In the end, I believe, Kierkegaard would have accepted with grace and some amusement the unraveling of a mystery he took such pains to create.

CHAPTER 1

Lines of Influence

What matters is to find a purpose, to see what it really is that God
wills that I shall do; the crucial thing is to find a truth which is a
truth for me, to find the idea for which I am willing to live and die.
—Kierkegaard, *Papers*, 1835.[1]

How much did Kierkegaard know about Kant? Did he ever formally study Kant while in secondary school or at the university?
Did he read Kant on his own? If so, which works interested him,
and which aspects of Kant's thought most captured his attention? Surprisingly, there is little direct or certain information at
hand to answer these questions. Neither Kierkegaard nor any
biographer ever discussed his familiarity with Kant. As a result,
if we are to obtain a picture of Kierkegaard's education in Kantian philosophy, we must fashion it out of many indirect but
intersecting hints and suggestions. Sixty years ago, D. Torsten
Bohlin, in his excellent study of Kierkegaard's thought, observed
that the task of clarifying Kierkegaard's relationship to Kant had
not yet been undertaken.[2] What follows, somewhat delayed, is
the beginning of that task.

Evidence about Kierkegaard's knowledge of Kant falls into
three distinct categories, ranging from the least to the most
authoritative. In the first category fall the assumptions it is reasonable to make about the intellectual formation of a young man
born scarcely a decade after Kant's death. In a second category we
may place the information available in the historical record concerning Kierkegaard's university career, including the formal lectures he attended and the examinations for which he prepared.
Finally, there is the evidence of his reading. This must be constructed out of a variety of sources: the record of books in his possession, direct quotations or explicit allusions in his writings, and
the many less explicit indications that he was familiar with one or
another of Kant's works. Since the category of reading is the most

important for our understanding of Kierkegaard's knowledge of Kant, it will occupy most of our attention in this chapter.

BROAD CULTURAL INFLUENCES

Unfortunately, there is little we can say for sure, although much we might suppose, about the impact of Kant and Kantianism on Kierkegaard's intellectual formation and upbringing. Kant had died only nine years before Kierkegaard's birth in 1813. His two landmark works in epistemology and ethics, the *Critique of Pure Reason* and the *Foundations of the Metaphysics of Morals*, were published only three decades before. According to Anders Thuborg, the decade 1790–1800 marked the distinctly Kantian period in Danish philosophy, with several Danish Kantians, among them A. S Ørsted, Christian Hornemann, and Johan Erik Berger dominating the university scene. Although, as Thuborg observes, this enthusiasm for Kant soon waned under the impact of an emergent romanticism that made many Danish thinkers uncomfortable with the austere bounds of knowledge set by Kant,[3] the formative first decades of Kierkegaard's life were precisely the years during which the thought of a revolutionary thinker like Kant would have begun to percolate through popular culture via the educational system and the press.

Was Kierkegaard exposed to Kantianism in his home environment? We know that Kierkegaard's father, Michael Pedersen Kierkegaard, played a major role in young Søren's upbringing. The elder Kierkegaard, who had retired from commerce in 1797 partly to busy himself with intellectual pursuits, was a devotee of Wolffian rationalism, the position taken by Kant before his critical period. The elder Kierkegaard, who also shared with Kant a background in pietism,[4] might well have been interested in Kant's intellectual peregrinations and communicated some idea of Kantian philosophy to his son.

Kant's efforts to provide a rational foundation for ethics could not have escaped the attention of any literate individual during the 1820s and 1830s. The *Foundations of the Metaphysics of Morals* was to become a standard part of gymnasia curricula throughout Europe during the nineteenth century, and there is reason to think that Kierkegaard was exposed to it before beginning his university career. There also may be several hints to this effect in his later writings. In *Either/Or*, for example, Judge William, who represents the "ethical" stage of existence in its purest form and boasts in passing of his familiarity with the "Aristotelian and the Kantian views of the ethical,"[5] offers a colorful account of his youthful education in ethics. He speaks of the ethical seriousness imparted to him by his father. "I did not have many duties," he observes, and was thus spared being "overwhelmed by a whole ritual of duties" that spoil life for most children and deprive them of the chance for ethical maturity and independence. As a result, "I received a very profound impression that there was something called duty and that this had eternal validity."[6] As this account proceeds, it resonates with Kantian ideas and terms. The young William develops an ethical rigorism marked by "unconditional respect" and "reverence" for the moral rule and disdain for the moral exception; in his ethical consciousness, he becomes aware of his "eternal nature" and finds "the true demonstration of the immortality of the soul"; he sees duty as an "eternal task" and is prepared to discourse on the multifariousness of duty in both its negative and positive forms. He believes each individual has his "teleology within himself"[7] and also must be his own moral teacher.[8]

Judge William, of course, is a literary creation, and it is possible that this account of his moral education represents nothing more than Kierkegaard's version of "the Kantian ethicist as a young man" or, even more generally, a depiction of the upbringing of any young person in the ethically rigorous environment of Lutheran piety in that period.[9] However, when we note the important biographical parallels in this account, especially the warm and respectful portrait of the father, and when we consider the proliferation of technical terms reminiscent of Kant's ethics, it is easy to believe that Kierkegaard is here offering us a picture of his home education in Kantian ethics.

Another possible link to Kant in this home environment was Kierkegaard's father's lifelong friendship with Jakob Peter Mynster. During Kierkegaard's youth, Mynster was curate of the prestigious Church of Our Lady, which the Kierkegaard family attended (in alternation with its continued attendance at the pietist Herrnhutter congregation). From 1834 until his death in 1854, Mynster also served as primate of the state church of Denmark. Later in his life, Mynster became known as a foe of both Grundtvigian sectarian enthusiasm and cultured "rationalism" in religion, but, as Bruce H. Kirmmse shows, Mynster's religious position was always grounded in an Enlightenment-oriented moral deism.[10] Following his university examinations in 1794, Mynster spent eight years as a private tutor for a wealthy family, and during this period he immersed himself in Kantian philosophy.[11] The impact of Kant on the writings and sermons that established Mynster's enduring theological outlook is apparent. "Deep within us," he writes, "our conscience unites its holy voice with...God's word to give witness that he is righteous." Conscience is "the stamp of our higher destiny" and must be obeyed "without exception."[12] Neither consequences nor rewards must govern our moral life, but only a purity of moral intention. "I will do my duty as fully as I am capable, willingly and without concern leaving everything else to him, who alone is able to rule. Whoever says this seriously has thereby become a new man."[13] The Enlightenment-oriented (and possibly Kantian) shape of Mynster's formative theology is also shown in the relative absence in his sermons of themes of sin, grace, and redemption and his stress on Christ's role as teacher and reminder of truths "grasped by every human understanding and felt by every human heart."[14] Although later in his life Mynster was to earn a reputation as a critic of "rationalism" because of his public differences with writers like H. N. Clausen or the Hegelian J. L. Heiberg, Mynster's lifelong position remained a personally appropriated ethical religiousness similar to the "religiousness A" of Judge William in *Either/Or*. We know that, besides his role as their pastor, Mynster was a frequent visitor to the Kierkegaard household and that Kierkegaard retained a personal relationship with Mynster until Kierkegaard began his "attack on Christendom" in the late 1840s. In view of this, it is reasonable to suppose that, directly or via Michael Pederson Kierkegaard, Mynster was responsible for some of the Kantianism Kierkegaard may have picked up in his home environment.

The impact of this early upbringing shows itself in a letter to his brother written in 1835. There Kierkegaard states, "The life by virtue of reason [*Fornuft*] and freedom has always interested me most, and it has always been my desire to clarify and solve the riddle of life."[15] Reason and freedom were by no means the exclusive property of Kant. To some extent they remained the cultural ideals of post-Enlightenment youth everywhere. Nevertheless, it seems to me unlikely that a bright and largely self-educated young man, who traced the passion for these ideas to his earliest years, would have failed to read Kant, the foremost philosopher of reason and freedom.[16]

UNIVERSITY YEARS

The long period comprising Kierkegaard's university training and the beginning of his *Journals* offers the first solid evidence of his familiarity with Kantian thought. Kierkegaard had prolonged his undergraduate career at the University of Copenhagen for almost ten years (from 1830 to 1840). Somewhat far along in this period, during the winter semester of 1837–1838, he seems to have attended a series of "Introductory Lectures on Speculative Dogmatics" offered by H. L. Martensen.[17] Much later, in the 1850s, during the last phase of his life, when he embarked on the "Attack on Christendom," Kierkegaard came into sharp personal opposition to Martensen, and even earlier he had come to view Martensen as a symbol of the intellectual disaster represented by Hegelian philosophy. But the Martensen of 1837–1838 still appears to be a respected teacher, and the careful notes taken by Kierkegaard and entered into his *Journal* form a thorough overview of modern German philosophy, especially Kant's thought, viewed from a somewhat Hegelian perspective. (In the first semester of the following year Kierkegaard also may have attended a series of lectures by Martensen entitled "The History of Philosophy from Kant to Hegel." The *Papers* include a notebook for these lectures, the manuscript for which is not in Kierkegaard's handwriting.[18])

These notes on Kant, extending over thirteen of the nineteen pages in the first series of lectures and over eleven of the fifty-one pages in the second, contain nothing surprising: they are virtually a synopsis of Kant's positions on epistemology, ethics, and the philosophy of religion. They present Kant as a major continuer of the tradition of critical doubt begun by Descartes and as a representative of Protestant subjectivism. Nor do the notes themselves tell us anything very certain about Kierkegaard's own knowledge of Kant. Although it is unlikely that he would have attended these lectures without also having done a good deal of the reading the lectures presumed, Kierkegaard would not be the first student in history to rely on good lecture notes rather than doing the "course" reading. What we can conclude from this collection is that Kierkegaard was well versed in the main outlines of Kantian philosophy. This was one of the very few collections of lecture notes he either made or preserved.[19] Its presence, and the fact that he seems to have drawn on it in later work—the organization for his never published book *De omnibus dubitandum est*, for example, almost follows the syllabus of Martensen's lectures[20]—testify, if nothing else, to Kierkegaard's interest in Kantian philosophy. Supplementing this impression are the many references to Kant found in his reading notes of this period, especially his notes to works by Franz Baader, Johannes Falk, Johann Erdmann, and Julius Müller.[21]

Kierkegaard might have had good reason to be interested in boning up on Kant's philosophy. In the summer of 1838, at the time of his father's death, he made the decision to complete his university degree in preparation for a career in the ministry. He already had spent several years in "aesthetic" dissolution, and he now dedicated himself to making up for lost time. The candidature examination or "Attestats" took place in two parts, a written portion in June 1840 and an oral examination on July 3 of the same year. *Journal* entries during the preceding two years give us an idea of how seriously Kierkegaard prepared. He saw this as "God's will" for him at this moment in his life.[22] The rigor of this preparation led to a suspension of his journal entries during the last nine months of this period and caused him to joke that he was "destined to study for the examination *in perpetuum*."[23]

As Josiah Thompson observes, we can only speculate on what Kierkegaard read during this period.[24] But if the questions that confronted him on July 3, 1840, when he took the crucial oral portion of this examination, are any indication, he must have been thoroughly immersed in Kant. The notary's record of the examination shows that three of the five members of the theological faculty, Professors Scharling, Engelstoft, and Hohlenberg, questioned Kierkegaard.[25] In keeping with the practice of rotating duties among the five regular members of the faculty, Martensen was not present at the exam, although the questions put by Engelstoft, the specialist in the Hebrew Bible, seem to have come from Martensen.[26] The questioning began with Professor Scharling, who put approximately twenty-six questions to the candidate on matters of the history of dogma and church history. Engelstoft followed, with twenty-three questions on the Hebrew Bible and fifteen questions on ethics and the philosophy of religion. Hohlenberg concluded the exam with thirty-five questions on New Testament and early church topics.

Engelstoft's (Martensen's?) fifteen questions on ethics and philosophy of religion are particularly fascinating for our purposes. In the order stated, they are as follows:

What is the basic idea behind any attempt to establish a moral principle?

Is a moral principle from all points of view equally necessary now?

How does one represent the moral principle as a goal?

[What are] the primary characteristics of a *eudaimonistic* system?

What principal thought is the point of departure?

In which moral principles does it manifest itself?

Kant's argument against that?

Kant's and Fichte's views of morality?

Accordingly, how must we grasp the concept of the moral principle?

The relationship to religion?

How does the categorical imperative lead to religion?

How is the philosophical position distinguished from the Christian positive one?

Where in particular?—How were positive laws viewed in Luther's system?

How is the necessity of duty regarded? By Lutheran theology?

How could it be regarded in a different way?

The importance of Kantian ethics to these questions is obvious. Beginning with a preliminary foray into eudaimonism (whose very concept results partly from Kant's critique of eudaimonism in ethics), they seem to move toward an understanding of the categorical imperative, Kant's own supreme principle of morality, as he developed this in the *Foundations* and first half of the *Critique of Practical Reason*. This is followed by the questions probing the link between ethics and religion, a link established by Kant in the second half of the *Critique of Practical Reason* and in the *Religion*. The questioning concludes with some attention to orthodox alternatives to a Kantian approach.

Sadly, for our purposes, there exists no record of the content of Kierkegaard's answers to these questions. Nor is there a record of his reply to the written examination questions in June, at least two of which, as we'll see shortly, have some relationship to Kant.[27] The notary's report of the exam provides only a brief evaluative notation on Kierkegaard's response to each question. These suggest that his performance on the questions about ethics was his best of the exam.[28] Overall, his performance on the exam, if not outstanding, was very good: Kierkegaard was one of forty-five candidates who received a grade of *laudabilis* ("with distinction"); fifty-nine received *haud illaudabilis* ("not without distinction"), and eleven were awarded a modest *non contemnendus* ("passing").[29] It is hard to believe, given the nature of these questions, that Kierkegaard could have done so well on this examination if his long and arduous period of preparation had not involved him in a careful study of Kant's writings on ethics and religion.

This period of scholarly preparation ends with what may be the only negative note by Kierkegaard on Kantianism we find in the historical record. This is recorded in a later remark in the *Journals* explaining the long delay in Kierkegaard's coming to an appreciation of the work of Trendelenberg, the philosopher and logician whose writings on the categories became a particular object of Kierkegaard's fascination during the mid-1840s. Trendelenberg had lectured in Berlin during Kierkegaard's first visit there in 1841, but the young scholar had neglected to attend his lectures. Writing in 1847, he explains this lapse: "The first time I was in Berlin, Trendelenburg was the only one I did not take the trouble to hear—to be sure, he was said to be a Kantian. And I practically ignored the young Swede traveling with me who intended to study only under Trendelenburg. O, foolish opinion to which I was also in bondage at the time."[30]

How can we assess an isolated critical comment like this? Does it reveal an abiding dislike of Kantian philosophy, or is it the understandable reaction of a young man who has just spent two years studying Kant for a degree examination? Does it reveal a dislike of Kant himself or only of later German "Kantians" who had turned the philosopher's living thought into a dead monument?[31] Does it possibly reflect the prejudices of his Hegelian teachers? Whatever its meaning, this comment is unique in Kierkegaard's authorship. His work is hardly a polemic against Kantianism. We'll see that in the period 1841–1845, perhaps because of the enormous intellectual momentum imparted by his several furious years of degree preparation, Kierkegaard's writings vibrate with Kantian themes, terms, and assumptions.

KIERKEGAARD'S READING IN KANT

The surest basis for our knowledge of Kierkegaard's familiarity with Kantian philosophy remains the record of his reading of Kant's texts. As I have said, we have to reconstruct this record out of a variety of intersecting considerations. Foremost among these are the direct quotations from Kant's writings, of which we have only a handful—perhaps as few as five. To these we might add the dozen or so explicit allusions to Kantian texts and the more numerous but less certain unacknowledged borrowings from these texts that bespeak a firsthand knowledge of Kant's writings. Finally, there are the books we know Kierkegaard to have owned. The Auctioneer's Sales Record (*Auktionsprotokol*) of the books in his library at the time of his death lists these. However, this listing of books is by no means a sure guide to Kierkegaard's reading in

Kant. To begin with, it does not include everything Kierkegaard read. As H. P. Rohde, editor of the Sales Record, observes, there are many indications that Kierkegaard's reading ranged far beyond the limits of his collection. He borrowed many books from the libraries of the student association, the Athenæum, the University Library, and elsewhere. Booksellers' bills preserved among his papers contain mention of volumes purchased by Kierkegaard but not in his library at the time of his death, and although these invoices mention no books by Kant, the bills themselves hint at his wider acquisitions.[32] Finally, there is the fact that, under economic pressure toward the end of his life, Kierkegaard also apparently sold many books in his library, making the *Auktionsprotokol* an even less reliable guide to his reading. As Rohde observes, "The sales catalogue represents a collection stripped of many of its books."[33] Neither can we assume that Kierkegaard surveyed or carefully read every book he owned. The Tieftrunk edition of Kant's *vermischte Schriften* contains over thirty-one essays, treatises, or collections of letters by Kant, many dating from Kant's precritical period or dealing with themes in natural science. As a rule, I think, it is reasonable to suppose that Kierkegaard paid most attention to those essays dealing with ethics or religion, but in the absence of quotations or allusions, there is no reason to assume he paid attention to everything in this edition.

What follows, then, is a critical reconstruction of Kierkegaard's reading in Kant. On the basis of these three intersecting considerations—direct quotations, allusions, and ownership—I range the following Kant books or treatises in an order of declining certainty with respect to his familiarity. First come those items with which he was certainly familiar. Second are those essays or treatises he very likely read carefully. Finally there are writings of which we can say nothing, either positively or negatively, with respect to his familiarity. As I mention works, especially those I believe it is most likely Kierkegaard read with care, I'll offer reasons for my judgments.

Works of Certain Familiarity

The Conflict of the Faculties, 1798   This late work by Kant[34] heads up the category of Kant's writings we can be certain

Kierkegaard read. I base this judgment on the presence of this essay in the Tieftrunk edition, the existence of an explicit quotation from it that appears in a *Journal* entry for 1850, and, as we'll see later, an extensive pattern of involvement with *The Conflict of the Faculties* in Kierkegaard's writings. The *Journal* quotation evidences Kierkegaard's appreciation of Kant's wit: "From his standpoint it is jaunty of Kant to say (in one of his small dissertations): It is all right with me for philosophy to be called the handmaid of theology—it must be that she walks behind to carry the train—or walks ahead and carries the torch."[35]

That Kierkegaard read this work with enough attention to copy out a passage is important, since *The Conflict of the Faculties* recapitulates much of the argument Kant develops in the *Religion* and represents Kant's most mature statement of his philosophy of religion. It also contains Kant's most direct criticism of revealed faith, historical salvation, and the symbolization of it in God's command to Abraham to sacrifice his son, themes that figure centrally in Kierkegaard's pseudonymous writings.

Dreams of a Spirit-Seer, 1766   It may seem odd that this early and little read work by Kant should appear on the list of writings with which we know Kierkegaard to have been familiar. In part, this results from the fact that there are two explicit quotations from this work, which appears in the Tieftrunk edition, in Kierkegaard's *Papers* and at least one likely unacknowledged borrowing. But we should not suppose that the ranking of this work is merely a quirk of the historical record. In the third chapter I'll suggest that this eccentric treatise in Kant's authorship may have had a major impact on Kierkegaard, serving as a model in some ways for his own method of indirect discourse and impressing him with the value of irony as a philosophical tool.

Kierkegaard's two quotations from the *Dreams* appear, without further comments, in the *Papers* for the year 1844.[36] The references are to two witticisms by Kant that appear respectively in the preface and first chapter of the *Dreams*. One is Kant's remark "Later on and in old age, we are sure to know nothing of that which was very well known to us at an early date, as children, and the man of thoroughness finally becomes at best a sophist in regard to his youthful delusions."[37] The second is the

comment: "What philosopher has not at one time or another cut
the queerest figure imaginable between the affirmations of a reasonable and firmly convinced eye-witness, and the inner resistance of insurmountable doubt? Should he wholly deny the truth
of all the apparitions they tell him about? What reasons can he
quote to disprove them?"[38]

These quotations are intriguing for several reasons. First,
they further attest to Kierkegaard's appreciation of Kant's sense
of humor. Kierkegaard's repeated criticism of Hegel and the
Hegelians for taking themselves too seriously does not apply to
his estimate of Kant.[39] Second, they also begin to suggest a pattern of Kierkegaard's use of Kant's material. An idea similar to
that in the first of these quotations reappears twice in
Kierkegaard's writings, once in a journal entry,[40] and once in a
long, humorous passage in the "Diapsalmata" of *Either/Or*,
Kierkegaard's first published work. Here the narrator tells us
that he wishes he had kept his youthful prize essays proving the
existence of God and personal immorality. They would be useful,
he says, in helping captivate his now doubting soul, and he
advises all "parents, superiors, and teachers" to caution their
young charges "to keep the Danish compositions written in the
fifteenth year."[41] There is no reference to Kant's witticism here,
nor would one be appropriate for a literary adaptation of this
simple idea. Nevertheless, we'll see this pattern repeated in
Kierkegaard's authorship: ideas, terms, or images, many far
clearer and of far greater importance, are picked up from Kant
and adapted to Kierkegaard's literary or philosophical purposes.

Dreams provides another illustration of these same two phenomena: the appreciation of Kant's humor and the unacknowledged utilization of it. This involves a vulgar joke made by Kant
near the end of the volume. Having at length demolished the pretensions of the mystic and visionary Emanuel Swedenborg, and
with him the metaphysicians whom Kant believed shared Swedenborg's essential faults, Kant applies to the whole lot of them
the judgment of "sharpsighted" Hudibras. They are, he concludes, the sort of hypochondriacs for whom, when they have
wind in their intestine, everything depends on the direction it
takes: "If it goes downward," Kant writes, "it becomes a f___. If
it goes up, it becomes a vision or holy inspiration" [so ist er eine

Erscheinung oder eine heilige Eingebung].[42] Writing in a journal entry in 1854, Kierkegaard seems to apply this same vulgarism to Luther:

> Although it is true that for some years he [Luther] was salt, his later life was not devoid of pointlessness. The *Table Talks* are an example: a man of God sitting in placid comfort, ringed by admiring adorers who believe that if he simply breaks wind it is a revelation or the result of inspiration [at blot han slær en Fjart saa er det en Aabenbaring eller Følge af en Indskydelse].[43]

Given the attention Kierkegaard seems to have paid to *Dreams of a Spirit-Seer*, it is reasonable to suppose that he recalled this pungent remark by Kant more than a decade later when he wrote this entry.

"An Answer to the Question: What Is Enlightenment?" 1784 Again, two explicit *Journal* references, dated 1850, allow us to establish with certainty that this brief essay, which also appears in the Tieftrunk edition, formed a part of Kierkegaard's reading.[44] Both references concern the distinction Kant makes here between the public and private use of reason. In keeping with this distinction, Kant would limit the right of public officials such as teachers or pastors to express unauthorized personal views on religious or political matters when operating in their official capacity, while also defending the right of such officials, especially professors, in their capacity as "scholars" to publish studies containing unorthodox views. Kierkegaard seems to draw on at least the first of Kant's distinctions in his 1846 work *The Book on Adler*. In the third chapter we'll see that Kierkegaard appears to employ other Kantian ideas in this book, which also marks the beginning of his explicit opposition to the Danish state church. It is interesting to consider, therefore, that Kant's own wrestling with questions of individual conscience and established religion attracted Kierkegaard's attention.

Works Very Likely Read

Critique of Pure Reason, 1781, 1794 (4th ed.) Only the most conservative criteria for selection force me to include this major work in the category of those "very likely" rather than those "certainly" read by Kierkegaard. In all Kierkegaard's writing there is no explicit quotation from the first *Critique* like those we have seen for the previous works. However, there is ample reason to conclude that Kierkegaard was not only familiar with Kant's major writing on epistemology but intimately familiar with it. First, there is the fact of ownership. The *Auktionsprotokol* lists the first *Critique* with the *Critique of Judgment* and the Tieftrunk edition of the *vermischte Schriften* as in Kierkegaard's library at his death.[45] Second, there is the record of his attendance at Martensen's lectures, in which Kant's various demolitions of the traditional rationalist arguments for God were a major focus.

Third, and very important, are the several major points in Kierkegaard's writings where, usually without attribution, he repeats aspects of Kant's criticism of the ontological proof. One of these appears in a long section of the *Philosophical Fragments* where Kierkegaard rejects efforts to prove God's existence. Observing that "I never reason in conclusion to existence, but I reason in conclusion from existence," he adds, "For example, I do not demonstrate that a stone exists but that something which exists is a stone. The court of law does not demonstrate that the criminal exists but that the accused, who does indeed exist, is a criminal. Whether one wants to call existence an *accessorium* [addition] or the eternal *prius* [presupposition], it can never be demonstrated."[46]

Presupposed in this remark is the idea that existence is not a predicate but the affirmation of the reality of the object with its predicates, an idea at the heart of Kant's criticism of the ontological argument in the "Transcendental Dialectic" of the first *Critique*. Again without attribution to Kant, Kierkegaard makes this same point in the *Concluding Unscientific Postscript*, when he brings under criticism the argument for God's existence that proceeds from the assumption that existence is a perfection necessarily possessed by an all-perfect being. This argument, Kierkegaard concludes, involves a serious confusion of reality with the realm of pure thought.[47] That Kant is on Kierkegaard's mind in these related comments is further illustrated by a *Journal* entry on the same topic included by the Hongs in the Supplement to their edition of the *Fragments*. In this entry, dated 1844, Kierkegaard explicitly attributes to Kant the idea of existence as an *accessorium*.[48]

This entry puzzles the Hongs, who rightly point out that Kant does not use the term *accessorium* in the way Kierkegaard suggests. Thulstrup says flatly that this term "is not employed by Kant," and Drachman, editor of the third edition of Kierkegaard's *Samlede Værker,* says that Kant seems not to have used the term.[49] In fact, although Kant does not use this term in the first *Critique* at all, it appears twice in his writings, once in *The Metaphysics of Morals*[50] in connection with a discussion of property rights, and once in a passage in *The Conflict of the Faculties*.[51] The first of these uses is irrelevant to Kierkegaard's concerns, but the passage in *The Conflict of the Faculties* immediately follows Kant's stinging rebuke of Abraham for having placed obedience to an alleged divine command to sacrifice his son over the clear prohibition on such slaughter that issues from rational conscience. Kant then distinguishes the universal and essential element of biblical teaching, its moral content, from what is merely secondary and associated with it, the revealed statutory precepts. These secondary elements he terms an *accessorium*. Remarkably, Kierkegaard picks up this precise sense of the term in the *Postscript* in connection with a criticism of the Hegelians for their preoccupation with historical detail at the expense of personal ethical commitment.[52] In the *Fragments*, however, Kierkegaard takes a position on the importance of history, specifically our need for a historical savior, that is diametrically opposed to Kant's. In the fourth and fifth chapters, we'll see that the issue of the importance and reliability of historical revelation, especially as it pertains to the Atonement, is the single and central point of contention between Kierkegaard and Kant. We'll also see that the Abraham and Isaac episode is the complex symbol for this disagreement. In some ways, therefore, this passage in *The Conflict of the Faculties* is at the very heart of Kierkegaard's involvement with Kant. Above all, Kierkegaard's two uses of the term *accessorium* evidence his tendency to appropriate key aspects of Kant's thinking, including the primacy of ethical commitment over concern with external, historical considerations, while rejecting Kant's christology and soteriology. An interesting question is why Kierkegaard should have picked up a term used by Kant in *The Conflict of the Faculties* in connection with the issue of historical existence and then have used that term himself in a context involving Kant's key argument against traditional religious metaphysics. One answer to this, we'll see, has to do with the complex ways in which Kierkegaard, especially in the *Fragments* and *Postscript*, selectively combines elements from Kant's epistemology and philosophy of religion to fashion his own religious argument for faith in a historical redeemer.

The *Journals* provide additional evidence for the claim that Kierkegaard had at least read with great care Kant's criticisms in the first *Critique* of the traditional rationalist proofs of God's existence. In many places Kierkegaard alludes to Kant's observation that "a hundred real thalers do not contain the least coin more than a hundred possible thalers."[53] Kierkegaard seems genuinely to have appreciated this famous remark, Kant's consummate illustration of the claim that existence adds nothing to our concept of an object, since he refers to it several times in connection with his criticisms of the later Idealist philosophers, whom he accuses of having spent and squandered "Kant's 100 dollars" by becoming fantastic.[54] Kierkegaard's frequent open and veiled allusions to this passage[55] not only reinforce our impression of his familiarity with the *Critique*; they further confirm that Kierkegaard greatly appreciated Kant's honesty and wit.[56]

These allusions do not exhaust the evidence about Kierkegaard's knowledge of the *Critique of Pure Reason*. There are also some important but smaller terminological borrowings to which I shall return in the third and fourth chapters, when I try to point up the significance of Kierkegaard's dependence on Kant's epistemology. Lee Capel, translator of Kierkegaard's dissertation, *The Concept of Irony*, also identifies a passage in the thesis where, he believes, a humorous image used by Kierkegaard concerning polemical opponents uselessly beating the air is drawn from a passage in "The Discipline of Pure Reason in Respect of Its Polemical Employment" in the first *Critique*.[57] Although I am less sure about this, since we also can trace this image back to Paul (I Cor. 9:27), if Capel is right, we can establish Kierkegaard's use of this work at least as early as 1840, when he was preparing his thesis. In any case, it is reasonable to assume that Kierkegaard's familiarity with this *Critique* dates from his student days and well precedes the commencement of his authorship.

The Critique of Judgment, 1790   Again, a definite if very elliptical reference helps us to locate this major work, the third of Kant's great *Critiques*, in Kierkegaard's reading. In a *Journal* entry dated 1842–1843, Kierkegaard mentions this *Critique* and Kant's conception there of beauty as involving "disinterested satisfaction."[58] Beyond this, it is impossible to say how extensively Kierkegaard delved into this book. One brief statement in an "Edifying Discourse" of 1843 calls to mind a powerful passage in the second part of this work, the "Critique of the Teleological Judgment," where Kant develops his "moral proof" of the existence of God.[59] It also seems to me very unlikely that, having examined the first part of this work, the "Critique of the Aesthetical Judgment," Kierkegaard would have neglected Kant's important treatment of religious and moral themes in the second part.

Religion within the Limits of Reason Alone, 1793   With this work, we move beyond the Kant texts we know Kierkegaard owned. Despite this, various considerations allow us to place this book high on the list of works with which Kierkegaard was very familiar. First, there are the detailed reading and lecture notes about Kant's arguments in the *Religion* that we find in the *Papers*. Not only in Martensen's lectures, but also in those by H. N. Clausen, Ph. Marheinecke, and Schelling, and also in his reading notes on works by Franz Baader and Johannes Falk,[60] Kierkegaard records references to aspects of Kant's discussion in the *Religion*. Overall, Kant's writings receive more attention in these materials than those of any other thinker, and the treatment of the *Religion* bulks large even among the Kant material.[61] Is it reasonable to suppose that Kierkegaard would have so often found Kant near the center of his teachers' concerns without being stimulated to study this volume himself?

Second, there are at least five explicit references in Kierkegaard's writings and in his *Papers* to Kant's idea of "radical evil,"[62] an idea that seems to have fascinated Kierkegaard and that Kant developed only in the *Religion*. Since the earliest of these entries to his *Journal* dates from 1837, we may assume that the *Religion* had attracted Kierkegaard's interest at least from the time he attended Martensen's winter-semester lectures on Kant.

Finally, there are the many places in his writings where

Kierkegaard seems to draw on ideas, themes, or phrases in the *Religion* to develop important ideas of his own. In Chapters 3 and 4 I'll examine the content of these borrowings, which, taken together, constitute in my view Kierkegaard's deepest engagement with Kant's thought.

***Foundations of the Metaphysics of Morals*, 1785**   Surprisingly, there is little external evidence to suggest that Kierkegaard read this work. The *Auktionsprotokol* does not mention it, and there is no explicit reference to it in his writings. True, Judge William in *Either/Or* claims to be able to discourse on "Kantian views of the ethical,"[63] and the employment in this same context of Kantian terms or ideas—including the distinction between negative and positive duties in a manner corresponding to Kant's distinction between perfect and imperfect duties and the repeated allusions to autonomy in ethics or to persons as ends in themselves[64]—suggest a familiarity with the *Foundations*. Nevertheless, these distinctions are not altogether unique to Kant, and, in any case, we cannot equate Judge William's knowledge and education with Kierkegaard's. This absence of overt references may be why Niels Thulstrup concludes that Kierkegaard "showed no overwhelming interest in Kant" and "apparently neither owned nor had any form of direct knowledge of the epoch making principal ethical works of Schleiermacher or Kant."[65]

Be this as it may, for reasons I have already mentioned, I believe Thulstrup is mistaken in this judgment. Because of the central place given to the idea of the categorical imperative on Kierkegaard's degree examination, it is inconceivable to me that he would have failed to study this text with considerable care. Kierkegaard's repeated use of the term *categorical imperative* from his youthful writings forward also suggests a long-standing familiarity with Kant's presentation of this norm.[66] To this, I would add the substantial indications, developed in Chapter 3, that the ethical position set forth by Kierkegaard in writings like *Purity of Heart* and *Works of Love* shows an exceptionally strong degree of influence by Kant's discussion in the *Foundations*.

There is also one instance of what seems to be unacknowledged borrowing by Kierkegaard from the *Foundations*. Compare the following two passages. The first is from the *Founda-*

tions, the second from *The Sickness unto Death*. The italics are my own.

> Man feels in himself a powerful counterpoise against all com-
> mands of duty which reason presents to him as so deserving of
> respect; this counterpoise is his needs and inclinations, the
> complete satisfaction of which he sums up under the name of
> happiness. Now reason issues inexorable commands without
> promising anything to the inclinations. It disregards, as it were,
> and holds in contempt those claims which are so impetuous
> and yet so plausible, and which will not allow themselves to be
> abolished by any command. From this *a natural dialectic* aris-
> es, i.e., a propensity to argue against the stern laws of duty and
> their validity, or at least to place their purity and strictness in
> doubt and, where possible, to make them more accordant with
> our wishes and inclinations. This is equivalent to corrupting
> them in their very foundations and destroying their dignity—a
> thing which even common practical reason cannot ultimately
> call good.[67]

> *Willing is dialectical* and has under it the entire lower nature of
> man. If willing does not agree with what is known, then it does
> not necessarily follow that willing goes ahead and does the
> opposite of what knowing understood (presumably such strong
> opposites are rare); rather, willing allows some time to elapse,
> an interim called: "We shall look at it tomorrow." During all
> this, knowing becomes more and more obscure, and the lower
> nature gains the upper hand more and more; alas, for the good
> must be done immediately, as soon as it is known (and that is
> why in pure ideality the transition from thinking to being is so
> easy, for there everything is at once), but the lower nature's
> power lies in stretching things out. Gradually, willing's objec-
> tion to this development lessens; it almost appears to be in col-
> lusion. And when knowing has become duly obscured, knowing
> and willing can better understand each other; eventually they
> agree completely, for now knowing has come over to the side of
> willing and admits that what it wants is absolutely right. [68]

We'll see that Kierkegaard's most intense use of Kant's writings seems to have occurred during the period of the early
pseudonymous works, roughly from 1841 to 1844. If the similarities in these two passages are not happenstance but rather
indicate, as I believe, careful attention by Kierkegaard to the text

of Kant's work, this instance of borrowing suggests that Kierkegaard continued to refer to Kant's writings, or at least the *Foundations*, as late as the end of the 1840s.

Critique of Practical Reason, 1788   What I have said about the *Foundations* applies as well to this volume. In *Either/Or*, Judge William twice alludes to a moral proof of the immortality of the soul,[69] suggesting that Kierkegaard was familiar with Kant's argument in the second *Critique*. Kant develops this proof most thoroughly there, and it fades from his attention, to be replaced by a doctrine of grace, in the *Religion*. The evidence of Kierkegaard's candidature examination also has importance here. A question on that exam, "How does the categorical imperative lead to religion?" is the central focus of the "Dialectic of Pure Practical Reason" that forms the second half of the second *Critique*.

To this evidence I would add at least two possible allusions to this *Critique* in Kierkegaard's writings. The first, and least compelling, relates to Kierkegaard's affirmation in his journals that the greatness of genius, its "honesty in the deepest sense," lies not in the fact that it produces something new, but only in that it serves "to reexamine the universally human, the fundamental questions."[70] This point, reiterated by Kierkegaard more than once in different ways in his writings, brings to mind a famous remark by Kant in a footnote of the second *Critique*. There, in reply to a reviewer of the *Foundations* who had criticized it for containing "no new principle of morality...but only a new formula," Kant states that this critic "had really done better than he intended" in this remark. For who, asks Kant, "would want to introduce a new principle of morality and, as it were, be its inventor, as if the world had hitherto been ignorant of what duty is or had been thoroughly wrong about it?"[71] In view of Kierkegaard's evident appreciation of Kant's honesty and sense of humor, this footnote may have caught his eye and confirmed his understanding of creative genius in intellectual matters.

A second possible allusion or borrowing appears in the *Papers* in an entry where Kierkegaard criticizes Christianity, in its effort to please "childlike souls," for transforming God into such a "fabulous monstrosity" (fabelagtig Monstrum) that "everything the most dissolute Arabian fantasy has hit upon, is but a bagatelle compared to this conglomeration."[72] This remark is reminiscent of an important passage in the "Dialectic" of the second *Critique* where Kant, having allowed reason to transcend the limits of experience to fulfill its urgent practical (moral) needs, also seeks to set limits on this permission by ruling out such transcendent moves for lesser reasons:

> In fact, so long as practical reason is pathologically conditioned, i.e., as merely regulating the interest of the inclinations by the sensuous principle of happiness, this demand [that theoretical reason should yield primacy to practical reason] could not be made on the speculative reason. Mohammed's paradise or the fusion of the deity of the theosophists and the mystics, according to the taste of each, would press their monstrosities [Ungeheuer] on reason, and it would be as well to have no reason at all as to surrender it in such a manner to all sorts of dreams.[73]

There are other signs that this passage by Kant may have captured Kierkegaard's attention. In a series of remarks in the *Fragments* dealing with the "unknown," Kierkegaard, in terms very similar to Kant's treatment of the problem, discusses the difficulties of working beyond the boundaries of knowledge and the need to place limits on such excursions:

> What, then, is the unknown? It is the frontier that is continually arrived at, and therefore when the category of motion is replaced by the category of rest it is the different, the absolutely different...If the unknown (the god) is not solely the frontier, then the one idea about the different is confused with the many ideas about the different. The unknown is then in διασπορά [dispersion], and the understanding has an attractive selection from among what is available and what fantasy can think of (the prodigious, the ridiculous, etc.).[74]

This remark also may have been influenced by a passage in Kant's *Conflict of the Faculties*, a work certainly studied by Kierkegaard.[75] Nevertheless, some of Kierkegaard's most important ideas, especially his understanding of the relation between practical and theoretical reason, are also found in Kant's discussion in these several pages of the second *Critique*, so it is worth noting here that Kierkegaard's familiarity with this *Critique* at this point might have extended to an absorption of the very images used by Kant to illustrate his points.

"On the Failure of All Attempted Philosophical Theodicies," **1791** This fascinating little essay by Kant appears in the Tieftrunk edition. It is hard to imagine that Kierkegaard, who always took a skeptical view of natural theology and of efforts to reason away the problem of evil,[76] would have ignored this brief essay. The written examination for his theological degree, which took place in June of 1840, also included among its six questions the following: "What is understood by 'theodicy', and how does Christianity solve the problem of theodicy?"[77] Once again, unfortunately, we have no record of Kierkegaard's answer to this question. But given the importance of this issue to his teachers, I believe Kierkegaard probably regarded himself as well advised to read this essay by Kant during his exam preparation.

Besides these general considerations, there are several possible borrowings from this work suggesting that Kierkegaard gave it serious attention. One is based on a footnote in Kant's treatise where he discusses the matter of oaths and uses the opportunity to protest the stupidity of forcing people in courtroom proceedings not only to swear that they will tell the truth but to require them also to affirm solemnly that they believe in God. "If the first attestation cannot prevent a lie," Kant observes, "a second false one will not be any more successful."[78] In an entry in his *Papers* for 1854 Kierkegaard expresses a similar thought in the same derisory tones: "Every police officer, policeman, every night watchman's report is under oath—but sometimes the party concerned is permitted to take another oath once again; consequently he affirms under oath that which he affirmed under oath. Glory be to humanity, justice, the police lieutenant, and all of them together."[79]

A second parallel is also to a footnote in the essay. Decrying the "seeming lack of *justice*" in the world as a major obstacle to belief in God, Kant suggests that the impunity of the wicked— even more than the seeming abandonment of the righteous—is a particular source of concern:

> In the charge about the lack of justice found in the distribution of men's lot here on earth, the complaint is not that the good

ones are not well but that the evil ones are not in woe (although to add the first statement to the second increases the scandal even more). For in a government of things established by God, the best man cannot make his wish for happiness rest upon divine justice but only upon God's goodness; and he who does all his duty cannot have any claim upon divine benevolence.[80]

Similarly, in a journal entry for 1842, Kierkegaard observes:

> It certainly would not be appalling that I should suffer punishment which I deserved because I had done wrong; but it would be appalling if I or any man should be able to do wrong and no one punished it. It would not be appalling that I should wake up in anxiety and horror to the deceit of my heart; it would be appalling if I or any man should be able to deceive his heart in such a way that no power could awaken it.[81]

I include the latter portion of this entry because its mention of self-deceit connects to the third and final item of evidence suggesting that Kierkegaard studied Kant's treatise carefully. In a long portion of this essay Kant turns to the Book of Job to illustrate his own thinking about the problem of evil. In this discussion, which stretches over three pages of the essay, we find a fascinating parallel to Kierkegaard's own treatment of Job in *Repetition*.

For Kant, the arguments between Job and his "friends," or the conclusions arrived at, are less important than the "character" exhibited by each party to the debate. Job's friends, on the one hand, "spoke as if they were overheard by the Almighty" and "as if they cared more for winning his favours by passing the right judgment than for saying the truth."[82] Their dishonesty thus contrasts sharply with "Job's free and sincere outspokenness." Even when God intervened to remonstrate him, Job confessed "not that he had spoken sacrilegiously for he was sure of his good faith, but only that he had spoken unwisely about things that were above his reach and which he did not understand."[83] A principal lesson of this text, Kant concludes, is that

> only the uprightness of the heart, not the merit of one's insights, the sincere and undisguised confessions of one's doubts, and the avoidance of feigned convictions which one does not really feel (especially before God, where dissemblance

would never work), these are the qualities which caused the
upright man Job to be preferred in the eyes of the divine judge
to the pious flatterers.[84]

Kierkegaard's treatment of Job in *Repetition* is surprisingly
similar. For Kierkegaard, too, the focus of attention is not on the
larger theological issues raised by this book but on the character
of Job himself. It is Job's "steadfastness with which he knows
how to avoid all cunning ethical evasions and wily devices" that
makes him the hero he is. Sometimes, when seemingly unmerited
sufferings assault a person, he may concede that "misfortune has
struck him because of his sins." But this admission is often
demonically dishonest and dissembling. "In such a case, for
example, a person will admit that God is in the right, although
he believes that he himself is. He wants, so to speak, to show
that he loves God even when God is tempting the lover. Or, since
God cannot remake the world for his sake, he will be sufficiently
noble to go on loving him."[85]

In contrast, Job "affirms that he is on good terms with God;
he knows he is innocent and pure in the very core of his being,
where he also knows it before the Lord."[86] The result is that "in
freedom he still has something of greatness, has a consciousness
that even God cannot wrest from him even though he gave it to
him."[87] In a journal entry for 1841, Kierkegaard expresses the
same idea: "It still holds that in order to pray in truth to God out
of an honest heart we cannot deceitfully hide anything in the
secrecy of our being—not that we are trying to deceive God, but
we do not have the courage to confide in him."[88]

The Book of Job has been subject to an almost infinite variety
of interpretations. Among these the themes of Job's inner integrity
and his moral reluctance to compromise his own inner judgment
of personal uprightness to deceive both himself and God are not
the most common. Yet these form the essential themes of Kant's
treatment of Job in the essay on theodicy. That Kierkegaard
dwells on these same themes and applies them to his purposes in
developing the idea of demonic self-deception before God strongly suggests to me a familiarity with Kant's discussion. When we
add this to the other evidence, it seems reasonable to place this
essay among those which Kierkegaard carefully scrutinized.

"The End of All Things," 1795   With this little essay on eschatology we descend into those works by Kant in which, although evidence exists to warrant including them in the category of "very likely read," this evidence grows more and more circumstantial. Apart from the fact that this essay appears in the Tieftrunk edition and deals with a subject of obvious importance to a religious thinker like Kierkegaard, there are only a series of textual or conceptual parallels of varying degrees of persuasiveness to suggest that this particular piece by Kant caught Kierkegaard's eye or influenced his thinking. Later, in the third and fourth chapters, I hope to develop the important connections between the views expressed in this essay by Kant on the matters of eternity and predestination and the views held by Kierkegaard. But for now, the textual parallels are our strongest evidence that Kierkegaard actually read this essay.

A first parallel occurs in connection with a remark about eternity made by Kant in this essay. A proper conception of eternity, he tells us, involves not a continuing in time but the *end of all time*. This way of thinking is foreign to us, he suggests, and it allows us no conception but a negative one. Kant then adds,

> But that some time a moment will make its appearance when all change—and with it time itself—will cease is a notion that revolts our imagination. Then, of course, the whole of nature, as it were, will grow rigid and petrified; then the final thought, the last feeling will remain stationary in the thinking subject and ever the same without variation. For a creature which can be conscious of its existence and the magnitude of it (viewed as duration) in time only, such a life, if, indeed, it may be called life, must seem equivalent to annihilation.[89]

A journal entry by Kierkegaard for 1850 seems to presume a similar sense of dread before the limitless stasis of eternity:

> While he is alive, the natural man does not fear death more than he fears stopping. Well, death and stopping have much in common…The natural man fears this limitlessness as he fears death. To a person whose element is "up to a point," the limitlessness, the infinitude, the stationariness of the eternal in the stopping is just like being killed.[90]

Two other possible parallels appear in connection with points made by Kant in this essay in the course of his comparative evaluation of what he terms "Unitarianism" and "Dualism" in theories of election. The former for Kant is the view that all are ultimately saved; the second is the view that some may be utterly damned. Although Kant denies that we can theoretically settle this dispute, he sees moral advantages in each position. The dualist view, for example, seems to agree with our own sense of the necessity of rigorous self-judgment: "So far as we can see it, so far as we are able to investigate it ourselves, the Dualistic system indeed possesses...a preponderance in the practical sense for every man as he has to judge himself (although not as he is empowered to judge others)."[91] Compare this remark with a brief statement by Kierkegaard in the *Postscript*: "A genuine religious personality is always mild in his judgment of others, and only in his relation to himself is he cold and strict as a master inquisitor."[92]

A related parallel appears directly in connection with the issue of election and predestination. Concluding his treatment of "Unitarianism" and "Dualism," Kant observes that the theoretical issues raised by this matter must remain unresolved for us, although the practical implications are clear: "From a practical point of view...the system to be embraced will have to be the Dualistic one, especially since the Unitarian system seems to be too much lulled asleep in complacent security."[93] Again, compare the series of ideas presented here with the more succinct, but conceptually very similar, remark made by Kierkegaard in a journal entry for 1849: "They argue about whether God intends the salvation of all or only some—almost forgetting the far more important theme: You, O God, intend my salvation; would that I might intend it also."[94]

"On the Supposed Right to Lie from Altruistic Motives," 1797

This small essay constitutes, for many of his modern readers, one of the more peculiar moments in Kant's authorship. Here Kant seems to defend a virtually exceptionless rule against lying. He presents the case of a deranged individual who appears at your front door and demands to know whether you are harboring someone, whom he intends to kill. Despite the powerful incentive to make an exception to the duty of truth telling here, says Kant, it would be morally wrong in any way to deceive the potential killer. Our larger duty to humankind to preserve the veracity of spoken utterances, he maintains, outweighs considerations of duty or benevolence to our friend.

Apart from the sheer notoriety of Kant's position here, there are bits of evidence to suggest that Kierkegaard was familiar with this essay. First, the essay appears in the Tieftrunk edition. Second, his written degree examination contained a question on the duty of truth telling. This question, the second in order and the only other one of the six besides the question on theodicy having a possible relation to Kant, reads as follows: "How have attempts been made to present the duty of truthfulness and its limit, and how must that concept of duty be substantiated in order that the collisions originating in it may be solved?"[95]

In view of this question, it seems to me reasonable to suppose that Kierkegaard read this essay, whether in the period before his exam preparation or sometime thereafter. Indeed, the rigoristic view Kant defends here may have even made a deep impression on him. In a journal entry in 1843, for example, he asks, "Christ hid something from his disciples because they could not bear it. He did it out of love, but is it ethical? This is one of the most difficult ethical doubts—if by suppressing something I can save another from pain, do I have the right to do it, or am I trespassing on his human existence [*Existents*]?" To this remark he adds the following intriguing marginal comment: "Right here lies the paradox of my life; in relation to God I am always in the wrong, but is it a crime in relation to men?"[96]

There is no doubt that Kierkegaard took the duty of truth telling very seriously. For example, it seems to have played a role in his break with Regine Olsen. In the *Journals*, Kierkegaard explains this decision as necessary because marrying Regine would have morally compelled him to reveal to her all the details of his tormented private life.[97] In view of this ethical rigorism, may we suppose not only that Kierkegaard read Kant's little essay on "altruistic lying" but also agreed with it enough for it to have influenced his personal decision making?

"Conjectural Beginning of Human History," 1786   This little essay appears in the Tieftrunk edition. Because it contains an effort by Kant to develop the possible anthropological significance of the biblical account of the Fall, it is reasonable to suppose that Kierkegaard read it. Kant returns to this topic, of course, in the *Religion within the Limits of Reason Alone,* so it is impossible to trace any of Kierkegaard's discussions of the Genesis account uniquely to this essay, but since there is evidence that Kant's treatments of original sin interested Kierkegaard, it would be surprising if he did not look carefully at this little treatise.

It is also possible that we find in this treatise a major stimulus to an important aspect of Kierkegaard's religious thought, his understanding of human anxiety. This theme emerges in Kant's discussion in the course of his treatment of the Fall:

> He [Man] discovered in himself a power of choosing for himself a way of life, of not being bound without alternative to a single way, like the animals. Perhaps the discovery of this advantage created a moment of delight. But of necessity, *anxiety* and alarm as to how he was to deal with this newly discovered power quickly followed; for man was a being who did not yet know either the secret properties or the remote effects of anything. He stood, as it were, at the brink of an abyss. Until that moment instinct had directed him toward specific objects of desire. But from these there now opened up an infinity of such objects, and he did not yet know how to choose between them.[98]

Commenting on this passage, Mark C. Taylor characterizes it as a "remarkable anticipation" of Kierkegaard's view of dread, especially his insight that anxiety results from the "possibility of freedom."[99] I agree. If it is true that Kierkegaard actually drew on Kant's essay, then we have perhaps identified a major source of influence. In general, Kant's writings lack the rich development of psychological themes that we find in Kierkegaard's work, especially in studies like *The Concept of Anxiety* or *The Sickness unto Death.* Where Kierkegaard is often an "existential psychologist," Kant is mostly an epistemologist and moral philosopher. Yet there are moments when Kant explores the most diverse areas of human experience, and it may be that his treatment of anxiety in this little treatise caught Kierkegaard's eye and helped shape his thinking.

Works for Which Evidence Is Lacking

Into this category, and as an exercise in caution, I would put all other writings by Kant. These include several interesting and religiously important essays in the Tieftrunk edition, including "What is Orientation in Thinking" (1786) and "On the Common Saying: 'This May be True in Theory, but it does not Apply in Practice'" (1793). This category also includes Kant's *Lectures on Philosophical Theology*, published in different editions in 1817, 1821, and 1830.[100] In these writings, Kant reiterates or restates, often in a summary way, arguments developed at greater length in the first and second *Critiques* and in the *Religion*. It is intriguing to think that Kierkegaard might have deepened his knowledge of Kant's ethical and religious position by examining these essays. But there is enough reason to believe that he was knowledgeable of Kant's views in these areas independently of his familiarity with these writings.

The same conclusion must be drawn for such important writings as Kant's *Prolegomena to Any Future Metaphysics* and *The Metaphysics of Morals*. It is true that some Kierkegaard scholars have maintained that Kierkegaard reveals familiarity with these works,[101] but they offer no evidence for these claims beyond the mention of epistemological or ethical points that were equally familiar to Kierkegaard from the first and second *Critiques*.

Of course, acknowledging that we must place all other writings by Kant in a category about which we can say nothing for sure concerning Kierkegaard's familiarity rules out negative as well as positive conclusions regarding these works, that is, certitude concerning *either* Kierkegaard's familiarity or nonfamiliarity with these texts. This genuine absence of knowledge leaves us free to speculate on whether Kierkegaard's unrecorded encounter with other works by Kant may not help explain some of the more recondite or perplexing features of his writings.

The preceding discussion traces the outlines of Kierkegaard's education in Kantian philosophy and begins to illustrate his tendency to carry over from Kant's writings a variety of materials, ranging from major ideas to concrete expressions. Subsequent chapters will significantly deepen this impression of borrowing by Kierkegaard from Kant. This record suggests to me that Kierkegaard immersed himself in Kant's writings during his exam preparation and that he maintained the momentum of this involvement during the period 1841–1845 when he was furiously composing the major books of his pseudonymous authorship. Indeed, I do not regard it as an exaggeration to say that during this creative period the Tieftrunk edition of the *vermischte Schriften* (especially the volume including *The Conflict of the Faculties*) and several other works by Kant, notably the *Foundations* and the *Religion,* may often have rested beside Kierkegaard's papers on one of his high desks. Only something approaching this degree of utilization of Kant's works, I think, explains the shared series of ideas and occasional terminological parallels at which this chapter hints and which subsequent chapters develop.

Before leaving the topic of Kierkegaard's familiarity with Kant's writings, an intriguing question suggests itself. How can we explain the fact that at least three of Kant's major writings in the philosophy of religion were missing from Kierkegaard's library at the time of his death? I have already noted that the Sales Record (*Auktionsprotokol*) of Kierkegaard's library provides no evidence that Kierkegaard owned Kant's *Foundations of the Metaphysics of Morals,* the *Critique of Practical Reason,* or the *Religion within the Limits of Reason Alone.* In view of the depth of Kierkegaard's borrowings from these works that we will be reviewing and their importance for his degree examination, can we really believe that he did not own copies of them? If they were lost, sold, or misplaced, why just these works by Kant? H. P. Rohde, the foremost student of the Sales Record, observes that it was Kierkegaard's custom thoroughly to mark up and dog-ear the books he most used.[102] From this observation it is only a short step to the conclusion that Kierkegaard may have taken pains to shape the historical record of his life and writings by jettisoning those volumes that would document his reliance on one thinker or another. Rohde comes to just this conclusion about Kierkegaard's library at the time of his death. Noting its incompleteness, even after deductions are made for books likely to have been sold under economic duress or slipped away after Kierkegaard's death by close relatives, Rohde comments:

> If one were to believe the sales catalogue, Kierkegaard's library consisted of only a couple of thousand volumes. But he may have had—and did have—books which cannot be identified today. Secretive as he was, it is not impossible that he, for example, in certain cases got rid of books which could tell pos-

terity more about him than was good for it. Significant tracks can have been obliterated. The sales catalogue is certainly an important source of information about Kierkegaard's collection, but, at the same time, a somewhat untrustworthy one.[103]

Niels Thulstrup upbraids Rohde for this suggestion. In a review of Rohde's study, he asks sarcastically whether Rohde wants us to believe that Kierkegaard's night table contained frivolous or titillating books that might have embarrassed Kierkegaard if his taste in them had become known.[104] But we need not suppose such trivial motives on Kierkegaard's part. We know that Kierkegaard was deeply concerned about others' interpretations of his life and authorship and that he actively strove to shape and edit posterity's understanding of him. His repeated tearing out of pages from his journals suggests this, as do remarks like the following:

> After my death no one will find in my papers the slightest information (this is my consolation) about what really has filled my whole life, no one will find the inscription in my innermost being that interprets everything and that often turns into events of prodigious importance to me that which the world would call bagatelles and which I regard as insignificant if I remove the secret note that interprets them.[105]

In view of this record and this attitude, is it unreasonable to suppose that Kierkegaard may have taken pains to eliminate the unwanted physical signs of his dependence on Kant? I raise this provocative question as background to the remarkable record of unacknowledged borrowing by Kierkegaard from Kant I plan to trace in the chapters ahead.

CHAPTER 2

Kant's Philosophy: An Overview

> Responsibility for and toward words is a task which is
> intrinsically ethical.
> As such, however, it is situated beyond the horizon of the visible
> world, in that realm wherein dwells the Word that was in the
> beginning and is not the word of Man.
> I won't explain why all this is so. It has been explained far
> better than I ever could by your forbear Immanuel Kant.
>
> —Vaclav Havel, speech to the German Booksellers' Association,
> October 15, 1989[1]

The claim that Kant's thought exerted a great influence on Kierkegaard raises an important question. Why has this influence been so little noticed? Why is it not common knowledge that Kierkegaard was deeply steeped in Kant's writings? Part of the answer has to do with the gaps we noted in the record of Kierkegaard's familiarity with and use of Kant's works. Another part of the answer stems from an oddity of the sociology of knowledge: Kierkegaard scholars are rarely Kant scholars and vice versa. In Europe and the United States, Kierkegaard's writings were initially discovered by thinkers interested in the religious and personal implications of his existential position, and these people were usually not attracted to the starchy formalism and elaborate architectonic that seems to characterize Kant's philosophy. On their side, Kant scholars were not likely to be interested in a thinker whose name was linked with radical "subjectivity" and a love of paradox and the absurd.

In this instance, the tendency of scholarly camps to divide into self-enclosed enclaves and to rely on stereotypes of the other was particularly unfortunate, because Kant's thinking about religion already represents one of the most perplexing and least available aspects of his philosophy. It is not even adequately appreciated by many Kant scholars, some of whom have regarded it as a late or misguided direction in his work. Because of this,

33

we can understand why students of Kierkegaard, who perhaps knew Kant only through a reading of selected passages in the first *Critique* or a cursory reading of the *Foundations*, saw little relationship between the two thinkers.

Tracing the lines of the influence of Kant on Kierkegaard, therefore, requires us first to overcome these stereotypes. To do this, we must retrace the complex intellectual journey that took Kant away from religion, as the religious orthodoxies or rationalist theologies of his day understood it, and then back to it via a wholly new approach furnished by his analysis of practical reason. In some ways Kant planned this journey. As early as the first *Critique* he made known the religious objective of his critical philosophy: his aim, as he says in the Preface to the second edition of the *Critique*, was "to deny *knowledge*, in order to make room for *faith*."[2] In other ways, however, even Kant failed to anticipate the outcome of this journey. I believe he had no idea when he began his work in the philosophy of religion that he would end by rationally vindicating aspects of the orthodox Christian doctrines of original sin and justification by grace. That the early writings point in only a general way to religion and give no hint of the radical ideas to come is a further reason many students of Kierkegaard are unaware of how similar the mature views of both thinkers are.

To begin to grasp the impact of Kant's thinking on Kierkegaard, we can trace the answers to the three famous questions for philosophy Kant set forth in the first *Critique*. These are, "What can I know?" "What ought I to do?" and "What may I hope?" To the first question belongs Kant's ground-clearing critical work in epistemology contained in the first *Critique*, the *Prolegomena to Any Future Metaphysics*, and, to an extent, the second part of the third *Critique* (the "Critique of the Teleological Judgment"). The intriguing explorations of aesthetic judgment in the first part of the third *Critique* probably also fit here. To the second question corresponds his work on ethics, primarily contained in the *Foundations of the Metaphysics of Morals*, the *Critique of Practical Reason,* and *The Metaphysics of Morals.* Important appendages to this body of work are his many shorter but influential writings on political philosophy, law, and philosophy of history, including such essays as "Perpetual Peace," "On the Common Saying: 'This May be True in Theory, but it does not Apply in Practice,'" and the "Idea for a Universal History with a Cosmopolitan Purpose." To the third question correspond Kant's writings on religion. These include the second half of the *Critique of Practical Reason*, portions of the *Critique of Judgment*, all of the *Religion*, and the many shorter essays on religious subjects, most of which appear in Kierkegaard's edition of the *vermischte Schriften*. One of these, eventually published as *The Conflict of the Faculties*, deserves special note since it appears to have particularly attracted Kierkegaard's attention.

EPISTEMOLOGY

The problem facing Kant in the *Critique of Pure Reason* was one that had bedeviled philosophers for centuries but that had become particularly acute in his day: to what extent is it possible to assert that human beings have knowledge a priori, knowledge developed *independently* of experience?[3] From Plato onward, philosophers and theologians had tried to transcend the limits of the sensory world by finding within the human intellect a mode of access to and logical proof of the reality of intelligible objects such as God and the immortal human soul. In Kant's day, the powerful new empiricism of Locke and Hume had brought this position and the rational arguments used to defend it under attack. Asserting that the human mind is a tabula rasa filled only by the play of sensory impressions, empiricism had undermined the traditional foundations of rational theology and ethics.

In this conflict, Kant saw his role as that of a peacemaker, or more precisely, a policeman.[4] By carefully investigating the nature of the human intellect, he would set limits to the claims and pretensions of each of these opposing positions and establish the true scope of human cognition. This task proceeded in two stages. First, by showing that human beings have a priori knowledge as a condition of "knowing" the sensory world, he would refute the radical empiricists. Second, by connecting knowledge inseparably with sensory experience and showing that we may not legitimately extrapolate it, as the rationalists had done, to a knowledge of "intelligible" reality or "things in themselves," he would put an end to speculative flights of fancy and expose the root error in all previous rationalist metaphysics.

The first of these tasks preoccupies him in the first division or "Transcendental Analytic" of the *Critique*. Here, using a method of "transcendental deduction" to derive the conditions logically presupposed in experiencing and knowing, Kant identifies a series of a priori elements in cognition. He develops two of these elements in the "transcendental aesthetic" of this section by identifying the presuppositions of our sensory apprehension (or "intuition") of reality. These elements are space and time, the former applying to our intuition of outer reality, the latter involved in the "inner sense" by which we measure and coordinate experience. Kant's deduction of these two "forms of intuition" involves the insight that space and time cannot be derived from experience alone, as the radical empiricists claimed, for without space or time no coherent or knowable experience would be available to us in the first place. Without presupposing the "inner sense" of time, for example, familiar aspects of outer or inner experience such as sequence or motion would be uncognizable. In defiance of experience as we have it, the array of thoughts and perceptual objects would present themselves to us simultaneously, creating utter discord. Similarly, without the mental assumption of space as a form for the ordering of outer reality, our experience of the world around us would be an ever shifting chaos lacking fixed points of reference. Space and time are a priori, therefore, not in the sense that they exist apart from and before any experience. On the contrary, they are given with and through experience. But they must be thought of logically as prior to experience, for without them there would be no coherent "experience" at all.

Cognition is not limited to a receptivity for sensory intuition. In addition, the intellect relates and manipulates intuitions by means of concepts. We not only perceive objects but *think* them. In Kant's view, conceptualization and intuition are both necessary parts of human knowing: "Thoughts without content are empty, intuitions without concepts are blind."[5] The task of conceptualization belongs to the faculty of the human mind Kant calls the "understanding." In the "transcendental logic" of the *Critique*, he continues his search for a priori elements in cognition by asking what aspects of the understanding's conceptualization process must logically be thought of as existing independently of experience.

One element he identifies is the overarching unity of consciousness and thought that makes it possible for us to connect the data of intuition into a coherent body of knowledge. Kant terms this the "transcendental unity of apperception." In one sense, it is the "I" that is at the center of all my experiencing and knowing and without which my knowledge would not properly be my own. More precisely, it is the active *process* of synthesizing information by means of concepts and in relation to a constant and unified knowing subject. Without this synthetic activity, says Kant, we would not have knowledge at all but a "rhapsody of perceptions" that would not form a completely interconnected consciousness.[6]

This synthetic activity of consciousness in turn proceeds through a series of twelve a priori concepts that define its activity. Kant calls these the "pure concepts of the understanding" or "categories." They include such concepts as "unity," "plurality," "totality," "possibility," and "existence."[7] Together, they represent the ways in which the understanding formally relates and organizes the objects of intuition. As such, Kant insists, these categories must be thought of as logically prior to any experience. One category, for example, is causality, the connection of two occurrences in such a way that when one comes to pass, the other is thought to follow from it *"necessarily and in accordance with an absolutely universal rule."*[8] The empiricist Hume had argued that our concept of causality results from a habit of mind that tends to see events that are repeatedly associated with one another as necessarily linked. Causality, Hume maintained, is thus nothing more than an imagined idea occasioned by the fact of repeated association.[9] In opposition to this, Kant contends that we cannot derive causation from experience because it is the rule we require even to have the experience of causation. How else would we be able to distinguish mere association from what we regard as causation? If we did not initially proceed into experience in a search for "necessary connection" as opposed to mere association, how would we begin the rudimentary "scientific" process that allows us to distinguish genuine causation from association, however repeated and seemingly invariant the latter might be? Causation, therefore, in Kant's view, is one of those indwelling concepts without which our very experience of causation as "necessary connection" could not take place.

This "deduction" of the category of causality represents Kant's approach to the other eleven categories he identifies. In each case, he develops formal concepts that cannot be thought of as derived from experience but that serve instead as the ground and basis of experience. In Kant's words, "The objective validity of the categories as a priori concepts" rests on the fact that "through them alone does experience become possible."[10]

Kant accomplishes his first major epistemological task by proving in this way the existence of a priori elements in cognition. He thus rebuts the claims of the empiricists. His second task, curbing the flights of speculative fancy associated with traditional metaphysics, continues in the "Transcendental Dialectic." Kant had established the key idea here in his deduction of the a priori categories by showing that these categories "have no other possible employment than the empirical" and serve "only to subordinate appearances to universal rules of synthesis."[11] In Kant's view, the unpersuasive and often contradictory conclusions of traditional metaphysical arguments all stem from the fact that human reason, the faculty of the mind that seeks to secure the highest unity of the rules of the understanding, mistakenly employs a priori elements of cognition apart from their proper application to the domain of experience.

The misuses of the category of causality furnish a good illustration of Kant's point. Reason, Kant tells us, naturally seeks the totality of conditions, the final *why*, for any conditioned object or state.[12] In this quest for a completed series of causes or conditions, however, reason is almost unavoidably tempted to transcend the domain of sensory experience in order to determine the ultimate "ground" of things in a noncontingent, transcendent reality. But this is a fatal misstep that leads inevitably to error or "dialectical illusion." In a long section of the "Dialectic" entitled "The Antinomy of Pure Reason," Kant demonstrates this error by presenting a series of rational arguments and counterarguments concerning some of the traditional objects of metaphysics such as freedom and God (understood as an absolutely necessary being). One argument defends spontaneous freedom on the grounds that we cannot think a series of causally related states without also thinking of a cause or beginning of these states. But if this "original" cause is not to be reduced to yet another relative beginning, it must be thought of as free, spontaneous, or unconditioned. In opposition to this rationalist "thesis," Kant advances the equally powerful empiricist "antithesis" involving the claim that a causality that is not itself caused is unthinkable, since our intellects always compel us to ask for the cause of every state or event.

That these equally impressive arguments can lead to absolutely contradictory conclusions stems, in Kant's view, from their seeking to employ a concept tied to experience in a way that transcends our possible experience. Rationalist metaphysicians, for example, take the idea of necessary connection between events within experience and seek to trace these back conclusively to a first cause whose own causation we need not presume. What the metaphysicians seem to gain here by way of explanation, however, comes about only because they apply causality to a realm not thought of as subject to causation in the ordinary sense and in which the notion of an "uncaused cause" initially seems plausible. Empiricists catch this rationalist error by arguing that experience does not admit the possibility of an uncaused cause, but empiricists then commit their own error by turning this into an absolute and dogmatic denial of the possibility of the kind of uncaused or spontaneous causality that freedom represents. No less than the rationalists, they seek to apply a concept of causality applicable to our experience to the way things really are "in themselves."

The a priori forms and concepts Kant discovers thus serve to identify the limits of human knowledge and to eliminate both metaphysical and empiricist pretensions to knowledge of ultimate reality. In the "Transcendental Dialectic," Kant further employs this basic insight about the limits of human knowledge to critique a variety of traditional metaphysical proofs. In the "Paralogisms of Pure Reason," for example, he brings under criticism rationalist psychology, which tries to move from the knowledge of an abiding subject in all cognition—the "unity of apperception" Kant had identified—to the claim that each of us has a nonmaterial soul that continues to exist even after our physical existence has ended. For Kant, this again confuses what is merely a condition of experience with an aspect of ultimate reality.

In a long section of the "Dialectic" entitled "The Ideal of Pure Reason," Kant also systematically brings under critical review all the traditional metaphysical proofs of God's existence. At the center of these proofs, Kant observes, is the so-called ontological proof with its demonstration of the existence of an absolutely necessary and perfect being or *ens realissimum*. Without this idea, says Kant, neither the "cosmological" or "physico-theological" proofs would be able to arrive at a determinate idea of God. The former proof argues from the existence of contingent reality to the existence of a noncontingent, necessary being as reality's ground, and the latter argues from the world's seeming order and purposiveness to the existence of a wise and benevolent Creator. Kant maintains that in the end both proofs rely surreptitiously on the ontological argument to prove that a supreme causality really has the qualities of a perfect and necessary being.

In turn, the ontological proof makes the mistake of confusing existence, a category of the understanding, with a quality or predicate of an object. Once we regard existence as one predicate among others, it is natural to assume that an all-perfect being in the totality of its qualities also possesses the quality of existence, as the ontological proof assumes. But existence is not a predicate. It is the category of the understanding we apply to possible objects of cognition. For something to be *thought* under this category merely establishes its logical possibility, whereas *real* existence requires the further judgment that the object, with all its predicates, is actually presented to us in experience. As Kant puts it, "The small word 'is' adds no new predicate, but only serves to posit the predicate *in its relation* to the subject."[13] This conception of existence underlies Kant's famous jest that although a "hundred real thalers do not contain the least coin more than a hundred possible thalers" their real existence has a very different impact on one's financial position.[14]

Since statements about real existence always involve the affirmation that something is given to us (posited) in experience, it also follows that we cannot say that any real object exists with necessity. Necessity belongs to the domain of concepts, not experience. Things either are or are not a part of our experience; they are not necessarily so. A further implication is that we can never "prove" the existence of God. To prove that something really exists is to show that it is given to us in experience, but God, by our very concept, transcends the sensory world and can never be an object of experience for us. We will eventually see that this radical implication of Kant's epistemology profoundly shapes Kierkegaard's own approach to religious knowledge.

In some respects, it may seem as though Kant's thinking ends by falling more on the empiricist than the rationalist side of the epistemological debates of his day. Human cognition is inseparably bound to the domain of sensory experience, what Kant terms the world of "appearances." Even our a priori concepts are only conditions of sensory knowledge and provide no knowledge of "things in themselves." Despite this, it does Kant a serious injustice, and misses the important religious direction his thinking was meant to take from the start, to regard him merely as an empiricist. True, Kant had set impassable limits to speculative reason. But these limits apply as well, and are equally constraining, to an empiricism that purports to have knowledge about the way things "really are." Thus, although it might be impossible to prove the existence of God, it is equally impossible to use any sort of empirical information to disprove God's existence. Again, although the assumption of human moral freedom runs contrary to our sure sense that all events in our experience are causally conditioned by events that precede them, empiricists cannot prove that moral freedom does not exist, for to do so would require showing that our time-space world of "appearances" is the only kind of reality there is, rather than the limited domain to which our cognition is confined. If there were now warrant on other grounds for affirming the reality of God or moral freedom, a warrant Kant will find in the operations of practical or moral reason, then no objections from the cognitive side will suffice to overrule these beliefs. Hence, in Kant's view, the net effect of his theory of knowledge is as liberating as it is constraining. Indeed, he signals this almost at the beginning of his critical enterprise in a remark in the Preface to the second edition of the *Critique*: "So far, therefore, as our Critique limits speculative reason, it is indeed *negative*; but since it thereby removes an obstacle which stands in the way of the employment of practical reason, nay threatens to destroy it, it has in reality a *positive* and very important use."[15] Kant's epistemology is thus not an end but a beginning. It prepares the way for his powerful insights in ethics and religion.

ETHICS

Kant's discoveries in ethics spring from an application to moral questions of the same procedure he applied in epistemology. He asks whether there are any a priori elements logically presupposed in our moral experience, and, if so, what these might be. In this domain, as well, Kant had to contend with the empiricists' claim that there are no such elements, that experience is the sole source of our moral knowledge. Hume, for example, traced our moral judgments to the feelings of sympathy we have toward others. Somewhat differently, but also with a reference to empirical experience, the Greco-Roman tradition of ethics had connected morality with each individual's personal search for happiness and fulfillment (*eudaimonia*).

In Kant's view these empiricist accounts miss key aspects of our concept of morality. One is our conviction that people who act wrongly are morally blamable or "imputable" for their conduct and may be subject to punishment. This crucial element of our moral judgment would make no sense if morality were a function of sympathetic feelings, for how could we blame an individual for lacking appropriate feelings? Nor would it be reasonable to condemn people for failing to pursue their own happiness. Such conduct might be foolish or misguided, but hardly blamable. There is, in other words, an imperatival element, an "ought" in morality, not adequately comprehended by empiricist accounts.

Kant also sees that morality cannot be narrowly connected to promotion of any particular and empirically determinable human objectives, such as the personal *eudaimonia* that figures so centrally in Greek ethics. Although morality may ultimately enhance human well-being as a whole, we cannot allow either personal happiness or any other particular goal to serve as the supreme "determining ground" of anyone's moral willing, for if this were the case, the plurality and discordance of these private objectives would ensure that "the most arrant conflict" and "savage disorder" would ensue.[16] Instead of involving the promotion of specific and empirically given objectives, therefore, morality is more properly thought of as involving restraint on the pursuit of private objectives in keeping with some generally recognizable standard of conduct.

These considerations lead Kant to the identification of a single, overarching, and purely formal principle at the heart of our moral consciousness, the famed "categorical imperative," whose main formulation, as given in the *Foundations*, is "Act only according to that maxim by which you can at the same time will that it should become a universal law."[17] This principle, Kant observes, sets limits on all merely particular ends and is the source of the "ought" residing in our moral consciousness. An a priori judgment of reason, it is known by and applicable to all rational beings. As the rule of reason we apply to all merely empirical volitions, it also furnishes a necessary and sufficient test of those intended courses of action or policies (maxims) we would raise to the status of morally acceptable conduct.

Although we can relate Kant's derivation of the categorical imperative to his kindred moves in epistemology, determining the exact meaning and import of this imperative is more difficult. Probably no effort to provide a fundamental guide to moral choice has been regarded as being as provocative as this one, but also has been as subject to criticism. Many commentators, for example, have viewed this imperative as imposing a logical requirement of noncontradiction on the processes of thinking and willing that moral reasoning involves. As such, they concede, it furnishes a necessary condition for rational choice. But these commentators deny that this minimal requirement takes one very far in resolving difficult issues of choice. They argue that although the categorical imperative may constitute a necessary feature of moral decision, it is not, as Kant believed, a sufficient one.

Kant's own famous examples in the *Foundations* are sometimes adduced to support this criticism. One example involves the question of whether we may morally make a promise with the intention of breaking it. In this and other cases, the categorical imperative initially requires us to "universalize" our choice.

That is, as a rule of reason, it prohibits us from making an unwarranted exception for ourselves and compels us to regard what we propose to do as a public practice—or "law"— open to all other similarly situated persons. The universalized maxim here, says Kant, immediately annihilates itself. Nonbinding promises are not really promises, and if everyone acted in this way, no one would accept such promises when they were made.

Although Kant's reasoning seems persuasive here, there are instances of moral choice involving something more than logical contradiction where the constraint imposed by the categorical imperative seems more obscure. Another of Kant's examples involves the case of the self-sufficient and unsympathetic individual who does not wish to inconvenience himself by helping others in need. In Kant's view, this individual's "maxim" of refusing aid is not logically contradictory: a world of such cold and independent beings is thinkable in the way that a rule of promise making/promise breaking is not. Nevertheless, Kant believes that this maxim also leads to self-contradiction when raised to the status of a universal law because it involves what he terms "a contradiction in willing." No matter how convenient it might be to avoid having to offer aid to others, he maintains, a person who raises this maxim to the status of a rule for all runs the risk of depriving himself of vital assistance at some future moment of great need. Because an individual would desperately want help when these circumstances arise, his universalized maxim sets his will at odds with itself.[18]

Although Kant's argument here, which reminds us of the "golden rule" with its requirement that we do unto others as we would have them do unto us, is initially plausible, it grows doubtful under closer scrutiny. For example, why can't an individual not reasonably decide to forego the advantage of mutual aid? Many choices involve a trade-off between competing goods. Since the practice of mutual aid involves some sacrifice of freedom and convenience, why can't some especially independent persons reasonably choose to sacrifice future assistance instead? More serious is the fact that many people with peculiar or even bizarre desires might reasonably accept their eccentric maxims being raised to the status of "universal laws" in this sense. R. M. Hare provides an example in his mention of a genocidal fanatic who would willingly fall victim to his own policy should he turn out to be a member of the group he hates.[19] In view of these cases, it appears that Kant's argument for the adequacy of the categorical imperative fails. In general, although it may be rationally necessary that we submit our maxims to this test, the imperative will not always provide a sufficient guide to conduct. It sometimes seems to permit types of conduct we consider morally objectionable or abhorrent.

These familiar criticisms assume that the imperative involves nothing more than a rule of universalization and a test of logical or volitional self-contradiction. But there is good reason to think that Kant's conception is more complex. Without launching into a complete defense of Kantian ethics, let me briefly suggest a way we can rescue Kant's claims for the categorical imperative. This is important because it is suggestively picked up by Kierkegaard in moments when he employs something like the categorical imperative as a measure of moral willing. One way of making sense of Kant's position is to see that the imperative, besides a requirement of universalization and the test of noncontradiction, also imposes a constraint of strict impartiality on each choosing agent. That is, after universalizing our maxim, we are also required to assess it from a common human standpoint and apart from a knowledge of our own special needs, preferences, or interests. Without fully doing so here, I think it can be shown that this mode of reasoning rules out the bizarre and eccentric preferences the choice of which, as we just saw, poses a threat to the adequacy of this principle. For what rational persons would risk having the genocidal fanatic's dangerous maxim raised to the level of a general practice if they did not know whether this preference was their own? And who would forego a practice of mutual aid if they had to reason from the standpoint of a common or "generic" human nature, without knowledge of any of their special abilities, strengths, or weaknesses?

Several major themes in Kant's writings on ethics support this interpretation of the categorical imperative. For example, there is Kant's important distinction between hypothetical and categorical imperatives. Hypothetical imperatives always involve the assumption of particular desires, what Kant calls "subjective conditions,"[20] as the first premise in a practical argument (e.g.,

"If you wish to be wealthy then act in the following way"),
whereas a categorical imperative makes no provision for such
particular ends or interests and works with the ends common to
rational moral agents generally.[21]

This interpretation also finds support in the alternate formulations of the categorical imperative offered by Kant in the *Foundations*. One requires us to treat "humanity," whether in our
own person or that of another, "always as an end and never as a
means only."[22] Often, this formula is taken as a noble but vague
admonition to treat others with respect, but Kant offers it as a
precise statement of the "material" dimension of the moral law.
That is, it identifies the "matter" or substantial values that must
inform the choices of a rational agent employing the imperative.
Where human beings are concerned, this "matter" turns out to
be "human nature" understood as the generic and common qualities possessed by all who are human. To treat others as "ends in
themselves," therefore, is not to respect all their empirical wishes
(which, in any case, is impossible). Instead it is to respect their
will as "generic beings," who, deprived of particular knowledge,
reason to protect their basic and shared human interests. This is
why Kant can come to the conclusion that punishing a criminal
offender is to treat him as an end, not as a means.[23]

Finally, this interpretation also finds support in the "autonomy" formulation of the imperative. To be autonomous, in Kant's
view, is to be free in the sense that one is governed only by a reasoned law one gives oneself. Heteronomy, its opposite, involves
dictation not by reason but by outer constraints or inner drives.
The heteronomous individual may be moved by fear of punishment at the hands of some authority or by the powerful inner
compulsion of various needs and desires. If to be autonomous,
therefore, is to be free from such constraints, in its most complete sense autonomy is to be free of determination by even our
private needs, wishes, or wants and to be directed by nothing
more than a law we give ourselves as impartial, rational beings.
Kant also expresses the idea of autonomy through the metaphor
of a "kingdom of ends," where each moral agent is both maker
of and subject to common rational laws.[24] We can think of this
kingdom, I believe, as a kind of "intelligible" or "noumenal" leg-
islature of impartial rational agents, similar to the hypothetical

choice situation of various "contract" theories, old or new.[25] To elevate one's maxims to the level of universal law, to reason autonomously and to exhibit one's membership in a "kingdom of ends," therefore, amount to the same thing: a willingness to subordinate all one's private interests, including the pursuit of one's own happiness if necessary, to the common ends and purposes of the entire community of rational agents.[26]

Viewed in these ways, Kant's ethics assumes a coherence and sensibleness sometimes eclipsed when it is reduced to a rule of purely formal universalization and rational willing. For one thing, it is crucial to see that Kant does not oppose human happiness or the pursuit of personal objectives per se. On the contrary, Kant sees our preoccupation with personal happiness and private fulfillment as an unavoidable part of our sensory human nature. "To be happy," he insists, "is necessarily the desire of every rational but finite being."[27] His many criticisms of ethical positions that proceed from happiness or aim at the fulfillment of human "inclinations," therefore, do not bespeak some kind of austere rejection of worldly well-being. Instead, they reflect the understanding that private pursuits can never be the final determinants of the conduct of rational members of a social order. Above and beyond any personal willing must stand the supreme law—the categorical imperative—that makes possible an impartial assessment and ordering of individual volitions.

Put another way, Kant's entire ethical theory aims at the possibility of a harmony or even "unity" of social willing. We already saw this theme in Kant's epistemology, where a "synthetic unity of apperception" is logically presumed as necessary to make possible coherent individual knowledge. In a sense the categorical imperative is the analogue of this synthetic unity on the level of practical reason and of social, as opposed to individual, existence.[28] Its purpose is to transform society from a mass of contending wills, whose peace results at best from transitory coalitions of power, into a harmonious community of beings freely respecting common laws they have made for themselves.

I have dwelt on this interpretation of the categorical imperative because I think we must have a sense of the full power of Kant's ethical thinking, and not reduce it to one or the other popular caricature, if we are to appreciate its possible impact on

Kierkegaard..I am not saying that Kierkegaard understood Kant in precisely the way I've outlined here. There are moments, especially in journals entries, where Kierkegaard seems to reiterate the standard criticism of Kant's ethics as empty and formal.[29] But there are also moments when Kierkegaard is not only far less critical of Kantian ethics but even seems to appreciate some of the themes we have just examined. This is particularly true, as we'll see, in *Purity of Heart*, where Kierkegaard's extended discussion of "willing one thing" seems to me a brilliant restatement of Kant's profound insight that the categorical imperative is the sole condition of harmonious willing in self and society.

Before concluding this brief interpretive review of Kant's ethical theory, there are two other matters pertinent to Kierkegaard I should mention. One concerns the role Kant gives intentionality and willing as a measure of moral worth. This, of course, is a familiar motif in the *Foundations*, where Kant, in a preliminary discussion based on "popular" moral conceptions, identifies the morally good will as the only thing that is "good without qualification."[30] Since Kant soon turns his attention to defining the good will as respect for the categorical imperative, the principal focus of his ethics is on the delineation of this basic principle of conduct. Nevertheless, it remains true that beyond the matter of right or wrong deeds, Kant is also concerned with questions of personal "virtue" and moral worth. In this connection, he correctly perceives that judgments about the moral worth of persons must focus, not on actions, but only on the quality of the intentions that lie behind them. Since we necessarily judge intentions in terms of the seriousness with which efforts are made to realize them, this focus does not amount merely to an ethic of "benevolent feelings." But Kant recognizes that we cannot finally judge finite sensory beings, who lack complete control of their environment, beyond a consideration of what they sincerely and strenuously set out to do. This focus on intention, we'll see, is a major point of contact between Kierkegaard's ethics and Kant's.

A second matter concerns Kant's emphasis on "duties to oneself." The reader whose knowledge of Kant's ethical writings is confined to his major published works might miss this motif since it appears most clearly in *The Metaphysics of Morals* and the posthumously published *Lectures on Ethics*. In both works

Kant rejects the common opinion that one cannot properly have duties to oneself or the view that such duties are secondary to our obligations to others. "Far from ranking lowest in the scale of precedence," says Kant, "our duties toward ourselves are of primary importance and should have pride of place; for...nothing can be expected from a man who dishonours his own person."[31] The discussions in these works reveal the traditionalist nature of Kant's applied ethics, with forms of sexual vice, self-neglect, and suicide condemned as expressions of disrespect for the dignity of human nature in one's own person.[32] As we might expect, Kierkegaard shared many of these specific moral opinions, whether he was familiar with any of Kant's views on ethics or not. But when we turn to the issue of Kierkegaard's relationship to Kantian ethics, it is important to keep in mind that Kant's position was not confined to the other-regarding ethic largely developed in the well-known *Foundations* (although even there duties to oneself make an appearance), but contained, as well, an important emphasis on personal discipline and self-development.

PHILOSOPHY OF RELIGION

Critique of Practical Reason

Kant's critical philosophy exploded like a bomb on the cultural scene of late eighteenth century Europe. One fragment of that explosion is the philosophical atheism found in the following century in thinkers like Feuerbach, Marx, Nietzsche, and Freud. Major and readily apparent aspects of Kant's epistemology and ethics pointed in this direction. These included not simply his criticism of traditional metaphysics, but also his discovery and uprooting of the source *within human cognition* of this persistent impulse to religious speculation. It also included his convincing defense of autonomy in ethics. To accept a law from without, whether from religious authority or directly from God, without first submitting it to the test of one's own moral reason, Kant insisted, was to abandon one's vocation and responsibility as a rational, moral being.

If this atheistic, antitheistic side of Kant's philosophy was apparent, the deeply religious side of this critical "explosion," the side that would lead to the work of thinkers like Ritschl, Hermann, Schleiermacher, and ultimately Kierkegaard, was initially harder to discern. Kant reserved only a few pages for it at the end of the first *Critique* in the "Canon of Pure Reason." He hinted at what was to come in the third section of the *Foundations,* where he dealt with the possibility of moral freedom, but this discussion was not yet openly religious in nature. Only in the second half of the *Critique of Practical Reason,* entitled the "Dialectic of Pure Practical Reason," do we find Kant's first sustained effort to develop the religious dimensions of his philosophy, and even here, as we'll see, he only suggests a fuller position to come.[33]

Kant's argument in the "Dialectic" of the second *Critique* would surprise anyone who had taken his previous writing on ethics as a decisive banishment of personal happiness from the sphere of the moral life. Now we learn that happiness plays an important, indeed indispensable, role, in moral reasoning. In addition to the categorical imperative, Kant tells us, practical reason has as its presupposition and requires belief in the attainability of the "highest good," understood as the proportionate and exceptionless union of virtue with happiness. Without this idea, he says, morality would lack a complete object and moral striving itself would become empty and vain. Although happiness cannot be the supreme determinant of any rational person's willing—only the moral law is that—"to be in need of happiness and also worthy of it and yet not to partake of it could not be in accordance with the complete volition of any omnipotent rational being."[34]

Kant's argument here is far from clear. True, he has not relinquished his insistence on the priority of morality over merely private willing. In the "synthesis" of concepts that make up the highest good, moral virtue comes first. It is the supreme condition of one's worthiness to be happy and must be thought of as related to well-being as cause to effect. It would be a total subversion of this idea to believe that persons who are able to make themselves happy, by whatever means, should be thought of as morally virtuous. But if we concede that Kant has not abandoned his understanding of the necessary ordering role of reason, why does he now give happiness such an important place in the world of moral ideas?

In replying to this question I feel we must go beyond Kant's own peremptory answer and seek a fuller understanding of what he is trying to say. Kant's answer is that the "highest good," understood as the exact and proportional union of happiness to virtue, is the necessary object of striving of every rational being. This is because each of us, as a rational but also finite worldly being, wants to see happiness conjoined with virtue, and feels ourself to be morally required to strive toward this end. If this goal were unattainable, if virtue and happiness could not be conjoined in this fashion, our striving would be in vain. Ought implies can. Since we feel strongly impelled to further this goal, to make sense of this experience of moral obligation we must assume that the highest good is ultimately attainable.[35]

This argument has several problems, but to me the most serious and most basic is that it is not clear why moral reasoning leads to such an impassioned insistence on the *perfect* union of virtue and happiness. We'll see in a moment that rather than give up this idea as unrealistic, Kant abandons his strong aversion to metaphysical speculation and argues for the need to postulate certain "transcendent" realities, foremost among them God, as a means of ensuring the eventual exact union of virtue and happiness. But why is this kind of complete union of virtue and happiness necessary? Why not give up this idea and its corresponding obligation in the face of the adversity of worldly experience? Or why not accept a lesser ideal and lesser duty, for example, one involving the idea of *general* progress toward the union of virtue and happiness? Why must we believe in the kind of complete and perfect attainment of this goal that only a supremely powerful and just God can ensure? Since morality is generally more conducive to human flourishing than egoism and injustice, it would seem adequate to content ourselves with this and remain in the immanent domain of human moral experience. We thus could dispense with religious ideas and rationally urge one another to strive onward toward a morally better world in the reasonable hope that an expected future growth in both virtue and happiness will provide a sufficient warrant for the rationality of our efforts.

In my view, the answer to all these questions has to do with the fact that the idea of the highest good emerges in Kant's thinking, not in connection with an assumed duty to promote its attainment, but as a result of a serious conceptual problem at the heart of moral reasoning. Let me sketch the problem. We have already touched on Kant's argument for the necessary priority of impartial moral reasoning over the merely private pursuit of happiness, the necessary supremacy of morality over "prudence." In general terms, this argument is powerful and convincing: surely happiness cannot be thought of as the supreme goal of finite persons' willing, for if this were so, chaos would result and everyone's happiness would be in jeopardy. Just as a strict system of law in the political domain is the necessary condition of individual liberty, so the supremacy of the moral law is the condition of everyone's pursuit of happiness.

So far so good. We have developed a general "transcendental deduction" of the categorical imperative. But is this deduction really convincing to the individual whose obedience to the moral law may foreclose his or her happiness? As finite beings, we always face this possibility. Although wartime experience offers the most graphic examples of the conflict between duty and personal happiness, this conflict is endemic to morality, which places no limit on what it may demand of individuals in the name of the common good. But when the choice is this stark, when my happiness is seriously imperiled, how can I or any rational person be rationally persuaded to do what duty requires? How can I convince myself that my commitment to morality is not just a foolish, imprudent indulgence that risks my welfare and the security of those who depend on me? Obviously, the argument that morality is the condition of my future happiness will not do, since my happiness is what morality now threatens. Equally unconvincing is the argument that I am not fully rational if I abandon morality. Ordinarily, I have every reason to want to be rational, since one who is irrational cannot adequately pursue the satisfaction of his or her desires. But is it clear that I want to be rational in this special moral sense if it leads to the destruction of all my hopes for personal fulfillment? We could continue on in this way reviewing possible rational arguments for moral obedience, but I think the essential point has been made: in the end, all such arguments are either circular or beg key questions that a rational individual may ask.

Thus, Kant's own general deduction of the priority of the categorical imperative exposes in a new and disturbing way a problem at the heart of moral reasoning: *we cannot necessarily justify the strict priority of duty over happiness to an individual whose own happiness is in peril.* This is the problem, I believe, that underlies Kant's introduction of the idea of the "highest good" in the "Dialectic" of the second *Critique.* Having developed the logic of duty more precisely than ever before, Kant now also sees the failure of this logic where individual commitment is concerned. This is why, in the context of a discussion of the "totality" of conditions required for morality, he now insists that every impartial rational person must hold out as an object of his or her will, and as really attainable, the perfect and exceptionless union of virtue and happiness. For if it were true that not a single discrepancy between these two were possible, then the problem of justification would vanish. Each moral agent could obey whatever the moral law commands without facing the possibility of doing something that any aspect of reason might brand as irrational. Human reason, in both its prudential and moral employments, would thus become "harmonious with itself."[36]

Putting matters this way, however, merely moves the problem to another level. For now the question becomes: is it reasonable to believe in the attainability of the highest good, this exceptionless union of virtue and happiness? This is the question to which Kant's attention turns as the argument of the "Dialectic" proceeds. He begins by dismissing as misleading "analytic" answers. These hold virtue and happiness to imply one another logically, either because virtue produces its own reward of inner contentment and well-being or because real happiness is unthinkable without virtuous conduct. These were the views of the Stoics and Epicureans, respectively, Kant observes, but, however noble these views might be, they are fundamentally mistaken.[37] Virtue and happiness are two essentially different things, and we cannot connect them in these ways. The Epicureans made the mistake of inverting the proper order of virtue and happiness. The refined satisfactions whose pursuit they counsel are not the same thing as obedience to duty. The Stoics confused the self-satisfaction of virtue, what Kant calls "contentment," and the joys of a good conscience, with happiness. But happiness is not the same thing as moral self-approval: it is the experience over the course of life where "everything goes according to one's wish and will."[38] The Stoics make a further mistake in urging these satisfactions of virtue as a reason for being moral. Since these satisfactions derive from a prior acceptance of the authority of the moral law and conscience, can one really recommend them to persons who want to know why they should be moral in the first place?[39]

The moral law and happiness, therefore, are not linked analytically, and relating them like this does not help with the problem of justification. Instead, we must regard virtue and happiness as independent concepts, and if we connect them at all, we must do so within our experience as a "synthetic" unity of cause and effect. Virtue must somehow produce happiness for those who are upright. With the nature of the highest good thus clarified, Kant now poses the problem of the highest good in sharpest terms as an "antinomy of practical reason" reminiscent of the antinomies of the first *Critique*. On one side of the antinomy is the assertion that happiness and virtue may be thought of as linked to one another as cause to effect. On the other side is the assertion that the relationship is the reverse, that virtue is the efficient cause of happiness. The first proposition or thesis, Kant states, is absolutely impossible since we can never regard our ability to pursue happiness as the ground of our moral worth. But the second proposition, the antithesis, also seems impossible, since "every practical connection of causes and effects in the world...is dependent not on the moral intentions of the will but on knowledge of natural laws and the physical capacity of using them to its purposes."[40] In other words, not morality but strength and cunning are what seem to determine people's worldly fortunes.

We thus seem to face a complete refutation of the possibility of the "highest good" and, as a result, are forced to accept the "falsity of the moral law."[41] We are led to this conclusion, Kant continues, only if the second proposition, that a virtuous disposition necessarily produces happiness, is *absolutely* false. But we have no grounds for asserting this with certainty. For one thing, as the first *Critique* has shown, we cannot say that our experience of cause and effect is the only kind of causality there is in the world: it is possible that worldly events may ultimately be governed by an intelligible or "noumenal" causality actuated by morality. Indeed, Kant adds, in our own irrefutable experience of moral freedom and our ability to be determined by only the categorical imperative, we already encounter a limited form of moral causality, and this warrants our belief that a more powerful causality of this kind may be at work in the world.[42] Kant devotes much of the "Analytic" of the second *Critique* and long portions of the third section of the *Foundations* to a transcendental deduction of freedom as a condition of our activity as rational and moral beings.[43] Because freedom is both presupposed and given in our intellectual and volitional experience, he concludes, the second part of the antinomy is not absolutely false. Therefore, to the extent that we refuse to limit our understanding of the nature of reality to worldly experience, we have grounds for believing in the attainability of the highest good and, with this, for rationally upholding our commitment to the moral law.

Kant's honest wrestling with the difficult problem of moral justification exposed by his own work in ethics, therefore, culminates in the admission of religious belief as a necessary presupposition of rational moral commitment. As his discussion proceeds, Kant vests the supreme moral causality to which his argument points with the qualities of understanding and will, and it becomes recognizable as the God of traditional faith. Kant also introduces the idea of the possible immortality of the soul, not to guarantee eschatological reward, but to provide the limitless opportunity for the self-perfection needed to attain perfect virtue. But these matters are refinements. Already at the conclusion of the antinomy of practical reason, moral reasoning has become religious, obliged, as Kant puts it, "to seek at such a distance...in the context of an intelligible world"[44] the warrant for those concepts needed to ground and complete its activity.

A final major problem tackled by Kant in the "Dialectic" returns us to epistemological matters. It concerns which aspect of reason, the moral or theoretical, has "primacy" when the interests of the two seem to conflict. We can state the problem as follows: given the first *Critique*'s strong emphasis on the experiential rootage of our knowledge and Kant's criticism of traditional metaphysics, is it not now peculiar to insist that moral commitment must find its grounding in admittedly transcendent ideas?

Does this not violate the important "interest" of theoretical reason in restricting knowledge to the domain of experience (or its attendant a priori concepts) and in preventing speculative inquiry beyond the bounds of sensory experience? After all, if human wishes and needs were taken as a legitimation of nonempirical beliefs about reality, where would it stop? Would not all sorts of dreams and illusions swarm forth to eclipse rational knowledge of the world?

Kant is obviously sensitive to these objections, since they reflect the position he developed in the first *Critique*, but he is unwilling to allow them final say. If purely subjective needs were the motivation for this transcendental movement of reason, he observes, it would not be allowed. In that case, "Mohammad's paradise or the fusion with the deity of the theosophists and mystics...would press their monstrosities on reason and it would be as well to have no reason at all..."[45] But we are not here dealing with a merely subjective need. We confront ideas "belonging imprescriptibly to the practical interest of pure [moral] reason," ideas inseparably linked to the validity of the moral law. To reject these ideas out of deference to the "interest" of theoretical reason, in Kant's view, would fail to respect the proper ordering of the interests of reason. For pure practical (moral) reason also has an interest. This is in guaranteeing the totality of conditions needed to warrant its imperatives. When this interest conflicts with that of the theoretical reason, the latter must give way "because every interest is ultimately practical, even that of speculative [theoretical] reason being only conditional and reaching perfection only in practical use."[46]

Like so many of Kant's best insights, this defense of the "primacy" of practical over theoretical reason is brief and opaque. But I think I can suggest the meaning and power of his elliptical argument here by restating it in my own terms. To begin with, the "limiting" interest of theoretical reason is certainly important. Since reason is human beings' unique way of relating satisfactorily to the world, we can well understand why theoretical reason ordinarily wishes to prohibit flights of speculative fancy that threaten to lead us dangerously away from an adequate comprehension of reality. But practical reason also has its interests, and supreme among these is its interest in facilitating rational, moral commitment. Without such commitment, all our efforts, even those involved in knowing the world, are threatened by the anarchy of normless egoism that would replace moral conduct.[47] True, this grounding of morality may require some modest trespass beyond the normal limits of theoretical knowledge. But for theoretical reason to press its claims here regardless of the interests of practical reason would be deeply self-contradictory. Like an insistence on the absolute and unfettered right of journalistic freedom in time of war, it would lead to its own undoing. It would end by undermining not just moral reason but theoretical reason as well. For all reason is "ultimately practical," and even theoretical reason both presupposes and aims at a moral ordering of the world.

By a careful analysis of the nature and dictates of practical reason, Kant thus opens a narrow aperture in the restraining wall of human cognition he built in the first *Critique*. He shows the need for and legitimacy of certain very limited conceptual forays beyond the confines of sensory experience into the intelligible word or realm of "things-in-themselves." In the closing pages of the second *Critique*, Kant goes out of his way to ensure that these expeditions beyond the restraining wall are as limited as possible. He limits transcendent concepts to those few absolutely needed for the operation of moral reason: the "postulates" of God, immortality, and freedom. He also denies that, in affirming the reality of these objects for its practical purposes, reason attains knowledge in any theoretical sense. None of these postulates may be the object of any "intuition." Together, they are neither "knowledge" in the full sense nor merely subjective opinion, but an intermediate form of conviction that Kant variously terms "moral belief," "faith," or the "faith of pure practical reason." Since this faith lacks grounding in objective experience, it is never entirely certain, although its important relationship to moral commitment and its nonempirical content also render it immune to refutation. As a result, says Kant, this faith "can therefore often waver even in the well disposed but can never fall into unbelief."[48]

One might think that the limited certainty of this practical faith is unfortunate and constitutes an obstacle to the ambitions of practical reason. But in a closing series of remarks, Kant denies this. It is in every way desirable that the objects of practical faith remain distant and uncertain. For what would happen if the opposite were true? Then, Kant observes,

> instead of the conflict which now the moral disposition has to wage with the inclinations and in which, after some defeats, moral strength of mind may be gradually won, God and eternity in their awful majesty would stand unceasingly before our eyes...Thus most actions conforming to the law would be done from fear, few would be done from hope, none from duty.[49]

The terminological worlds of Kant and Kierkegaard are in many ways very different. Kant does not call faith a "leap," and we shall see that he sometimes even uses this term pejoratively to describe illegitimate religious moves. Nor would he call the content of faith "paradoxical" or "absurd." Nevertheless, in his understanding of this "faith of practical reason" as a self-postulated and always uncertain movement beyond the sphere of possible knowledge, Kant anticipates Kierkegaard.

Religion within the Limits of Reason Alone

In Kant's philosophy of religion, *Religion within the Limits of Reason Alone* deserves a place of its own. Whereas some aspects of the *Religion* are in direct continuity with the argument of the second *Critique*, others move in surprisingly new directions. This becomes apparent if we contrast Kant's discussion in the *Religion* with a parallel work by J. G. Fichte, the *Critique of All Attempts at Revelation*. Kant's *Critique of Practical Reason* directly inspired this youthful study by Fichte. It was published anonymously in 1792, and many readers even wrongly took it to be Kant's long awaited definitive statement on religion. But, although Fichte's study is a perceptive and intelligent extrapolation of the *Critique*, it moves in thoroughly predictable directions by carrying the morally interpreted ideas of God and immortality forward to create a rational framework for assessing revealed religion. In contrast, Kant devotes only a few pages in the Preface of the *Religion* to restating the argument of the second *Critique*. He then embarks on a long and penetrating discussion of human sinfulness and the possibility of moral redemption. Themes not even mentioned in the *Critique of Practical*

Reason move to the fore, making the *Religion* a very different work from Fichte's.

In stressing the novelty of Kant's discussion in the *Religion*, I don't wish to suggest that he departs from his previous position. On the contrary, the main argument in the *Religion* pivots absolutely around an insight already developed in the second *Critique* concerning the degree of human *rational* freedom to be moral and immoral. But whereas this idea was merely an implication of the argument in the *Critique*, it now becomes the point of departure for a fresh new approach to religious issues. Nothing so well illustrates Kant's philosophical honesty and the continuing vitality of his mind (Kant was sixty-nine when he published the *Religion*) than the way he allows his own logic to lead him down paths in this mature work that are not fully anticipated in earlier writings. In the decades following publication of the *Religion* it became fashionable among liberal critics of traditional religion to contend that this work represented a cowardly effort by a philosopher in his dotage to curry favor with political authorities or popular opinion by reinstating religious views his earlier work had repudiated.[50] This interpretation is based not only on a complete misreading of Kant's moral character, but also on a serious misunderstanding of the leading directions of his critical philosophy.

Kant devotes the first book of the *Religion* to an examination of what he calls the "radical evil" in human nature. He begins by observing the ancient and repeated complaints in so many cultures about human iniquity. Are these complaints justified, he asks? Are human beings morally evil, as so much opinion and experience seem to attest, or are we basically predisposed to good, as some more modern thinkers contend? If the less favorable opinion is true, and human beings are evil, how can we explain this? How can we account for the fact that beings who know the good become corrupted?

A first issue Kant proposes to examine is whether these debates about human nature have put the question properly. Maybe it is a mistake to render things so absolutely. Perhaps human beings are neither entirely good nor entirely evil, but a bit of both. "Experience," he says, "actually seems to substantiate the middle ground between these two extremes."[51]

Nevertheless, Kant replies, it is of great importance in ethics to avoid intermediate judgments that threaten to compromise clarity and precision. There is also no reason to focus here on the varied pattern of deeds, since, in evaluating a person's moral integrity, we must look not to exterior acts but to the underlying and general direction of the will, to the basic rule or highest maxim (*oberste Maxime*) of rational choice that directs all specific choices. If persons are morally good, this maxim is one of unswerving obedience to the dictates of duty. If they are not, this maxim gives precedence to what Kant calls "self-love," his general term for any private willing, however altruistic or compassionate, not approved by the categorical imperative. But what is the maxim of the presumably morally intermediate person? To the extent that he or she has a maxim—and not having one is culpable—is it not to comply with duty sometimes or even *most of the time* so long as doing so is not greatly inconvenient? But if this is true, what ultimately determines when this kind of person suspends duty? Is it not the decision that the "price" of obedience has risen too high or that some personal interest has become overwhelmingly important? But this amounts to being directed by some higher maxim of "self-love." One cannot, therefore, really be "partly good." The supposed intermediate state is not a moral stance at all, but a disguised or dishonest form of selfishness.

Against the background of this "rigoristic" understanding of the moral demand, Kant returns to the question of human nature. On the basis of experience, he observes, there is ample reason to believe that human beings commonly fail to live up to this standard, and hence we must view ourselves as having wills essentially not oriented toward morality. In this sense, everything we can tell about our species supports the opinion that we are evil by nature. Why is this so? Why do we regularly put self-interest before the requirements of duty? Part of the answer has to do with the active conflict we experience between the demands of duty and the pressing needs of our sensuous nature. The tug of sensuous inclinations furnishes an occasion for immoral willing, Kant observes. Nevertheless, he hastens to add, we cannot regard these inclinations as the cause of human immorality. This is so, first, because these natural inclinations are as much involved in good willing as in bad. They compose the "stuff" of our morally legislative reason and, in the strictest sense, are morally neutral. Second, if wrongdoing were traceable to natural inclinations beyond our control, our conduct would not then be morally blameworthy ("imputable"). But we know ourselves to be always morally capable of controlling and directing these inclinations, so the failure to do so must be owed to a culpable act of willing on our part.

These points are a perceptive development of the role freedom has in our thinking about moral conduct and choice. They represent a decisive rejection of the tendency in classical Greek ethics to attribute moral evil to the force of natural impulses or desires and to their overcoming of reason, a tendency that contradicts this same tradition's insistence on the supremacy of reason in human choice. But if we must think of ourselves as free and determinable, not by natural forces, but by purely rational and moral concepts, why does it happen that we inevitably choose the course of self-love over morality? Why, if we are rational beings, is our behavior not more decisively shaped by reason's supreme expression, the moral law?

In the *Religion*, Kant offers no answer to this important question. In part, I believe, this is because all his previous work on ethics, particularly his argument in the second *Critique*, has already pointed to an "answer." There, we saw, Kant focused much of his attention on the difficult problem of moral justification exposed by his previous analysis of the moral law. If the moral law's supremacy derives from its logically necessary role as the guarantee of individual happiness, how do we justify moral obedience to individuals when their happiness (the consummate object of self-love) is jeopardized? Kant's "answer" to this question, we saw, was the introduction of transcendent, religious elements into the moral reasoning process, a series of warranted beliefs about ultimate reality that made self-love and moral duty correspond.

Kant's argument in the second *Critique* is sometimes called the moral "proof" of the existence of God, but although Kant uses this term himself in the "Critique of the Teleological Judgment,"[52] it is somewhat misleading. Kant's argument is in no way meant to "prove" either God's existence or the necessity of being moral to one who wishes to reject either or both. Instead, Kant's argument is a derivation of the logical presuppositions of fully rational action. On Kant's account, the individual who wants to act rationally faces a serious problem because the dictates of prudence and morality seem opposed. For example, one can opt to be immoral and to satisfy the demands of prudence, but one can never expect the approval of one's moral reason in doing so. Or one can choose morality, but then the voice of prudence, basing itself on the lessons of experience, seems to issue a veto. Faced with this impasse, how can one act in a fully reasoned way at all?

We know that Kant answers these questions by postulating religious realities that have the effect of ending the conflict between moral and prudential reason. If we suppose that worldly experience is not the only, nor even the definitive, kind of connection of causes to effects, then we have some reason to believe that moral choice is also always prudent. True, this belief rests on uncertain cognitive grounds. But the alternatives, choice in defiance of reason in one or another of its employments, or choice without reason, may be more unpalatable for a being who wishes to be rational.

Restated this way, we can see that Kant's argument is no "proof." It is not meant to demonstrate the reality of God or immortality to one who resists these beliefs because we cannot reasonably persuade such a person by nondemonstrable statements about objects transcending experience. Nor is it meant to show that one must be rational in the fullest sense of being committed to morality because it is just this commitment that lacks complete rational justification. Rather, for one who has already made the commitment to morality, this argument is an exploration of ways of doing so in a fully rational manner, and it presumes a wish to be completely rational in this way. Hence, in every respect, none of these commitments or beliefs is required. Belief in God, Kant observes, represents "a voluntary decision of our judgment...itself not commanded" by reason.[53] And if the position as a whole has any force, it is not because reason requires it but rather, as he says in the *Critique of Judgment*, "because no other expedient is left to make reason harmonious with itself."[54] As Allen Wood has put it, Kant's moral faith "is the choice of finite rationality to remain rational while confronted by its finitude, the choice of sober hope rather than wild despair."[55]

Against this background, we can see how dramatically and how radically Kant has exposed the degree of human freedom with regard to moral choice. It is not merely, as he shows in the *Religion*, that we cannot think of ourselves as necessitated by natural impulses. We are also not in any way necessitated by *reason* to act morally. *We are free to choose between the demands of impulse and reason.* Departing from a tradition of rationalist thought, Kant has shown that a deduction of the logic of rational morality does not amount to a justification of individual obedience to moral reason. By exploring the circularities and question begging of all such defenses, he has shown how nearly completely free we are to make a rational decision not to be moral. True, such a decision always invokes the protest of our moral reason. But apart from a prior commitment to reason and to the freely assumed religious beliefs needed to support it, this protest is unconvincing. Being moral and religious rests on a love of reason that cannot itself be rationally required, and being immoral is not irrational in every sense of the word. We can even see that reason, in its prudential and cognitive activity, can strongly lend itself to immoral choice.[56]

Immorality, then, has its source in the human will, in an undetermined, free choice to place our own interests above the demands of the moral law. But if this is so, why do we seem so persistently to exercise our will in this selfish fashion? Part, but only part, of the answer lies in the tug of our sensuous inclinations and finite nature. God, whose will we think of as holy, has no inclinations that contradict the moral law, and for him duty does not even take the form of an imperative.[57] Nevertheless, for all their force, these desires do not determine our conduct, and they can even contribute to upright behavior, since the moral law has as its aim the satisfaction of everyone's desires. Our radical freedom also plays a role in the process of wrongwilling. In its rigorous ideality, the moral law does not permit a single exception to its mandates, but in repeated choices made in utter freedom, a person may sometimes err. However, to trace wrongwilling to freedom in this way explains nothing, since, if we are free to be moral, what we must explain is why we knowingly choose, even once, to exercise our freedom in an immoral way.

Against this background, we can see why Kant deliberately refuses in the *Religion* to explain why we are immoral. Precisely because this "perversion of the will" rests on a misuse of freedom, he says, its origin must remain "inscrutable" to us. Our concept of causation, we must remember, involves the assumption that an occurrence is necessarily linked to its temporal antecedent. However, if our choice of a basic maxim of volition were "caused" in this way, if it were determined by some prior event in time and space, we would not be accountable for it. But we always know ourselves to be free to resist natural impulses, and we properly regard ourselves as blameworthy for failing to do so. Hence, we cannot trace our fundamental maxim of wickedness to anything but an unnecessitated choice, which, if we tried to explain it, could only be "referred back endlessly" to a series of free and unnecessitated maxims of choice.[58]

Having used moral concepts to develop the idea of the "radical evil" of the human will and its origin in an inscrutable free use of our will, Kant concludes his discussion of human nature with a modest rehabilitation and "demythologization" of the orthodox doctrine of original sin. To be sure, he insists, we cannot attribute human iniquity to a flaw inherited from our "first parents," for then we would not be responsible for it, as we know ourselves to be. Of all the explanations of human evil, says Kant, this emphasis on the inheritance of sin is "the most inept."[59]

Yet the myth of the Fall presented in Genesis conveys several important moral truths. In its attribution of guilt to the parents of our race it suggests the omnipresence of sin in each of us. For as they acted, so each of us acts on innumerable occasions. *Mutato nomine de te fabula narratur* ("Change but the name, of you the tale is told").[60] In its depiction of a free and culpable fall from innocence, it captures the essential nonnecessitation, the "originality" of each act of wrongful willing.[61] And in its tracing of human iniquity back to the beginning of history, it suggests a reality experienced in each of our lives: that our guilt is traceable to the earliest remembered exercise of our wills.[62]

Kant's assessment of human sin thus ends with a dramatic reappropriation of the orthodox religious doctrine of original sin. Because of even one instance of mischoice in the past, each of us has reason to believe (or "postulate," as Kant says) that our underlying maxim is corrupt and that we are guilty of what, from the unyielding perspective of reason's requirements, is equivalent to a total defection from the dictates of the moral law. This is the source of an "infinite guilt," which, says Kant, entails "endless punishment" and permanent "exclusion from the kingdom of God." This kingdom is Kant's religiously designated goal of all our striving: a commonwealth of rational creatures experiencing the union of perfect virtue and happiness. But if, in the second *Critique*, this goal was threatened primarily by the seeming unattainability of happiness, now it is jeopardized by the unattainability of virtue following even a single act of selfish willing.

This pessimistic conclusion is admittedly an odd one for a philosopher whose work began on the Enlightenment premise that human beings can know, and presumably do, what the moral law requires. Among some students of Kant's philosophy of religion, it is a common belief that in the *Religion* Kant's religious background came to predominate over his philosophy. William Peck expresses this viewpoint when he remarks that "Kant's moral convictions, but not his rationalist philosophy, lead him to insist on the reality of evil in human life and to emphasize its all-pervasive character and influence, its deep roots in human nature and conduct."[63] Against this popular viewpoint, I think we can now better see that Kant was led to these conclusions regarding human sin by the remorseless logic of his understanding of morality and the depth of human freedom with respect to it. *Kant's doctrine of radical evil is neither a well- nor ill-intentioned appendix to his critical philosophy. It is the inevitable result of that philosophy's discovery of the reality and structure of moral freedom.*

From this point forward in his work, if Kant is to defend the reasonability of continued moral effort, his deduction of the logical conditions of human willing must grow correspondingly more complex. Indeed, what we see at the end of the first book and throughout the second book of the *Religion* is a renewed "religious" effort by Kant to reestablish the possibility of rational moral striving in the face of the impasse he has just described. At the heart of this discussion is the idea that people who wish to be morally worthy must respond to their necessary sense of moral inadequacy with an act of deep repentance and change, what Kant calls a "revolution" or "rebirth" in the moral disposition.[64] They must seek to reorient their will to the moral law and continue their moral efforts in the hope that this renewed striving will mark the beginning of a long and continuing course of moral excellence. How is this possible? How can renewed effort overcome what seems to be an ineradicable basic flaw? "If a man is corrupt in the very ground of his maxims, how can he possibly bring about this revolution by his own powers and of himself become a good man?"[65]

Kant's answer to his own question is complex. First, there is the fact that "duty bids us do this."[66] No matter how paralyzed we may be by our sense of moral incapacity, duty's voice is clear, and its presence within gives us reason to believe that what we are called to do may be within our powers. Second, no human being can be absolutely sure about the basic maxim that determines his or her choices. As the timeless ground of all our phenomenal choices, this maxim belongs to the intelligible realm and is beyond the range of our phenomenally based cognition: "Not even does a man's inner experience with regard to himself enable him so to fathom the depths of his own heart as to obtain, through self-observation, quite certain knowledge of the basis of the maxims which he possesses."[67] As a result, each individual has reason to hope that what seems to us mere persistence in an "ever-enduring struggle" may really be a testimony to the revolution in our disposition, and we may also hope that for God, "who penetrates to the intelligible ground of the heart," this rededication and continued struggle bear witness to the innermost quality of our wills.[68]

But even with these confidences the individual who would effect this revolution of disposition faces some very serious further difficulties. For example, how can we be sure of the constancy and unchangeability of our disposition in all future choices? Given our freely chosen selfishness on even one past occasion, what warrants our thinking better of ourselves in the future? Equally serious is the problem posed by our past misdeeds and wrongful choices. This past record, says Kant, constitutes a debt we can never wipe out, for a person "cannot regard the fact that he incurs no new debts subsequent to his change of heart as equivalent to having discharged old ones."[69] Furthermore, since it is always our duty to do all the good that lies in our power, where are we to find the "surplus" needed to repay our past moral debts?

Kant responds to each of these problems and questions with a series of quasi-religious ideas involving heavily moralized interpretations of biblical teachings. To the problem of the demand for perpetual steadfastness of will, for example, he advances the idea that one who perseveres in uprightness over the course of his life has reason to regard this continuing rectitude as grounds for confidence in unending moral improvement, even into eternity. We may regard this "good and pure disposition," says Kant, as a "good spirit presiding over us," or as the "Comforter (Paraclete)" promised by scripture.

In response to the problem of past deeds, Kant advances the idea that we may regard the anguish caused by the consciousness of our past wrongs and our willingness to accept as punishments all future sufferings that come our way as forming an adequate satisfaction for prior misconduct. Morally speaking, however, there is a serious further problem. Since the individual who undergoes this moral revolution of repentance is, in a basic sense, no longer his old self, how can he be asked to suffer punishment for that previous person's wrongdoing? Kant's answer is that this punishment may be regarded as a form of vicarious suffering. In the moment of moral transformation, the morally good new man voluntarily undertakes sufferings due the old self (although these sufferings for him cease to be "punishments" in the strict sense of the word and become sufferings undertaken for the sake of moral improvement).[70] Kant finds this immanent moral conception biblically expressed in the idea of a single representative of all sinners, the Son of God, who renders satisfaction to the supreme justice through his suffering death.

In terms of the centuries-old debate on the role of works or grace in the economy of redemption, Kant's discussion maintains what Gordon E. Michalson, Jr., describes as a "fragile balance" between an appeal to "something 'outside' me that I seem to require for salvation, and the epistemological self-sufficiency of my own conscience."[71] On the one hand, Kant is unwilling to adopt a fully transcendent religious solution to the problem of persistent human evil he has identified. Jesus Christ is not here a "redeemer" whose suffering death atones for human iniquity and reconciles human beings to God. Instead, he is the mythological expression of an idea of moral purity always resident within our reason (the "archetype" of a morally perfected disposition), or he is the mythologized depiction of the process of vicarious suffering that must occur within each of our moral consciousnesses. Nor does Kant relinquish the demand that, despite repeated and seemingly insurmountable failures, we must always continue to renew our efforts at moral reform.

On the other hand, Kant is prepared to concede a substantial role in the process of redemption to factors that go beyond the recognized limits of our own moral striving. For example, to the extent that someone has made use of his original predisposition to good to become morally better, says Kant, that individual "can hope that what is not within his power will be supplied through cooperation from above."[72] This assistance takes several forms. First, we may look to God for that single intuitive judgment of our heart needed to transform what must always seem to us only an infinite *becoming* into the possibility of the actual possession of virtue.[73] Second, belief in God's presence in our will (in the form of a morally good disposition) sustains our confidence in the stability of that disposition through all our future willing.[74] Finally, it is divine grace, also present in this indwelling good disposition, that supplies the surplus needed to overcome our past defections from the moral law. By willingly assuming the punishments due the old man within us, this disposition makes satisfaction to God for the wrongs we have done.[75]

Another way of viewing Kant's "solution" to the problem of human iniquity here is to see that it follows the pattern established for the resolution of major rational antinomies in the first two *Critiques*. On the one hand, there is a "thesis" drawn from experience (in combination with moral reason) that points to the certitude of moral condemnation where there has been even one instance of wrongwilling. On the other hand, there is the rational "antithesis" derived entirely from the moral law. This involves duty's requirement that we morally press on and duty's refusal to accept the excuse of our persistent past failures as a reason for not doing so.

As with all the previous antinomies, Kant resolves this one with reference to a possible but unknowable intelligible domain beyond our experience. Within this domain, the supreme moral causality previously postulated as proportioning happiness to virtue is now regarded as sustaining our will and as accepting our penitent suffering as satisfaction for the wrongs we have done. Since this divine agency operates in a different moral domain than we do, it may be able morally to forgive what we cannot. And, since it makes itself known in and through our moral disposition and sense of moral requiredness, no direct contradiction with our moral conceptions or moral experience need be involved.[76] On our side, we must always place this disposition foremost in our thinking and strive to develop it. It is the point of departure and the object of our moral willing, and we may never substitute for it a passive reliance on divine grace. Nor may we replace it with morally hollow expiations, penances, ceremonies, or expressions of praise of God.[77] Belief in the divine support of our project of moral reform, therefore, does not alter our conduct or the "practical" side of our reasoned activity. This remains focused on moral willing. Whatever "comfort and hope" it provides serves only to answer the "speculative question" about the possibility of redemption despite the reality of sin. Nevertheless, as hemmed in as it is, this speculative question is not unimportant and should not be "passed over in silence." For without an answer to it, Kant concludes, "reason could be accused of being wholly unable to reconcile with divine justice man's hope of absolution from his guilt."[78]

Kant's discussion in the *Religion* continues in the third and fourth books with a lengthy treatment of ecclesiological matters, especially the development of a heavily moralized conception of the Christian church. This discussion offers Kant an opportunity to express his own sharp personal opposition to forms of historically revealed religion, "clericalism" and "pseudo-service" to God. Throughout, Kant speaks with the voice of the Enlightenment, and one senses in the swiftness and vigor of his discussion that he is on more familiar and more comfortable terrain examining these issues than he has been in the tortuous reasoning that marks the initial portions of his discussion. For in the first two books of the *Religion*, Kant has gone a long way toward dissolving some of the basic confidences that animated his earlier work as well as that of many of his rationalist predecessors. Developing and defending rational human freedom with such acuity, Kant has discovered that we are rationally free *from* the demands of the moral law. He has also illuminated, as never before, the demands of morality and has led us to the necessary human admission of our persistent failure to comply with these demands. Finally, in response to these problems, Kant has proposed a series of conceptual solutions which, though consistent with his epistemology and ethics, are strongly reminiscent of some classical Christian ideas about grace.

The Conflict of the Faculties

With this work, we conclude the development of Kant's mature philosophy of religion. Like the *Religion*, it began as a single essay published separately and later joined with related material to form a book. Unlike the *Religion*, however, this additional material does not form an organic whole. Under the premise of reconciling conceptual disputes among the various faculties of the university, Kant discusses in sequence conflicts between philosophy and theology, philosophy and law, and philosophy and medicine. Only the first of these three discussions is of interest to us.

In most respects, Kant's essay "The Conflict of the Philosophy Faculty with the Theology Faculty" offers nothing new. The essay lacks any significant philosophical development over the themes of the *Religion*. For example, although the problem of virtually ineradicable human sinfulness is accepted as a background assumption, there is no further discussion here of the origins of the problem. Instead, Kant chooses to intensify his polemic against a historical-revelational standpoint in religious matters and to deepen his insistence on the purely rational point of departure for all the concepts and confidences needed for moral-religious salvation.

Kant signals his mood and intention early in the essay in a key passage whose sharp tone is perhaps explained by Kant's own recent bouts with religious censors over the publication of the *Religion*:[79]

> The biblical theologian says: "Search the Scriptures, where you think you find eternal life." But since our moral improvement

is the sole condition of eternal life, the only way we can find eternal life in any Scripture whatsoever is by putting it there. For the concepts and principles required for eternal life cannot really be learned from anyone else: the teacher's exposition is only the occasion for him to develop them out of his own reason.[80]

Later, in Chapter 3, we will return to this passage and explore its dramatic impact on Kierkegaard's thinking and authorship. But for now, it is enough to signal Kant's strong position taking against any historical or revelational point of departure for human moral or religious improvement. Everything we need to know for salvation, he insists, resides within us.

Despite its sharp beginning, Kant means this essay to be a resolution of the dispute between the theological and philosophical faculties. In keeping with this project, he proposes a series of "principles of scriptural exegesis" for settling disputes between philosophical and theological readings of scripture. Foremost among these is a principle requiring any scriptural text containing theoretical teachings transcending (or defying) rational concepts to be interpreted solely in terms of the interests of practical reason. Thus, the scriptural teaching of the Incarnation, Kant tells us, should not be interpreted literally since "we can draw nothing practical" and can find no moral example in the idea of God dwelling incarnate in some particular historical person. Instead, we must think of the Incarnation in terms of the morally energizing "idea of humanity in its full moral perfection."[81]

Almost as an aside, in the course of offering further examples of his exegetical principles, Kant returns in this essay to the themes of grace and redemption. In doing so, he appears to intensify themes sketched in the *Religion*. As in the *Religion*, for example, Kant makes clear that human beings need grace to complete their religious and moral redemption. "If man's own deeds are not sufficient to justify him before his conscience (as it judges him strictly), reason is entitled to adopt on faith a supernatural supplement to fill what is lacking in his justification."[82] Now, however, Kant makes clear that this belief is not merely an option for some but an indispensable practical proposition of moral faith, since, as he says, "only by it can man cease to doubt that he can reach his final end (to become pleasing to God) and so lay hold of the courage and firmness of attitude he needs to lead a life pleasing to God."[83]

As strongly as he emphasizes the need for the presumption of grace in our moral thinking, however, Kant also returns to his insistence on the primacy of practical, moral striving in our progress toward redemption. As always for Kant, the foe is any kind of ecclesiastical encouragement to rely on grace instead of moral works. In terms of scriptural interpretation, this leads Kant to insist that "action must be represented as issuing from man's own use of his moral powers, not as an effect [resulting] from the influence of an external, higher cause by whose activity man is passively healed."[84] It also leads him to insist on the essential pointlessness and unimportance of any kind of theoretical investigation into the mechanisms by which grace works on or through the human will. Since such mechanisms are supersensible, we cannot know anything about them apart from their final effect on our own heightened sense of moral requiredness and rededication. It is these, rather than speculative questions, to which we should turn our attention through renewed moral striving.

A discerning reader of The Conflict of the Faculties may see a difficulty in Kant's position. Although his agnosticism regarding theoretical knowledge of the mechanisms of grace is fully consistent with his epistemological and moral views, it is not clear that such agnosticism can extend to the fact that grace has been bestowed. Kant himself appears to suggest that only a practically efficacious confidence in the fact that my sins have been forgiven can allow me to cease to doubt and "lay hold of the courage" needed for renewed moral exertion. In other words, just as I must believe in the reality of God to sustain rational striving in the face of the world's moral adversity, so I must believe in God's grace to ground my rational striving for virtue following the discovery of my sinfulness.

But if this is so, is it really true that all speculative questions can be put aside as one singlemindedly renews moral effort? Kant seems to think so, lumping together inquiry into the fact of grace with specific theological speculations on its various mechanisms and effects. At one point in this essay, for example, he considers a problem in his emphasis on the primacy of moral striving, placing in the mouth of an unnamed interlocutor the following objection:

> To believe that God, by an act of kindness, will in some unknown way fill what is lacking to our justification is to assume gratuitously a cause that will satisfy the need we feel (it is to commit a *petitio principii*); for when we expect something by the grace of a superior, we cannot assume that we must get it as a matter of course; we can expect it only if it was actually promised to us, as in a formal contract. So it seems that we can hope for that supplement and assume that we shall get it only in so far as it has actually been pledged through divine *revelation*, not as a stroke of luck.[85]

It is a measure of Kant's self-honesty that he should present this objection in all its force. It is a measure of his uncertainty on this new frontier of grace and moral reason that his reply to the objection is less than convincing. This reply embraces two familiar Kantian themes. First, we are unequipped cognitively to recognize a divine bestowal of grace: "A direct revelation from God embodied in the comforting statement 'Your sins are forgiven you' would be a supersensible experience, and this is impossible."[86] Second, there is his insistence that *knowledge* of such forgiveness is unnecessary and even undesirable. Since, as sinners, there is no way we can conceive the unyielding decrees of a holy and benevolent lawgiver unless we assume the possibility of forgiveness, we have all the practical certainty we need in the bestowal of his grace. Furthermore, "if without the aid of a definite, empirically given promise, we have a rational faith and trust in His help, we show better evidence of a pure moral attitude and so of receptivity to the manifestation of grace we hope for than we could by empirical belief."[87]

This last point is Kant's familiar insistence, encountered at the end of the second *Critique*, that the uncertainty of faith, by leaving room for free decision, is morally superior to knowledge. But although this point makes sense in the sphere of an untroubled commitment to morality, we can ask whether it is any longer applicable in the deeply unsettled region disclosed by the discovery of human sinfulness. For it is characteristic of this realm that it is permeated by the awareness of repeated false starts and complex self-deceptions. Is it really the case that in the

wake of the discovery of his or her sin any person can find sufficient confidence to renew moral exertion merely in the inner urg-
ings of the moral command and the unsubstantiated rational
"hope" for grace? Or is Kant's interlocutor right: that only a definite promise somehow rooted in experience and history is needed? As we'll see in the chapters ahead, this is the essential point
of disagreement between Kierkegaard and Kant. Again and
again, Kierkegaard will follow Kant's philosophy to this impasse
in *The Conflict of the Faculties* and will, in countless ways and
with intensified sophistication, reiterate the objection of Kant's
interlocutor.

Kant's whole critical effort thus concludes at the doorstep of
some of the major premises of Christian orthodoxy. Whether or
not Kant actually took the step into Christian faith, he pointed
the way for those who wished to do so. Furthermore, Kant's
work lent enormous credibility to those who would defend the
validity of orthodox teachings in the face of its cultured despis-
ers. For here was Kant, the philosopher whom Kierkegaard
regarded as standing "at the pinnacle of scientific culture,"[88]
wrestling seriously with some of these same orthodox teachings.
In the chapters ahead we'll see that the encounter with Kant's
mature thought sustained Kierkegaard's own keen sense of the
limits of philosophy and ethics. Kierkegaard may ultimately have
disagreed with Kant on the matter of the significance of historical revelation. In doing so, however, he did not merely abandon
Kant's philosophy but used its entire structure of epistemological, ethical, and religious categories to complete in Christian
terms the project Kant had begun.

CHAPTER 3

Points of Contact

> If one were to concentrate in one single descriptive word the delusion and confusion of modern science and scholarship—or essentially the delusion and confusion of the modern age, especially since it abandoned Kant's honest way and paid the well-known 100 dollars in order to become theocentric, then one might say: it is *dishonest.*
>
> —Kierkegaard, *Papers*, 1847[1]

Kierkegaard's debt to Kant extends to all three major areas of Kant's critical writings: epistemology, ethics, and philosophy of religion. In each of these areas, Kierkegaard's relationship to Kant ranges from direct appropriation of Kant's ideas (or his terms and illustrations) to substantial disagreements and arguments with the philosopher. In this chapter I explore a number of matters in which we can perceive this process of appropriation-argument. None of these matters is central to Kierkegaard's authorship. Together they represent only important "occasional pieces" in the furnishing of his intellectual house. In the next chapter, in contrast, we'll explore ideas that are crucial to the development of Kierkegaard's thinking, that constitute the "main timbers" of his intellectual edifice. Here, even his disagreements with Kant, which are both more focused and more important, evolve out of a sustained engagement with Kantian philosophy and make it legitimate to regard Kierkegaard's entire viewpoint as deeply Kantian.

EPISTEMOLOGY

Kierkegaard's involvement with Kant's epistemology has a manifest side composed largely of expressed disagreements with Kant's conception of the *Ding an sich* and a latent side where Kierkegaard takes over from Kant a number of key insights. The disagreements figure importantly among the few overt references to Kant in Kierkegaard's writings. Taken by themselves, these references seem to place Kierkegaard in opposition to Kant, although when we examine them closely and in their development, I think we can see that even here Kierkegaard's disagreement is subtle and places him far closer to Kant than to Kant's later Idealist followers.

An early entry in the *Papers* from 1837 expresses Kierkegaard's opposition to Kant's approach to religious knowledge:

> In the presentation of supernaturalism there is a difficulty, for what Kant pointed out is probably true, that if there is no theoretical knowledge, then this obviously means that the entire sphere of the *an sich* is excluded from human consciousness and therefore never comes to man through consciousness either, and I therefore readily concede to Goschel that nonknowledge consistently ends in nonfaith—but therefore the supernaturalist maintains also that there must be a complete change in consciousness, that a development must begin from the very beginning and [be] just as eternal in idea as the first. It is therefore probably a mistake for the supernaturalist to link his faith to the nonknowledge of Kant, because as stated, from the nonknowledge of Kant must come nonfaith, and the supernaturalist's faith is precisely a new consciousness. The error appears more clearly in rationalism, which remains within the very same limits of consciousness, yet without discovering that if nonknowledge is admitted in the Kantian sense, he can never get faith in his sense within the same consciousness, and that the only means of attaining faith in this way is a more profound investigation of the nature of consciousness.[2]

From this early remark, one might conclude that Kierkegaard envisions the possibility of fashioning some kind of epistemological response to Kant's skepticism about the possibility of knowledge of ultimate reality, perhaps by identifying, after the fashion of Schleiermacher, some special religious consciousness through which we might enter into relationship with God. But Kierkegaard never moves in this direction. As his authorship progresses, faith becomes for him a leap beyond knowledge, a leap into the absurd with its point of departure in ethical-religious experience. In view of this, it is interesting to observe that Kierkegaard's disagreement with Kant about knowledge of things-in-themselves assumes a different character in later remarks. Now the point is not that Kant's religious epistemology as a whole is wrong, but that Kant made an initial mistake in his discussion of the thing-in-itself by bringing the treatment of ultimate reality into connection with thought rather than moral experience. Since Kant had actually shifted the grounding of religion from theoretical knowledge to ethics, Kierkegaard's criticism is a modest one, and the full brunt of it is now reserved, as in the following remark in the *Postscript*, for the Hegelians, who have converted Kant's small misstep into a philosophical movement:

> Instead of conceding the contention of Idealism, but in such a manner as to dismiss as a temptation the entire problem of a reality in the sense of a thing-in-itself eluding thought, which like other temptations cannot be vanquished by giving way to it; instead of putting an end to Kant's misleading reflection which brings reality into connection with thought; instead of relegating reality to the ethical—Hegel scored a veritable advance; for he became fantastic and vanquished idealistic skepticism by means of pure thought, which is merely an hypothesis, and even if it does not so declare itself, a fantastic hypothesis.[3]

It is not clear, then, that, in his overt criticisms of the Kantian idea of the thing-in-itself, Kierkegaard is really signalling a fundamental difference with Kant. By stressing the priority of ethical actuality for religious faith, and by avoiding the "temptation" to indulge in any kind of speculative approach to the religious problem, Kierkegaard actually effects a movement "back to Kant" on the crucial matter of how the religious is to be approached.

This hint of a deeper but undeveloped affinity between Kant and Kierkegaard is accentuated when we look at a series of interesting similarities between the two thinkers on epistemological matters. Five specific parallels suggest themselves. A first one concerns the notion that human cognition has the inherent tendency to extend itself beyond its allowable limits. For Kant, this idea lies behind the unavoidable "dialectic of reason" he diagnoses in the first *Critique*; for Kierkegaard it constitutes the "passion" that contributes to thought's undoing and points the way to faith. Consider the following two remarks, the first of which serves as the opening passage of the *Critique of Pure Reason* and the second of which opens Kierkegaard's discussion of "The Absolute Paradox" in the *Philosophical Fragments*:

Kant:

> Human reason has this peculiar fate that in one species of its knowledge it is burdened by questions which, as prescribed by the very nature of reason itself, it is not able to ignore, but which, as transcending all its powers, it is also not able to answer.[4]

Kierkegaard:

> But one must not think ill of the paradox, for the paradox is the passion of thought, and the thinker without the paradox is like the lover without passion: a mediocre fellow. But the ultimate potentiation of every passion is always to will its own downfall, and so it is also the ultimate passion of the understanding [*Forstand*] to will the collision, although in one way or another the collision must become its downfall. This, then, is the ultimate paradox of thought: to want to discover something that thought itself cannot think.[5]

A second and related parallel to Kant's epistemology appears in Kierkegaard's treatment in this chapter of the *Fragments* of the problem of thought beyond the boundary of human knowledge, in the domain of religious or metaphysical reality. This parallel, incidentally, provides evidence that although Kant is not once mentioned in the *Fragments*, his philosophy plays a major role in shaping Kierkegaard's position there. Kant deals with the matter of religious speculation at the frontier of knowledge in two places in his writings. One is a key passage we have already examined in the *Critique of Practical Reason;*[6] the second appears in *The Conflict of the Faculties*. The first of these passages follows Kant's argument regarding our rational need to "postulate" the existence of God as a concomitant to dedicated moral striving. Kant would allow a religious transgression of the boundaries of knowledge but only for the strictest of moral reasons, and he warns of the dangers of other excursions into this cognitively unreachable domain:

In fact, so long as practical reason is pathologically conditioned, i.e., as merely regulating the interest of the inclinations by the sensuous principle of happiness, this demand [that theoretical reason should yield primacy to practical reason] could not be made on the speculative reason. Mohammed's paradise or the fusion with the deity of the theosophists and mystics, according to the taste of each, would press their monstrosities [*Ungeheuer*] on reason, and it would as well to have no reason at all as to surrender it in such a manner to all sorts of dreams.[7]

The second passage appears in *The Conflict of the Faculties* at the center of the section dealing with historical revelation versus rational religious knowledge. Here Kant rebuts the charge that rational interpretation of scripture leads to mysticism:

The sole means of avoiding mysticism (such as Swedenborg's) is for philosophy to be on the lookout for a moral meaning in scriptural texts and even to impose it on them. For unless the supersensible (the thought of which is essential to anything called religion) is anchored to determinate concepts of reason, such as those of morality, fantasy inevitably gets lost in the transcendent, where religious matters are concerned, and leads to an Illuminism in which everyone has his private, inner revelations, and there is no longer any public touchstone of truth.[8]

Compare both these passages with Kierkegaard's treatment of the "unknown" in the *Fragments*:

What, then, is the unknown? It is the frontier that is continually arrived at, and therefore when the category of motion is replaced by the category of rest it is the different, the absolutely different. But it is the absolutely different in which there is no distinguishing mark. Defined as the absolutely different, it seems to be at the point of being disclosed, but not so, because the understanding cannot even think the absolutely different... If the unknown (the god) is not solely the frontier, then the one idea about the different is confused with the many ideas about the different. The unknown is then in διασπορά [dispersion], and the understanding has an attractive selection from among what is available and what fantasy can think of (the prodigious, the ridiculous, etc.).[9]

Over the course of this chapter and the next, we'll see that much of Kierkegaard's argument in the *Fragments* combines elements of Kant's epistemology in the first *Critique* with his understanding of historical religious knowledge in *The Conflict of the Faculties*. This parallel with respect to the dangers of religious speculation beyond the boundary of cognition, therefore, hints at Kierkegaard's indebtedness to Kant's epistemology as a whole.

A third epistemological parallel appears in connection with the definition of truth. Several times in the first *Critique* Kant offers explicit definitions of truth as involving "the agreement of knowledge with its object"[10] or "the conformity of our concepts with the object."[11] These bring to mind Kierkegaard's remark in the *Postscript* that "Whether truth is defined more empirically, as the conformity of thought and being, or more idealistically, as the conformity of being with thought, it is, in either case, important carefully to note what is meant by being."[12] The idea that truth involves a conformity of thought and its objects is not unique to Kant. We find a similar view as far back as Aristotle.[13] Nevertheless, Kant's repeated statements of this definition in the *Critique* provide a clear and authoritative precedent for Kierkegaard's own confident utilization of a closely related definition in the *Postscript*. If we further consider that in the first two *Critiques* Kant defines the human will as the faculty *making actual* the objects of mental representation,[14] we may further see how important it is that Kierkegaard picked up this Kantian definition of truth. For by paying careful attention to Kant's understanding of human "being" as involving a time-bound willing that strives to make *real* what it thinks, and by unifying this with the Kantian definition of truth, Kierkegaard would be able to conclude that human beings arrive at truth, the "conformity of thought and being," only by temporal acts of decision. In other words, Kant's understanding of truth and willing points directly ahead to the outlines of Kierkegaard's doctrine of "truth as subjectivity." I would not insist that Kierkegaard's view results solely or even primarily from a reading of Kant. On the contrary, it draws on some of the deepest resources of his own experience and insight. But in the first and second *Critiques* Kierkegaard may have found some of the stimulus for his developed ideas in the *Postscript*.

Several minor allusions and borrowings suggest a fourth epistemological parallel between Kant and Kierkegaard: Kierkegaard's appreciation of Kant's analysis of time and space as a priori forms of sensible intuition. Various remarks by Kierkegaard suggest his familiarity with Kant's view. For example, speaking tongue in cheek of the young aspiring philosopher Johannes Climacus, whose career he recounts in his treatise *De omnibus dubitandum est*, Kierkegaard strikes a distinctively Kantian note: "When it was explained to Johannes that the accusative case, for example, is an extension in time and space, that the preposition does not govern the case but that the relation does, everything expanded before him. The preposition vanished; the extension in time and space became like an enormous empty picture for intuition."[15] Similarly, in the *Postscript* Kierkegaard seems to echo Kant's understanding in the first *Critique* that "the concept of alteration, and with it the concept of motion is...possible only through and in the representation of time" when he states, "It is impossible to conceive existence without movement, and movement cannot be conceived *sub specie æterni*."[16]

Another sign of Kierkegaard's reliance on Kant's epistemology at this point concerns both thinkers' interest in the issue of the simultaneous occurrence of causally related events. Despite Kant's insistence that our concept of causality involves the notion of the necessary antecedence of one event to another in time, he recognized that this concept also applied to simultaneously occurring events, such as the impression made in a soft cushion by a ball. Discussing this conceptual difficulty in the first *Critique*, Kant removes the problem by stating that it is the "order" of events in time, not the lapse between them, that is relevant to our determination of causality. A is the cause of B if we necessarily think of it as present *at the occurrence of B*, whatever the time lapse between them. "The time between the causality of the cause and its immediate effect may be [a] vanishing [quantity], and they may thus be simultaneous," Kant says, "but the relation of the one to the other will always still remain determinable in time."[17]

Against this background, consider the following remark by Kierkegaard in the *Fragments*:

> Everything that has come into existence is *eo ipso* historical, for even if no further historical predicate can be applied to it, the crucial predicate of the historical can still be predicated—namely that it has come into existence. Something whose coming into existence is a simultaneous coming into existence

(*Nebeneinander* [side-by-side], space) has no other history than this, but nature, even when perceived in this manner (*en masse*), apart from what a more ingenious view calls the history of nature in a more special sense, does have a history.[18]

Not only does this comment reflect Kant's concern with the issue of simultaneity, but it also shares Kant's view that all empirical events in nature belong to the realm of "historical" knowledge. In a long passage near the end of the first *Critique*, Kant bifurcates knowledge into the categories of the rational and the historical.[19] The former pertains to all necessary concepts of thought, and the latter comprises all empirically derived knowledge. Empirical knowledge is "historical" because it always concerns temporally conditioned causal events. By telling us that even simultaneously occurring events belong to nature and "have a history," therefore, Kierkegaard is merely combining Kant's treatment of simultaneity as causal with Kant's claim that all causal events belong to the sphere of historical-empirical knowledge.

A fifth epistemological parallel has to do with Kant's insistence on the role of judgment in perceptual knowledge. For Kant, we know, the mind plays an active role in empirical experience, ordering the flow of perceptions that would otherwise be a mere chaos or "rhapsody." Against this background the two following passages from Kierkegaard's and Kant's work become especially important. The first is drawn from the *Fragments*:

> Immediate sensation and immediate cognition cannot deceive. This alone indicates that the historical cannot become the object of sense perception or of immediate cognition, because the historical has in itself that very illusiveness that is the illusiveness of coming into existence.[20]

The second quotation is from the *Critique of Pure Reason*:

> For truth or illusion is not in the object, in so far as it is intuited, but in the judgment about it, in so far as it is thought. It is therefore correct to say that the senses do not err—not because they always judge rightly but because they do not judge at all. Truth and error, therefore, and consequently also illusion as leading to error, are to be found only in the judgment, *i.e.* only in the relation of the object to our understanding.[21]

Kant's point here is an unexpected, if impressive, implication of his view that the faculty of judgment plays a constitutive role in cognition. Although we ordinarily describe ourselves, in instances of optical illusion, for example, as being "deceived by our senses," it is just Kant's point that the senses never lie: they are accurate reporters of whatever input they receive. In cases of illusion, judgment, whose task it is to connect appearances in a unity, errs.

The counterintuitive quality of Kant's idea suggests to me that Kierkegaard's reiteration of it rests more on borrowing than on independent insight. Although Kierkegaard openly attributes the idea that the senses are not the source of error to the Greek skeptics, to Plato, Aristotle, and Descartes,[22] the citations he offers seem less relevant to his point than Kant's remark. That Kant's observation rests on a complete theory of the role of judgment in cognition and is stated in a section of the first *Critique* we know Kierkegaard studied carefully further supports the claim that it is the most proximate source for Kierkegaard's development of this idea in the *Fragments*. In any case, the parallel remains. At the heart of Kant's "Copernican revolution" in philosophy is a view of the human intellect, not as passive recipient of outer sensory data, but as the active and formative constructor of reality. What the remark by Kierkegaard here suggests is that in developing his complex understanding of the relationship between faith and history (and of the essential unimportance of eyewitness contemporaneity with Christ as a foundation for Christian faith), Kierkegaard drew on Kant's understanding that sense data are not the primary determinants in our knowing. The conceptualizing activity of the human mind shapes all sensory data, whether immediate or historical. In the next chapter we'll see that Kierkegaard's thinking on faith and history owes an even more apparent debt to Kant's ethics and philosophy of religion, but we should not overlook the importance of this possible epistemological link.[23]

A sixth and final intriguing epistemological parallel (although one that also pertains to ethics and religion) concerns Kant's and Kierkegaard's conceptions of eternity. Interestingly, although this topic is potentially of great religious significance, it receives relatively little sustained attention from either thinker. Kierkegaard distributes his remarks about eternity or the afterlife unsystematically throughout his published and unpublished writings.[24] Although Kant makes immortality one of the postulates of his rational religious belief, he never develops the content of this conception in his major published works, but reserves a discussion of it, and the issue of eschatology generally, for a short essay, "The End of All Things," published in 1795. Despite its peripheral place in Kant's writings, this essay's presence in the Tieftrunk edition of the *vermischte Schriften* gives us reason to think that Kierkegaard paid it close attention.

The influence of Kant's thinking about eternity on Kierkegaard reveals itself in two parallels. First there is the important understanding shared by both thinkers that eternity *not* be thought of merely as the infinite succession of time. Rather, it is the *end* of time, and, with that, the end of time's phenomenal expressions: change and movement. Kant reiterates this point several times in his essay:

> It is a common expression, particularly in pious talk, to have a dying person say he is *passing from time into eternity*.
>
> In point of fact, this expression would mean nothing if eternity were to be understood here in the sense of time progressing into infinity; for then surely man would never emerge from time, but would always merely be moving forward from one point in it to another. An *end to all time*, therefore, must...mean a quantity (*duratio noumenon*) completely incomparable with the temporal, a notion of which we can certainly form no concept—except, perhaps, a purely negative one.
>
> Now just as the last child of its parents is called the youngest child, so our language has chosen to refer to the Last Day (the moment which terminates all time) as the *Youngest Day*. The Last Day, therefore, belongs as yet in time, for something still happens on it (not relevant to eternity where nothing happens, since the passage of time would not pertain to it), namely the reckoning of men's accounts on the basis of their conduct during their entire life span.[25]

Compare this remark with the following two *Journal* entries by Kierkegaard:

> About eternal damnation. *eternal, continuous development* (*contrad. in adjectivo*) the eternal as the opposite of time, not an infinite succession of moments in time.[26]
>
> ...in eternity a person is not in the succession of time, and being *eterno modo* is the most intensive punctuality[27]

These comments also point toward a second intriguing parallel on this topic, the way in which, for both Kant and Kierkegaard, the changelessness of eternity is above all morally significant. For Kant this is true because eternity translates a human being from phenomenal to intelligible (or noumenal) reality. Since moral experience is the preeminent (if not the only) domain in which we have intelligible experience in the midst of phenomenal life, it follows that any future existence for us in eternity must be thought of as governed by morality. Because Kant also views the course of our moral choices over a lifetime as ultimately traceable to a single timeless and universal "maxim" of choice, eternity, in his view, involves a revelation to us of that which, in moral terms, we have always essentially been. Consider the following remarks in "The End of All Things":

> While we now follow up the transition from time to eternity...as reason itself makes this transition in a moral respect, we encounter the end of all things considered as beings in time and as objects of possible experience. But this end, in the moral order of purposes, is simultaneously the beginning of a duration of these self-same beings as supersensible, i.e., as not standing under the conditions of time. Consequently, this duration and its status will be susceptible of no other definition of its nature than a moral one...
>
> For we still see nothing ahead of us that could apprise us at the present time of our fate in a coming world except the judgment of our own conscience, that is, what our current moral state, so far as we are cognizant of it, permits us rationally to judge of the matter. That is to say, we must judge that those principles of our behavior in life which we have found governing in us (be they good or evil) until its end, will also continue to prevail after death, and we have not the slightest reason to assume an alteration of them in that future.[28]

Compare this with Kierkegaard's remarks in *Purity of Heart*, a work which, as we'll soon see, is otherwise saturated with Kantian ideas:

> Immortality cannot be a final alteration that crept in, so to speak, at the moment of death as the final stage. On the contrary, it is a changelessness that is not altered by the passage of years.[29]

For, after all, what is eternity's accounting other than that the voice of conscience is forever installed with its eternal right to be the exclusive voice? What is it other than that throughout eternity an infinite stillness reigns wherein the conscience may talk with the individual about what he, as an individual, of what he has done of Good or of evil, and about the fact that during his life he did not wish to be an individual?[30]

Kierkegaard's attitude toward eternity has been a source of confusion. At times, it seems as though he regards it as an immanent reality, experienced, not after death, but within transcendent moments of terrestrial experience. The first of the two remarks just quoted, for example, begins with the observation that for a creature to be judged immortal, "immortality must have been present at each instant of its life."[31] This mode of speaking has led some commentators to conclude that Kierkegaard, despite considerable evidence to the contrary—including his chosen gravestone inscription[32]—did not subscribe to the traditional Christian conception of an afterlife.[33] We can dispel some of this confusion, however, if we perceive Kierkegaard's deep indebtedness to Kant on this matter. For both thinkers, eternity begins *in existence* with the timeless judgments of conscience. This does not preclude the possibility of some kind of continued existence in an afterlife, although the conception of a such a "timeless" state of being necessarily defies the mode of cognition of creatures rooted in time and space. Both Kierkegaard's and Kant's emphasis on immanent transcendence and their relative silence on the nature of the afterlife, therefore, may be traceable to the fact that present moral experience remains our only portal to a domain whose reality, though by no means impossible, is, for us, literally "unthinkable" and "unknowable."

ETHICS

As we move from epistemology to ethics, a series of deep uncertainties about Kierkegaard's ethical position confuses the effort to identify his points of contact with Kant. Unlike Kant, Kierkegaard wrote no "metaphysics of morals," and we must glean his views on ethics from a variety of writings, some of which are pseudonymous and thus deliberately represent extreme or polemical positions.

We perceive the problem the minute we ask what these writings tell us about the relation between Kierkegaard's views on ethics and those of Kant. For some scholars, to the extent that Kierkegaard recognizes a philosophical ethics at all, it is Kant's ethics. But he does so, they contend, only to reject it. Those who hold this view tend to believe that Kierkegaard's ethic is fundamentally religious and is most graphically portrayed in *Fear and Trembling*, where we see defended, through the use of the Abraham and Isaac story in Genesis 22, the possibility of a divine command that can erupt into the midst of existence and require the suspension of the ordinary "duties" of rational ethics. Some commentators who share the view that Kierkegaard rejects rational ethics deny, however, that it is exclusively Kantian ethics he has in mind. They see the position he sets up (to demolish) in both *Either/Or* and *Fear and Trembling* as a mélange of Kantian and Hegelian ethical themes.

Others are less certain that Kierkegaard wholly repudiates Kant's ethics in favor of a religious view. They point to many Kantian themes running throughout Kierkegaard's writings, not just the pseudonymous works, and they perceive a deeply humanistic dimension to Kierkegaard's ethical thought. But some who read Kierkegaard this way still see substantial differences between Kant's and Kierkegaard's final ethical positions. This view is perhaps most forcefully stated by George Stack in his study *Kierkegaard's Existential Ethics*. In Stack's words:

> Despite the occasional echoes of Kantian sentiments in Kierkegaard's writings (especially in *Either/Or*), the bifurcation between his ethics of self-becoming and Kant's formalistic, metempirical ethics is, *mutatis mutandis*, complete...Since radical individuation, specificity, inwardness, and the development of subjectivity are central to Kierkegaard's existential ethics, it is clear, essentially, that the spirit and intention of his practical ethics is divorced from the formalism of Kant.[34]

Amidst this debate, sorting out the lines of relationship between Kant and Kierkegaard—including the full range of borrowings, debts, and matters of common interest but final disagreement—requires us to proceed step by step through a series of specific issues and questions. First, there are questions raised by *Fear and Trembling*. Is it Kantian ethics that the pseudonymous author, Johannes *de silentio*, has in mind in this book? (If so, then if *Fear and Trembling* finally rejects this ethic, we can nevertheless identify an important point of contact between Kierkegaard and Kant.) Is this ethic, in fact, rejected? Does the "teleological suspension of the ethical" Johannes describes amount to a repudiation of Kantian "autonomy" in ethics and its replacement with a "heteronomous" or "theonomous" ethic based on divine command? Finally, what is Kierkegaard's own view? Does Johannes *de silentio* represent Kierkegaard's considered position on the relationship between reason and religion in the moral life?

Second is a series of questions having to do with Kierkegaard's other, more general treatments of ethics, whether in the pseudonymous work *Either/Or* or in religious discourses like *Purity of Heart* and *Works of Love*. To what extent, for example, does Kierkegaard share the view of ethics put forth by Judge William in *Either/Or*? How does this view relate to that put forth in the religious discourses? And is it the case, as Stack maintains, that the emphasis on subjective decision, inwardness, and choice of "oneself" found in all these works represents a different style of ethics than that found in Kant's writings?

Let me state here in a general way what I believe to be the answers to these questions. Certainly Kierkegaard's thinking about ethics sometimes disagrees with Kant's. This is particularly true of the role of religion in the moral life, since Kierkegaard is clearly uncomfortable with Kant's conception of moral autonomy. Nevertheless, I think we'll see that the disagreements here are not as sharp as many commentators believe and that they take place within a much broader framework of agreement. Kierkegaard's ethic is also less "formalistic," as Stack maintains, than Kant's *seems to be*. But the emphasis here is on *seems*. Kant's ethics as a whole is considerably more "content filled" and humanistic than it is ordinarily taken to be, and there is evidence that Kierkegaard was aware of and even drew on this side of Kant's thinking. Finally, despite these points of difference, I hope to show that Kierkegaard's ethical thinking as a whole is saturated with Kantian assumptions.

We cannot answer the question about the presence of a Kantian ethic in *Fear and Trembling* with certainty because the ethical position presented there, without attribution, seems to combine themes from the entire rationalist tradition begun by Kant. In its broad lines, for example, it may derive from Hegel's discussion of "the good and conscience" in *The Philosophy of Right*, a discussion to which Kierkegaard explicitly alludes several times in *Fear and Trembling*.[35] But other themes have a definite Kantian flavor. These include the ideas that ethics is the "universal," that it requires the subordination of particular interests to the needs of the common good, and that, in this respect, its "telos" or goal takes precedence over all merely private ends. Although these ideas are present in Hegel's discussion, they are at the center of Kant's understanding of the categorical imperative. In Books 3 and 4 of the *Religion*, Kant repeatedly makes the point that ethics admits "no special duties to God" and that it views the fulfillment of human moral responsibility as the only legitimate means of obeying God's commands. These ideas constitute a major theme of Kant's thinking about religious ethics. In fact, the focus on Abraham in *Fear and Trembling* also may have been suggested by the *Religion*, since Kant there (and again in *The Conflict of the Faculties*) expresses doubt that Abraham acted rightly in endangering his son by placing an alleged and possibly spurious divine command before the clear, prohibitory voice of duty.[36] Finally, it is possible that Kierkegaard is also indebted to Kant for the conception of the "tragic hero," who must subordinate one form of duty to a still higher form. Kierkegaard illustrates this conception by presenting several classical instances of conflict between parental duty and the welfare of the state. Similarly, Kant, in his essay "Idea for a Universal History with a Cosmopolitan Purpose," which appears in the Tieftrunk edition, chooses to illustrate the concept of *casus necessitatis* by a case where a father must betray his son "in order to preserve the state from catastrophe."[37] Ordinarily, we would not expect this easing of moral rigor from Kant—recall that he does not permit lying even to save a life. His explicit qualification of parental duty here may explain Kierkegaard's confidence when he asserts that "ethics" allows us to subordinate parental duty in these circumstances. Taken together, these shared points suggest that the ethics Kierkegaard has in mind in *Fear and Trembling* is significantly Kantian.

Does Kierkegaard then reject Kant's ethic here in favor of one based on the divine command? This is a difficult question to answer. Apart from the usual problem of separating what might be Kierkegaard's views from those of his pseudonymous author, there is the deeper question of what *Fear and Trembling* is all about. It has often been read as a rejection of the Kantian notion of ethical autonomy in favor of a more traditional "heteronomous" or "theonomous" ethics of direct obedience to God. Nevertheless, I think there is good reason to regard this as only a "surface message" of the book. In Chapter 5, on the basis of a rereading of Kierkegaard's argument in connection with Kant's *Religion* and *The Conflict of the Faculties*, where Kant repeatedly discusses Abraham, I will argue that at its deepest and most important levels *Fear and Trembling* is really in dialogue with some of the central themes of Kant's philosophy of religion, not his ethics. If I am right about this, we should not simply view *Fear and Trembling* as a rejection of Kant's ethical theory. But judgment on this will have to await the treatment in Chapter 5.

To say that *Fear and Trembling*'s treatment of ethics is not necessarily anti-Kantian does not mean that Kierkegaard was comfortable with the themes of ethical autonomy developed by Kant. If we review the explicit remarks about Kant in Kierkegaard's *Papers*, we find that a substantial number of them—four out of thirty-one—directly criticize Kant's idea that each person must be thought of as his or her own lawgiver and judge. In Kierkegaard's view, this conception ignores the fact that, if allowed, people will be lenient in their own case, neither imposing the moral law in its full rigor nor properly convicting themselves of moral transgressions. One of these journal entries is worth quoting at length because it conveys the essence of Kierkegaard's criticism of Kantian autonomy:

> Kant was of the opinion that man is his own law (autonomy)—that is, he binds himself under the law which he himself gives himself. Actually, in a profounder sense, this is how lawlessness or experimentation are established. This is not being rigorously earnest any more than Sancho Panza's self-administered blows to his own bottom were vigorous. It is impossible for me

to be really any more rigorous in A than I am or wish to be in B. Constraint there must be if it is going to be in earnest. If I am bound by nothing higher than myself and I am to bind myself, where would I get the rigorousness as A, the binder, which I do not have as B, who is supposed to be bound, when A and B are the same self...

The maxim which I give myself is not only not a law, but there is a law which is given me by one higher than myself, and not only that, but this lawgiver takes the liberty of taking a hand in the capacity of tutor and bringing pressure to bear.

Now if a man is never even once willing in his lifetime to act so decisively that this tutor can get hold of him, well, then it happens, then the man is allowed to live on in self-complacent illusion and make-believe and experimentation, but this also means: utterly without grace.[38]

This entry is interesting because it unites Kierkegaard's defense of a heteronomous or theonomous normative position with the themes of self-judgment and human beings' need for grace. In the next chapter we'll see that it is on the last of these matters, the need for grace, that Kierkegaard differs most sharply with Kant: Kierkegaard is entirely willing to forsake moral autonomy to make room for the grace needed to effect human redemption from sin. It is natural, therefore, for Kierkegaard to buttress this position by emphasizing, as he does in all his critical comments on Kantian ethical autonomy, the greater rigor of an externally imposed moral law. This said, we will nevertheless see in the next chapter that Kierkegaard uses a Kantian idea of ethics to point up the rigor of the moral demand. Like Kant, he seems to perceive that a self-given law, however dishonestly evaded and qualified, may in the end furnish the sternest standard of judgment, precisely because of its immanence and inescapability. I mention this here because it helps explain why Kierkegaard, after registering his discomfort with Kant's autonomous ethic, never goes beyond this point. Apart from some suggestions in *Works of Love*, he never elaborates a religious ethic that can replace Kant's understanding of morality, and, as we will see, in most of his explicit discussions of the moral life, he draws on Kant's views. Kierkegaard undoubtedly saw Kantian autonomy as a threat to human moral redemption. But it may be that he hoped to replace this element in Kant's thinking while profiting from other major ethical aspects of the intellectual structure Kant built.

The question of whether the ethic put forth in *Either/Or* differs substantially from Kant's poses a different set of problems. Here we are dealing with an ethic that better represents Kierkegaard's own views on the moral life. Judge William is no straw man set up to be demolished but represents a position close to Kierkegaard's own conception of moral responsibility. For example, we learn in the *Postscript* that "the ethics which he champions...is quite the opposite of the Hegelian."[39] Themes Judge William voices, such as the need to choose oneself, are also upheld by Kierkegaard in the direct address of the religious discourses. True, the "ethical stage" of existence Judge William defends is meant to be transcended in the "religious," as the "Ultimatum" that concludes *Either/Or* suggests, but transcendence does not mean abolition. Rather, in the religious stage the ethical is reestablished—in its proper place. Dethroned from a central position and placed in the service of human beings' full spiritual completion (for which grace is needed), it nevertheless continues to impose its normative demands.

To what extent, then, is the ethics sketched in *Either/Or* similar to or different from Kant's? The case that it is very different rests on two claims. The first, already voiced in Stack's quoted remarks, is that Kierkegaard's/Judge William's ethic avoids the "rationalistic formalism" of Kant's. For example, it does not proscribe "aesthetic existence" and the joys and pleasures of human existence, but seeks to make room for them within a morally ordered life. Once I make the ethical choice of myself, says the judge, "the whole of the aesthetical comes back again in its relativity."[40] A second claim is that the fundamental norms of this ethic are very different from Kant's categorical imperative. They include above all the requirement of personal individuation, the demand that one move from the "aesthetic" stage of existence to the "ethical" by choosing a concrete mode of being that defines the self. In this ethic, it seems we are far from Kant's concerns with distinguishing right and wrong conduct. In the words of Peck, it seems that "Kierkegaard is not dealing with standard moral phenomena but with the ground and limit of morality, the birth of morality out of a pre-moral state."[41]

The first of these claims rests on a misapprehension of Kantian ethics, a misapprehension, however, that Kierkegaard may not have shared. The charge of excessive formalism simply does not square with a proper appreciation of the role Kant understands reason to play in the moral life. The categorical imperative works necessarily with "maxims," concrete expressions of human willing and desire. Its purpose is not to prohibit these expressions but to adjudicate among them and to permit only those forms of willing that are allowable in a universal community of wills. Kant's ethic is also not opposed to happiness. This unfortunate view results from confusing his repeated diatribes against making happiness the *supreme* determining ground of the will with an opposition to happiness generally. We've seen that happiness plays a central role in both Kant's ethics and his philosophy of religion. In fact, a statement by Kant himself is the best corrective for this generations-old misunderstanding of his ethical position. In the short essay "On the Common Saying: 'This May be True in Theory, but it does not Apply in Practice,'" a work appearing in the Tieftrunk edition, Kant directly confronts a statement by one of his critics that interprets him as teaching that the virtuous man "constantly strives to be worthy of happiness, but never, *in so far as* he is truly virtuous, to be actually happy." Kant replies to this interpretation as follows:

> The words *in so far as* contain an ambiguity which must be eliminated before we can go any farther: They can signify *in the act* of submitting, as a virtuous man, to one's duty—in which case the sentence is perfectly compatible with my theory—or they could imply that if he is never anything but virtuous, the virtuous man should not take happiness into consideration at all, even where the question of duty does not arise and where there is no conflict with duty—in which case the sentence is totally at variance with my statements.[42]

The point, of course, is that duty comes first. But duty is not opposed to well-being. It presumes concrete human goals. As a regulative and restraining conception, the categorical imperative issues its "no" only when the pursuit of some objective is incapable of being accepted as conduct open to all. In this respect, Kant would certainly agree with the following remark in a journal entry by Kierkegaard:

The ethical act of reflection is in the last analysis decisive. However great, however glorious everything else is, it does not help. Everything higher than the universal must first have tested itself in the ethical act of reflection, which is the measure of the universal. Briskly to follow a talent, to choose a brilliant distinction, even if one amazes the world ten times over, means to remain behind. Ethical reflection is the authorization; if it is secured, then the distinction can be celebrated.[43]

The second contention, that Kierkegaard's/Judge William's ethic of self-choice and personal individuation is different from Kant's, has more to recommend it. Certainly, we find nothing in Kant's writings on ethics like Judge William's admonitions to his young colleague to move out of the aesthetic into the ethical stage of existence, nor do we find the same kind of explicit advocacy of self-choice and individuation. Here, it seems, we find a series of important themes that are genuinely indigenous to Kierkegaard or at least not influenced by Kant.

Nevertheless, it is important to recognize that Kant's ethics does not oppose these themes. The choice of ethical existence is not something Kant writes about. In his mature thinking about freedom, however, he does assume the possibility of one's choosing to abandon moral responsibility entirely, and he would presumably agree with Kierkegaard's view that the choice of ethics is the first and most important ethical choice of all. Nor is the theme of self-choice and personal individuation opposed to anything Kant says. If we assume, as is true in Judge William's and Kierkegaard's expressions of this theme, that self-choice is always also "universal choice" in the sense of being a willingness to conform one's particularity to shared human limitations and needs, then Kant's ethic is not opposed to this Kierkegaardian idea.

In fact, if we pay careful attention to Kant's argument in the *Foundations* and supplement this with some of the things he says in *The Metaphysics of Morals*, we can go further: it may be possible to discern in these themes a measure of borrowing on Kierkegaard's part. As William Peck points out, in the examples dealing with sloth and mutual aid in the *Foundations* and in his "law of nature" formulation of the categorical imperative, Kant presents a "more substantive or material" understanding of his moral conception than he does elsewhere. In these instances, the choosing agent is asked, as part of the test of a maxim's suitability as universal law, to mentally create a world of persons in which he or she might be a member. As Peck observes, the idea that in this way one becomes, in a sense, "one's own creator" is not far removed from some of the things Judge William says about self-choice.[44]

In the *The Metaphysics of Morals*, especially the portion known as *The Metaphysical Principles of Virtue*,[45] this idea is supplemented by an explicit emphasis on responsibility *to* and *for* the self. Somewhat surprisingly, Kant devotes a large part of this document to the discussion of self-regarding duties. If we can assume that Kierkegaard, in the course of his exam preparation on matters of ethics, encountered the side of Kant's ethics evidenced in *The Metaphysics of Morals*, then, without insisting on the point, it becomes reasonable to suggest that the lines of connection between Kant's ethic and the ethic of self-choice presented in *Either/Or* are more direct.[46]

Up to this point, I have devoted most of my attention to seeming differences between Kant and Kierkegaard's ethical positions. Now, however, I want to emphasize the clear and unambiguous parallels. We find these throughout Kierkegaard's work, not only in the pseudonymous writings, and they are so basic to his ethics that whatever we judge to be the final direction of his thinking, whether, for example, it is theonomous or autonomous, religious or rational, these parallels reveal a deep imprint of Kantianism on his entire ethical viewpoint.

A major and overarching area of similarity between Kierkegaard and Kant has to do with their shared conviction that "the ethical is the universal."[47] Within this overarching conception, however, reside several specific points of agreement, corresponding to the various ways both thinkers employ the idea of universality. One has to do with Judge William's understanding that ethical choice requires one to convert oneself into a "universal man" or model of "essential humanity."[48] We just saw that this conception, although initially different from some of the ways in which Kant usually speaks of the categorical imperative, actually conforms to his mode of reasoning in several of his most important examples. In personally choosing whether to act on a maxim of mutual aid, for example, Kant suggests that we must mentally "create" a world with its own type of humanity and human existence. This seems very close to Judge William's conception of self-choice as universal choice.

Kant and Kierkegaard also share the idea that moral judgments cannot be merely private or particular, privileging one's interests above those of other members of the moral community. We meet this idea within even the familiar interpretation of the categorical imperative as requiring the "universalization" of maxims, but it also finds expression in Kant's repeated suggestions that moral reasoning must proceed without our being determined by particular needs or desires. This idea is basic to Kant's distinction between hypothetical and categorical imperatives.[49]

Kierkegaard shows his acceptance of this idea in both the pseudonymous works and the religious discourses. In *Either/Or*, for example, Judge William contrasts his deep love for his wife with the kind of love that will replace it in eternity. "The defect of earthly love," he remarks, "is the same thing as its advantageous quality, i.e. its partiality." In contrast, "spiritual love," the love found in eternity, "has no partialities and moves in the opposite direction, constantly abhorring all relativities."[50] In *Works of Love* this contrast between the particularity of human love and the universality of Christian love becomes a central theme.[51]

Another sense of universality employed by Kant and picked up by Kierkegaard has to do with the idea of ethics as a law for the entire human community. Ethics is not relative; in its most basic principles, at least, its laws are universally known and universally applicable. This understanding, of course, follows directly from Kant's "rationalistic" conception of the categorical imperative as an a priori principle of reason. It is perhaps less expected of Kierkegaard, whose alleged emphasis on revelation may seem more compatible with the claim that one's ethic depends on the religious community to which one belongs. Nevertheless, Kierkegaard repeatedly affirms the universality of ethics in this Kantian sense. In *Either/Or*, for example, Judge William criticizes "freethinkers" who seek to prove the relativity of ethics by pointing to the diversity of external practices across cultures, such as the fact that "savages have the custom of putting their aged parents to death." The mistake here, says the

Judge, is confusing outer practices with inner intention.[52] In a journal entry dealing with the same point, Kierkegaard adds that in instances like this "it is clear that savages do not intend to harm their parents but to do good to them."[53] The practice of parricide among certain nonliterate tribes has become a major focus in the discussion of ethical relativism in contemporary moral literature,[54] and the issues here may be more or less complex than Kierkegaard's brief rejoinder suggests. But there is no doubt that in this debate Kierkegaard, like Kant, defends the universality of ethics against relativist claims.

If the principles of ethics are universally applicable, and the moral community comprises all who are human, it follows that we may suppose that all human beings know the moral law, are accountable for obeying or not obeying it, and come under its protection as the bearers of moral rights. Kant supports this sense of the universality of the moral law by his insistence that rationality is the sole requirement for membership in the moral community: rationality alone imposes on persons the burden of moral responsibility, and it entitles them to the respect due those who are not means but "ends in themselves."[55] At its core, therefore, Kant's ethical position is profoundly egalitarian and contains an impassioned defense of equal human dignity. Although Kant's teachings about specific ethical matters do not always follow through on this promise of equality, it is one of his most important contributions to modern ethical thought, and, through its influence on radical or liberal thinkers from Marx to Rawls, it has had an important impact on modern political philosophy.

Repeatedly in his writings, Kierkegaard defends these same ideas. In *The Concept of Anxiety* and again in his *Journals*, for example, he approvingly alludes to various Greek myths that present the ethical as bestowed on all human beings equally, unlike various talents or abilities.[56] A journal entry for 1849 makes this same point in terms so deeply reminiscent of Kant's insistence that "ought implies can" and of Kant's distinction between categorical and hypothetical imperatives that it is worth quoting at length:

> In the realm of genius, the realm of natural qualifications, the realm of the esthetic, what counts is: to be able. In the realm of the ethical: to be obliged. Therefore the ethical is related to the universally human; whereas the esthetic is related to the differ-

ences between man and man. It would be a contradiction of
the ethical to speak of *being obliged* if every human being did
not have the conditions for being able if he himself only wills.

In connection with the ethical there are, therefore, no conditions; it is the unconditional ought which tolerates no conditions because it presupposes no conditions.

The esthetic presupposes the conditions and it is unconditional only where the condition is unconditionally present;
whereas the ethical is unconditional in that there is no condition and thus is unconditional everywhere or unconditionally
unconditioned.[57]

Kierkegaard is no less clear about the dignity that ethics con-
fers on all who are human. Kierkegaard was no democrat. Even
more than Kant, who combined a progressive political philosophy with more conservative social and economic views, Kierkegaard sought to maintain a sharp distinction between the spiritual and social implications of his ethical-religious position.
Nevertheless, for Kierkegaard, no less than for Kant, the universality of ethics also implied an absolute and equal human dignity.
In *Either/Or* Judge William seems to paraphrase Kant's "autonomy" formulation of the categorical imperative when he states
that each person, "even though he were a hired servant...has his
teleology in himself."[58] And in a journal entry for 1847 Kierkegaard remarks on the "kingly words" of a poor woman who
weeds the gardens of the rich and who can say, "I am doing this
work for a dollar a day, but I do it very carefully for the sake of
conscience." This phrase and thought *for the sake of conscience*,
Kierkegaard adds, represents "a transformation of language," an
"Archimedean point outside the world." When it is uttered "in
deep inward silence before God, the weeder-woman can say that
she moves heaven and earth."[59] These and many similar statements indicate that Kierkegaard was deeply committed to the
dignity and equality of all persons, regardless of their social position.[60] Although our understanding of Kierkegaard as a social
and political thinker is not yet complete, as Bruce H. Kirmmse
has convincingly shown, he was in many ways a foe of the smug-
ness and conceit of the bourgeois social order around him.[61] Here
I am suggesting that he owes this sensibility partly to Kant, as do
the left-wing social critics whose thinking Kant helped inform.

A final and related aspect of universality shared by Kant and Kierkegaard has to do with their idea that respect for the moral law is a condition and guarantee of unity and harmony among all human beings. In Kant's thinking, the impartiality and universality of perspective the categorical imperative requires are designed to effect the "harmony of wills" at which ethics aims.[62] In the previous chapter, we saw that in some ways this imperative is the moral and social analogue of Kant's idea of the "synthetic unity of apperception." Whereas the latter makes possible "experience" within a single mind, the former makes possible "social experience" for a community of rational wills. It does so by requiring persons to put aside private ends not conformable to the impartial assent of others and by making this assent the condition of individual conduct.

Kierkegaard, of course, does not speak in these terms. But in a remark in *Purity of Heart* he expresses the same idea when he affirms that "willing the Good" is the sole thing that unites human beings, whereas all other objects of volition divide them. This remark also brings to mind Kant's conception of a "kingdom of ends" as a purely ideal community linking all human beings who act freely as subjects and objects of laws they have made:

> For all clannishness is the enemy of universal humanity. But to will only one thing, genuinely to will the Good, as an individual, to will to hold fast to the Good, which things each person without exception is capable of doing, this is what unites. And if you sat in a lonely prison far from all men, or if you were placed upon a desert island with only animals for company, if you genuinely will the Good, if you hold fast to God, then you are in unity with all men.[63]

Kierkegaard's argument in *Purity of Heart* represents a complex play on the relationship that exists between unity and the Good. Not only does he believe the Good is the only thing that can be willed as a unity; it is also, as in this passage, the only single object of willing that creates unity. Taken together, as Jeremy Walker has observed, these are complex and "dark" claims.[64] In part, they have roots in a tradition going back to Plato and Augustine, and for Kierkegaard they seem to involve certain theological assumptions about the divine will. But Kierkegaard's claims in this book also make clear sense when "the Good" is interpreted in terms of the categorical imperative. We will see this again in a moment in connection with Kierkegaard's criticism of "double-mindedness" and his insistence that the Good excludes considerations of reward. Without insisting that he has only Kant's ethic in mind, therefore, we can perhaps see in these statements about the Good and human unity another important instance where Kierkegaard is significantly instructed by Kant.

If Kierkegaard's understanding of the universality of ethics forms one major area of parallelism to Kant, his opposition to eudaimonism in ethics forms a second. In the previous chapter we saw that a hallmark of Kant's approach to ethics is his unsparing opposition to thinking about duty as the pursuit of happiness, however nobly or altruistically "happiness" is conceived. For Kant, the supreme end of ethics cannot be any finite value because all such values lack universality. The only possible moral determining ground of the will is the formal requirement that whatever we will be valid for everyone in a possible community of wills. Not only is happiness generally inadmissible as the foundation of ethics, therefore, but we must never allow considerations of prudence or expedience to override duty in individual instances of moral willing.

We can presume from the record of Kierkegaard's degree examination that he was very familiar with Kant's critique of eudaimonism in ethics. Not surprisingly, therefore, throughout his writings he displays an essentially Kantian point of view on this matter. In the *Postscript* he states flatly that "The ethical never raises questions of prudence."[65] In *Purity of Heart*, he presents considerations of personal profit and well-being as absolutely inimical to morality. "To will the Good for the sake of the reward," he tells us, "is *double-mindedness*."[66] In the *Postscript* he rejects as "fictitious" any "transition from eudaimonism to the ethical within eudaimonism,"[67] and in a journal entry for 1844 he presents the qualitative transition from prudence to duty as an illustration of the role of the "leap" in ethical-religious thinking. In the next chapter we'll see that Kant's thinking and terminology contribute decisively to Kierkegaard's understanding of the leap of faith. This entry, therefore, provides preliminary evidence of how much the basic structure of Kant's philosophy informs Kierkegaard's whole approach to religious-ethical questions:

> The transition from eudæmonism to the concept of duty is a leap, or, assisted by a more and more developed understanding of what is most prudent, is one finally supposed to go directly over to virtue? No, there is a pain of decision which the sensuous (the eudæmonistic), the finite (the eudæmonistic), cannot endure. Man is not led to do his duty by merely reflecting that it is the most prudent thing to do; in the moment of decision reason lets go, and he *either* turns back to eudæmonism or he chooses the good by a *leap*.[68]

Interestingly, Kierkegaard, like Kant, is unwilling to relinquish entirely the idea of reward in ethics and of a possible relation between duty and personal welfare.[69] But, like Kant, he refuses to make this connection immanent within human experience. As in Kant's conception of the "highest good," duty and reward come together only eschatologically, and to put them together in the world, whether in crassly materialistic terms or in the elevated refinements of various Greek philosophical schools, misconceives the nature of the ethical demand. A comment in the *Postscript* expresses this idea:

> The actual interval of time separates the good and its reward so long, so everlastingly, that prudence cannot bring them together, and the eudæmonist begs to be excused. It is certain indeed that to will the good is the height of prudence, but not in the sense in which the merely prudent man understands it, but in the sense in which the good man understands it. The transition thus reveals itself clearly as a breach of continuity, even as suffering.[70]

In Kant's thinking, happiness is an unsuitable supreme determining ground of the will, not only because, like every finite value, it lacks universality, but also because it is an undefinable and indistinct object of pursuit. Kant concedes that in one sense happiness is a universal objective: definitionally, all persons seek the fulfillment of their wishes, which is what happiness represents. But this seeming unanimity of purpose is spurious: first, because the continually changing nature of one's ideas about personal fulfillment makes it unclear to any single individual what he or she really wants in the name of happiness; and second, because even when each of two people clearly understands in what his or her happiness consists and each resolves to pursue this happiness, the seeming unity of purpose may conceal the most acute discord. Kant makes the first of these points in a well-known passage in the *Foundations* where he remarks that what really constitutes happiness for each of us is so indeterminate and uncertain that it would require omniscience for us to know what will truly make us happy.[71] He makes the second point in a colorful passage of the *Critique of Practical Reason*:

> It is therefore astonishing how intelligent men have thought of proclaiming as a universal practical law the desire for happiness, and therewith to make this desire the determining ground of the will merely because this desire is universal. Though elsewhere natural laws make everything harmonious, if one here attributed the universality of law to this maxim, there would be the extreme opposite of harmony, the most arrant conflict, and the complete annihilation of the maxim itself and its purpose. For the wills of all do not have one and the same object, but each person has his own (his own welfare), which, to be sure, can accidentally agree with the purposes of others who are pursuing their own, though this agreement is far from sufficing for a law because the occasional exceptions which one is permitted to make are endless and cannot be definitely comprehended in a universal rule. In this way a harmony may result resembling that depicted in a certain satirical poem as existing between a married couple bent on going to ruin, "Oh, marvelous harmony, what he wants is what she wants"; or like the pledge which is said to have been given by Francis I to the Emperor Charles V, "What my brother wants (Milan), that I want too."[72]

In various places in his writings, Kierkegaard seems to pick up both aspects of Kant's criticism of happiness as a supreme end. For example, in *Purity of Heart* it is the essential variability and changeability of the worldly goods composing happiness that draw his attention:

> Pleasure and honor and riches and power and all that this world has to offer only appear to be one thing. It is not, nor does it remain one thing, while everything else is in change or

while he himself is in change. It is not in all circumstances the same. On the contrary, it is subject to continual alteration. Hence even if this man named but one thing whether it be pleasure, or honor or riches, actually he did not will one thing. Neither can he be said to will one thing when that one thing which he wills is not in itself one: is in itself a multitude of things, a dispersion, the toy of changeableness, and the prey of corruption![73]

In *Either/Or*, it is the essential unsociability of the private pursuit of happiness that receives emphasis:

If an esthete were not an egoist, he would—presuming that every conceivable favor had fallen to his lot—have to despair over all his happiness, because he would have to say: What makes me happy is something that cannot be given in the same way to another person and that no one else can acquire. Indeed, he would have to be anxious lest someone ask him wherein he sought his happiness, for he had become happy so that all the others would feel that they could not become happy. If such a person had any sympathy, he would give himself no rest until he found a higher point of departure for his life. When he had found it, he would not be afraid to talk about his happiness, because if he were to articulate it properly he would say something that absolutely reconciled him with every human being, with all mankind.[74]

Neither one of these ideas carries Kant's copyright. Each is in a way obvious, and the first, at least, is a staple of the philosophical-religious tradition. Nevertheless, this frequent reiteration of ideas expressed by Kant suggests to me an active process of appropriation and borrowing from the philosopher.

Before continuing with this examination of facets of Kant's and Kierkegaard's rejection of eudaimonism in ethics, I might parenthetically insert here the suggestion that Kierkegaard's ethical thought may owe a substantial terminological debt to Kant in its contrasting of the "aesthetic" and "ethical" stages of life. Kierkegaard's conception of "aesthetic" existence is somewhat peculiar. It contains, on the one hand, our accustomed sense of "aesthetics" as involving art and beauty. But Kierkegaard also sometimes thinks of "aesthetic" existence quite differently as a stage of "immediacy" or "immediate existence," in which the individual is governed by the play of outer or inner sensations (as opposed to the ethical sphere of "becoming," where choice and decision are required).[75] In fact, Kant's own utilization of the term embodies both these meanings. In the *Critique of Judgment*, for example, he uses the term *aesthetics* to designate judgments about objects of sensory and intellectual pleasure—especially artistic creations. But in the first *Critique*, as we saw, the "aesthetic" designates the entire domain of sense perception. Although Kant never speaks of "aesthetic" existence in Kierkegaard's terms—he prefers the term *pathological* for nonethical, feeling-oriented states of being: to the extent that one "lives" aesthetically, according to his larger use of the term, one would be, like Kierkegaard's "aesthete," governed by outer or inner impressions and not yet be in a sphere where concepts, reason, and true human willing pertain.

Kierkegaard's employment of Mozart's music in the first volume of *Either/Or* to symbolize the "aesthetic" stage is a further reminder of the link here to Kant. In the *Critique of Judgment* Kant tells us that music represents "sensuousness" in its purest form.[76] For Kierkegaard, too, music represents "sensuous immediacy" and the "genius of sensuousness."[77] That the young sensualist A in *Either/Or* is so attracted to Mozart's "Don Juan," and can effusively praise the way Mozart's music reveals the composer's "enviable" happiness,[78] is a sign that A still dwells in a realm of sensory impulsion and the extrinsically determined quest for well-being, rather than in the ethical realm of free resolve and personal decision. His is an aesthetic existence in both of Kant's senses of the term. Interestingly, there is another important dimension of Kierkegaard's use of the term *aesthetic* that goes directly back to Kant and about whose connection to Kant's writings we don't have to speculate, since Kierkegaard is explicit in confessing his debt. This has to do with Kant's provocative notion, developed at some length in the *Critique of Judgment*, that judgments of beauty involve "disinterested" satisfaction.[79] Although, in Kant's view, aesthetic judgments do not involve "concepts," they share with moral judgments the feature that they are made apart from any kind of personal or self-referential interest we may have in the object of the judgment. In this respect, they differ from judgments of pleasure. To say that something "pleases" me is to say that it is capable of satisfying one of my desires. But I can judge something "beautiful," according to Kant, even if I have no personal interest in it. There is no doubt that Kierkegaard was aware of and intrigued by Kant's idea. He makes reference to it once in a journal entry for 1842–1843.[80] In *Either/Or*, Judge William attributes this idea to the young aesthete.[81] And in *The Concept of Anxiety* and *De omnibus dubitandum est* Kierkegaard classes aesthetics, with mathematics and metaphysics, among the "disinterested" sciences, noting, as he does in *The Concept of Anxiety*, his borrowing of this idea from Kant.[82] Finally, a footnote in the *Postscript* explicitly likens the disinterestedness of art and poetry to the exercise of abstract thought and contrasts both with the passionate self-involvement of the existing individual.[83]

At first glance, we might think that this quality of disinterestedness would elevate the worth of the aesthetic. But if we keep in mind that Kierkegaard views the aesthetic not just as a form of judgment but as a whole mode of life, a "stage of existence," then we can see how pernicious it becomes in Kierkegaard's mind to live "aesthetically" and why he judges all such disinterestedness to be "simply a retrogression."[84] For to live this way is to be uninvolved with the stakes of existence and to believe that one can be as distanced from the outcome of one's own life as one may be in a dispassionate judgment of a work of art.[85]

In few places, I think, do we better see the creative side of Kierkegaard's appropriation of Kant than in this use of the concept of the aesthetic. Beginning with a series of penetrating, if recondite, ideas from Kant, Kierkegaard puts them together in a new way to form his own creative contribution to our understanding of the moral life. That Kierkegaard's creativity is consistent with the deepest lines of Kant's thought, yet builds on them, illustrates the fruitfulness of this meeting of minds.

Returning to the general issue of eudaimonism, we encounter another important parallel between Kant and Kierkegaard in the idea that the moral worth of persons resides in their inner intentions, not in their deeds or the outer consequences of their acts. In this respect, Kierkegaard effects a dramatic movement "back to Kant" by rejecting the Hegelian focus on individuals' "world-historical" significance or their contribution to the unfolding of "spirit" on the stage of history. In *Either/Or*, for example, Judge William remarks, "If I am contemplating a world-historical individual, I can make a distinction between the deeds of which Scripture says 'they follow him' and the deeds by which he belongs to history. Philosophy has nothing at all to do with what could be called the inner deed, but the inner deed is the true life of freedom."[86]

In the *Postscript*, this stress on inwardness finds expression in a remark by Johannes Climacus that again shows Kierkegaard's fascination with the qualitative difference between moral obligation and all other human concerns. The "truly great ethical personality," Climacus observes,

> would strive to develop himself with the utmost exertion of his powers; in so doing he would perhaps produce great effects in the external world. But this would not seriously engage his attention, for he would know that the external result is not in his power, and hence that it has no significance for him, either *pro* or *contra*. He would therefore *choose* to remain in ignorance of what he had accomplished, in order that his striving might not be retarded by a preoccupation with the external, and lest he fall into the temptation which proceeds from it. For what a logician chiefly fears, namely a fallacy, a μετάβασις εἰς ἄλλο γένος, that the ethicist fears quite as profoundly, namely a conclusion or transition from the ethical to something nonethical.[87]

Since, for both Kant and Kierkegaard, concern with consequences and preoccupation with reward are fatal distractions from the kind of willing that distinguishes moral choice, the best evidence for the "purity" of a person's moral disposition is that he or she sustains this resolve despite the absence of external rewards or accomplishments. In the *Foundations* Kant illustrates this point with the often misconstrued example of an individual who lacks a sympathetic nature but who nevertheless goes out of his way to help a fellow human being.[88] Kant's point, of course, is not that it is desirable to lack sympathy. Rather, it is the analytical observation that we best discern the purity of an individual's disposition in a case where no determinants other than duty are present to confuse judgment—in this instance even the satisfactions yielded a sympathetic person by an altruistic act. Although Kierkegaard is not concerned with analysis of this sort, he shares with Kant this emphasis on moral purity and the conviction that it is best developed without distracting external considerations. In *Purity of Heart* for example, he states, "In ancient times there was also a simple sage, whose simplicity became a snare for the impudent ones' sophistry. He taught that in order really to be certain that it was the Good that man willed, one ought even to shun seeming good, presumably in order that the reward should not become tempting."[89] Further on in the same volume, he adds, "*Let us properly linger over this, convinced that one may learn more profoundly and more reliably what the highest is by considering suffering than by observing achievements, where so much that is distracting is present.*"[90]

This last observation invokes a final important ethical parallel between Kant and Kierkegaard. In sharp contrast to the whole eudaimonistic tradition in its many forms, both maintain that, in this world, virtue and personal happiness are usually inversely related to one another. Several factors contribute to this shared point of view, what William Peck has called "the darkness of their moral outlooks."[91] One is the sense that duty often requires the suppression of personal "inclinations" or desires so that, where human beings are concerned, "nature" and morality are often painfully opposed. A second is the distinctive recognition that all aims not informed by duty lack moral worth. In opposition to the eudaimonistic tradition, which sought to grade and value human objectives in terms of their relative nobility or sociability, Kant divided the moral world into two sharply separated domains: on one side, the ethical, ruled by the categorical imperative, and, on the other, the realm of merely particular or private pursuits, all of which he regarded without distinction as forms of selfishness. For Kant, "all material principles are, as such, of one and the same kind and belong under the general principle of self-love or one's own happiness."[92] Similarly, Kierkegaard makes a sharp distinction between morality and natural human striving, no matter how altruistic or generous its motivation. "All love, erotic love, friendship, even mother love," he tells us, "is by itself only an expression of self-love."[93]

This rigorous distinction between the moral and the merely "natural" orders of human life produces, in both Kant and Kierkegaard's thinking, a deep moral pessimism about the world itself. Although this theme is less pronounced in the *Foundations* or first and second *Critiques*, it becomes a leitmotif of Kant's later writings, especially those dealing with religion. For example, *Religion within the Limits of Reason Alone* begins with a long analysis of the age-old complaint that "the world lies in evil."[94] The "Critique of the Teleological Judgment" contains a long passage recounting the bitter fate of virtue in this world.[95] And this theme resonates throughout the smaller essays dealing with religious topics. Thus, in "The End of All Things," Kant offers a rational explanation based on human moral experience for the common religious tendency to depict this world as ending in a cataclysmic day of judgment and doom.[96] It is true that in some later writings, such as the "Idea for a Universal History with a Cosmopolitan Purpose," Kant expresses a hope for human moral improvement. But, in a manner that anticipates Hegel's philosophy of history, he sees this progress as being brought about through the brutal clash and mutual checking of egoisms on an ever larger scale.

A reader of Kierkegaard does not have to be convinced of the similar darkness of his moral perspective. At least from the period of the *Postscript* forward and accelerating through the late 1840s, these themes begin to dominate Kierkegaard's writings. Again and again, as in the following journal entry from 1849, Kierkegaard sees the Christian as pitted against both the natural world and the false world of "Christendom":

> Only the Christian is *hated*; he must be destroyed and in the basest way, as no criminal is destroyed. If not, the secular mentality gets no peace and joy from things of the world, whose influence is weakened by the Christian, he who expresses that erotic love is self-love, that friendship is self-love, that honor and such are nothing and money less than nothing. Is this not mutiny, is this not the basest atrocity, should not Barrabas and all the others be released, almost honored and respected in comparison to such a vile criminal as a true Christian. For the secular mentality is not so secular that it cares about things of the world in and for themselves if they are not joined to the conception that it is earnestness and integrity to make money and gain honor and esteem—but it is precisely this idea which the Christian takes away. Nor would anyone care very much

for friendship if he had to confess publicly that it is self-love—
no, but the appearance that this relationship is true love, this
appearance the world wants—and it is this very appearance
which the Christian takes away.[97]

Kierkegaard's sense of the antagonism between Christianity,
with its demanding moral standard, and the world is not by any
means exclusively derived from Kant. Kierkegaard's whole life,
his rigorous upbringing, the familial tradition of "melancholy,"
and his bitter confrontation with midcentury Danish society
played a major role in shaping his views. But if Kierkegaard
wished an intellectual ally in this estimate of the world around
him, he could find no better one than Kant. Here, in the writings
of the most esteemed and revered scholar of his age, a man with
no personal axe to grind regarding his treatment by contemporaries, were recorded the darkest and most pessimistic estimates
of the fate of individual virtue in the world. This estimate had
two conceptual bases: one, the view that suffering and hardship
are not inimical to virtue but provide its truest test; the other, the
perception that human nature will always seek to avoid this test,
substituting crass egoism for virtue or, when it cannot do so,
engaging in the more elegant evasions of self-deception and
hypocrisy. These insights by the wisest and most respected moral
philosopher since Socrates must have contributed to Kierkegaard's own intellectual formation on this matter.

METHODOLOGY

The idea that Kant's method of treating philosophical subjects
might have influenced Kierkegaard seems initially preposterous.
What can Kant's philosophy, with its elaborate emphasis on system building, on architectonic, and on the remorseless and sometimes tedious exposition of concepts, have to do with the work
of a philosophical gadfly like Kierkegaard, who disdained all systems and whose writings are often a "dialectical lyric," as much
poetry and literature as they are philosophy? On almost no matter do these two thinkers seem further apart than on their
approach to philosophizing and philosophical writing. Yet here I
want to suggest that Kierkegaard may have owed a debt to Kant.

This debt concerns two essential elements of Kierkegaard's philosophical method: his addiction to irony as an essential philosophical orientation and his employment of "indirect communication" as a method of philosophical writing. These elements of
Kierkegaard's approach are deeply related to one another. The
standpoint of irony, as Kierkegaard observes in his doctoral dissertation dealing with this subject, is "negative."[98] The ironist
says what he does not believe or distances himself from the subject of his discourse.[99] As a philosophical method, in the manner
employed by Socrates, this becomes a pedagogical tool. By ironically accepting or appearing to believe the claims of his opponents, the ironist draws them out and enables them to see the
implications or shortcomings of their views.

An ironical approach also underlies Kierkegaard's use of
pseudonyms in the method of indirect communication. Rather
than merely presenting and then critiquing a philosophical-ethi-
cal position or "stage of life," Kierkegaard allows it to speak for
itself. In fact, he "speaks for it," lending his full literary and
philosophical talents to the pseudonymous author, allowing him
to develop his position to the limits of its coherence and sustain-
ability. Finally, just as Socrates requires his listeners to make
their own judgments regarding the adequacy of the fully defended views of a Euthyphro, a Thrasymachus, or a Callicles, so
Kierkegaard requires his reader to engage the pseudonym's position and make a decision for or against it.

If this is a fair statement of Kierkegaard's philosophical
approach, the question remains, what can it have to do with
Kant? Where do we find anything like indirect communication
and Socratic irony in Kant's work? The answer is that both these
elements are significantly present in Kant's 1766 treatise *Dreams
of a Spirit-Seer*. This is one of the few writings by Kant we are
certain Kierkegaard read carefully because he quotes from it
twice in his journals, a fact that makes the suggestion of influence here even more appropriate.

To understand what Kierkegaard might have drawn here
from Kant, a brief review of this unusual little work is in order.
The full title, *Dreams of a Spirit-Seer Illustrated by Dreams of
Metaphysics* ("Traüme eines Geistersehers, erläutert durch
Traüme der Metaphysik"), hints at Kant's intentions. On the one

hand, he would critique the work and position of a single "spirit-seer," the Swedish mystic and illuminatus Emanuel Swedenborg. More basically, he would use this critical assessment of Swedenborg's work to reveal the central defects of classical dogmatic metaphysics. Although *Dreams* is technically a "precritical" work, it belongs to the twenty-year period when Kant was distancing himself from the Wolffian rationalism of his youth and was developing the outlines of his mature critical position. In Swedenborg's reveries, Kant believed he found the perfect vehicle for his attack on classical metaphysical rationalism. By showing that Swedenborg's claims of intimate familiarity and communication with the spirit world rested on intellectual premises very similar to those of the metaphysicians, Kant could reveal the absurdity of the metaphysicians' views and suggest where uncontrolled speculation leads.

What is fascinating about *Dreams*, however, is that Kant does not make this point directly. Instead, beginning with the first chapter he assumes the sober and altogether reasonable tone of a metaphysical philosopher. Building on simple premises, some of which are remarkably Kantian (such as those affirming an "intelligible" aspect of human life found in moral experience) but adding others that are distinctly un-Kantian (for example, the view that some especially "sensitive" persons might have immediate access to a separate "spiritual" realm), by the end of the third chapter he leads the reader into an acknowledgment of the reasonability of some of Swedenborg's wildest claims, including his alleged communication with nonmaterial spiritual beings. At this juncture, Kant resumes his own voice and drives the lesson home. Either one can accept the claims of people like Swedenborg to be "half dwellers in another world" or one can judge his and similar metaphysical views, this "bottomless philosophy," as Kant calls it, to be a misguided result of reasoning from faulty premises. Or, even more simply, one can regard all these types as "candidates for the hospital" and spare oneself further investigation.[100]

As this last remark suggests, *Dreams* is a bitingly funny and sarcastic demolition of metaphysical pretensions. From its first words to its last it is filled with witty jibes at Kant's intellectual opponents. As M. Kronenberg remarks,

So entirely did Kant look down upon Swedenborg and his contemporaries the metaphysicians that he merely played with
them, handling them now with serious irony, now with sly
humour, sometimes pouring upon them his gallish scorn and
dealing them the sharpest blows of his cynical wit. Such a tone
is only assumed by one who sees his subject far beneath him.
So did Kant hold himself in regard to the metaphysicians, to
general philosophical knowledge, yea even to knowledge itself
as a whole.[101]

Against this background, we can speculate on several levels
of indebtedness by Kierkegaard to Kant's effort in *Dreams*. One
is somewhat unexpected. It is the possibility that in preparing his
own study of metaphysical pretension, *The Book on Adler*, written in 1846 and never published during his lifetime, Kierkegaard
may have drawn on the model furnished by Kant in *Dreams*.
This study is one of the most enigmatic of Kierkegaard's writings. It drew his energies for an extended period, and he seems to
have regarded it as one of his most important efforts, yet he
chose not to publish it. Part of the reason may be the appearance
of philosophical "overkill." *The Book on Adler* focuses on the
disordered claims to private revelation made by a mentally dis-
turbed priest in a small rural parish, Magister A. P. Adler. Adler's
teachings, often communicated in the scratchy whistling voice he
adopted when in direct communication with Jesus, ranged from
the claim that they contained a new revelation of authentic
Christian teaching to the claim that they involved a wholly new
revelation that somehow "went beyond" and extended the outlines of Christian truth.

Adler was surely a puny target for the dialectical cannons of
Søren Kierkegaard. Yet Kierkegaard chose to write this book.
Part of the reason seems to be that he believed Adler's thinking
represented a fundamental misunderstanding of the role of
authority in the religious life. Adler, on the one hand, claimed the
right to serve—and to receive his salary—as an orthodox Christian pastor. Yet he also vaunted that he was the source of a new
revelation transcending received and established church doctrines. Kierkegaard saw this confusion as one shared by many
less eccentric "Christian" teachers of his day. This issue drew his
attention in a section of *The Book on Adler* published separately

as an essay entitled "On the Difference between a Genius and an Apostle."[102] Adler's widely ridiculed excesses thus gave Kierkegaard a unique chance to present this confusion at its worst.

The same is true for a related but much deeper confusion betrayed by Adler's revelations. On the one hand, Adler purported that these revelations were directly inspired by Christ and contained essential and timeless Christian truths. On the other hand, they somehow were also supposed to "update" Christianity and "go beyond" traditional teachings. In Kierkegaard's view, that Adler could so blithely make these contradictory claims was not accidental. It was a manifestation of both the pastor's youthful immersion in Hegelian philosophy and the spirit of the times that he shared with some of its most respected teachers. For was it not the essential claim of the Hegelians that they had "gone beyond" Christianity? Was not Hegelianism supposed to be the philosophical culmination of what Christianity had only begun? If so, the difference between the ravings of Adler and that of some of the most distinguished "teachers" and pastors of the Danish church was only a matter of style and degree. They might not, like Adler, whistle as they talked, but the content of their teachings was no less disordered and un-Christian than his.

If we keep in mind Kierkegaard's main points in this book, we can discern a series of possible debts to Kant. First, there is a specific concern with issues of authority and the teaching of established religious doctrine. In the first chapter, I mentioned Kierkegaard's apparently great interest in Kant's discussion of this problem in his *Conflict of the Faculties,* which appears along with *Dreams* in the Tieftrunk edition of Kant's assorted works. Kierkegaard's favorable references to Kant's strict understanding of the duties of those in clerical positions (including the obligation to refrain from public disagreements with established doctrine)[103] shows that Kant's writings were on his mind as he approached the issue of authority and revelation central to *The Book on Adler.*

Second, and more important, is the use of an eccentric figure, widely regarded as on the edge of madness, as a vehicle for displaying the major philosophical errors of one's time. By inviting their readers to laugh with them at Swedenborg and Adler, but by then showing there to be no essential difference between the wild excesses of these pitiful figures and some of the fashionable teachings of the most respected thinkers of the day, Kant and Kierkegaard hoped to expose the pretensions of their eras' dominant intellectual and philosophical positions.[104]

Finally, there is perhaps Kierkegaard's specific debt to the indirect and ironical method used in the *Dreams*. Certainly, there are many differences between Kant's approach here and that developed by Kierkegaard in his pseudonymous works. But the example of *Dreams* is not unimportant. Apart from the Socratic corpus, Hume's *Dialogues Concerning Natural Religion,* and Voltaire's *Candide* (from which Kant appreciatively quotes in his closing remarks in *Dreams*), no philosophical effort employs irony so thoroughly and with such effect as this little treatise by Kant. In a journal entry for 1846–1847 in which he tries to define irony, Kierkegaard illustrates his point in terms that could as well apply to *Dreams* as to *The Book on Adler* (on which he was working at the time):

> The ironic subtlety lies in turning the attack into a self-revelation through a negative approach...Thus, when a man says something extraordinary about himself—for example, that he has had a revelation—it is ironically correct to believe him (the negative approach—not to contradict him directly, which only foolish men do) in order in this way to help him find out for himself that he has had no revelation.[105]

It seems to me reasonable to suppose that this small work had an impact on Kierkegaard's method of authorship. Whether Kant's *Dreams* directly stimulated Kierkegaard's approach or not, he must have seen in it a confirmation of what would become the governing style of his own writing. For here was the greatest philosopher of his time, a thinker who Kierkegaard acknowledged was "at the pinnacle of scientific culture," using humor and irony as a major philosophical tool.

SOCRATES AND KANT

A final point I wish to make in this chapter is less an observation of another parallel between Kant and Kierkegaard than a suggestion meant to stimulate our thinking about Kierkegaard. We know that within the philosophical tradition Socrates is the philosopher who plays the major role in Kierkegaard's intellectual formation. Socratic irony forms the focus of Kierkegaard's doctoral thesis, and Socrates is mentioned again and again in Kierkegaard's writings with genuine respect as an exemplar of the best that philosophy has to offer. Kant, in contrast, is rarely mentioned. Nevertheless, in this chapter we have begun to see the scope of Kierkegaard's debt to Kant. What I now want to suggest is that it is reasonable to suppose that Kierkegaard closely linked Kant and Socrates in his thinking and that when he refers to Socrates to make a point he often has Kant and Kantian philosophy in mind.

I have several reasons for making this somewhat unusual claim. First, there is the matter we just examined: Kierkegaard's possible debt to Kant in the use of irony as a philosophical tool. That Kierkegaard was primarily indebted to Socrates here goes without saying: the doctoral dissertation proves this. But Kant is the other great ironist in the immediately preceding philosophical tradition, and it was natural, in this respect, for Kierkegaard to comprehend *both* of them in his praise for Socrates' distinctive philosophical style. Kierkegaard's appreciative references to Kant's wit suggest that in his mind he distinguished both these thinkers from the self-important and stuffy Hegelians.

Second, a general confounding of Socrates and Kant might well be an outcome of Kierkegaard's own philosophical formation. Kierkegaard owed much of his knowledge of the history of philosophy, especially Greek philosophy, to Tennemann's eleven-volume *History of Philosophy*,[106] which he seems to have consulted often throughout the period he was writing the major pseudonymous works. Tennemann was a Kantian, and his history is saturated with Kantian terms and ideas. Kierkegaard thus viewed the philosophical tradition, including the world of Greek thought, through lenses heavily colored by Kantianism. A small sign of this is a reference to Socrates in the *Philosophical Fragments* in which Kierkegaard credits him with having advanced "the physico-teleological demonstration for the existence of God."[107] Now, although Socrates may have introduced this theological approach, *physical teleology* is one of Kant's preferred terms for this proof in the *Critique of Judgment*.[108] That the

Socrates who strides onto the stage of history in Tennemann's study looks remarkably like a disciple of Kant—he is the champion of ethical and religious purity and the foe of metaphysical excess—further suggests why Kierkegaard may have tended to conflate these two great philosophers in his mind.

Finally, I would observe that some of the major and most important claims Kierkegaard makes about Socrates apply equally well to Kant. Kant was even explicit about these matters and proudly defended his philosophy on these grounds. One such claim, perhaps the major one, concerns Socrates' famous "ignorance," his denial that he had any "knowledge" apart from knowing what he did not know. In the epigraph to *The Concept of Anxiety* Kierkegaard quotes Hamann to the effect that "Socrates was great in 'that he distinguished between what he understood and what he did not understand.'"[109]

Of course, it was also the whole point of Kant's critical philosophy to establish the limits and boundaries of human knowledge, to put an end to dogmatic metaphysics and dogmatic empiricism by making clear what human beings can never know. Nor was Kant silent about this central aim of his work. In the introduction to the first *Critique* he even makes the link to Socrates, completing a review of the value of his own critical approach by stating, "But, above all, there is the inestimable benefit, that all objections to morality and religion will be forever silenced, and this in Socratic fashion, namely, by the clearest proof of the ignorance of the objectors."[110] (It is interesting to observe that Kierkegaard directly quotes this remark by Kant in his notes of Martensen's lectures.[111]) In a similar vein, Kant concludes the *Foundations* with this memorable remark: "And so we do not comprehend the practical unconditional necessity of the categorical imperative; yet we do comprehend its incomprehensibility which is all that can be fairly demanded of a philosophy which in its principles strives to reach to the limit of human reason."[112]

A second major claim by Kierkegaard that applies as well to Kant as it does to Socrates concerns the indwelling nature of human knowledge. The *Philosophical Fragments* presents Socrates as the chief representative of a purely philosophical and nonrevelational cognitive standpoint. In Socrates' thought world, Kierkegaard observes, neither the "teacher" nor the moment of learning is decisive because each person is presumed to have the essential sources of knowledge within herself or himself. According to Kierkegaard, any thorough account of human knowing faces the difficulty that we must have a receptivity for truth and yet do not seem always to have the truth before us. Socrates, he says, "thinks through the difficulty by means [of the principle] that all learning and seeking are but recollecting."[113] As a result, "viewed Socratically, any point of departure in time is *eo ipso* something accidental, a vanishing point, an occasion [*Anledning*]. Nor is the teacher anything more."[114]

The same claim can and has been made for Kantian philosophy, where all religious knowledge and all response to revelation proceed from an inner, a priori structure of moral concepts. Indeed, the deep affinity between Kant's philosophy and the Socratic doctrine of "recollection" referred to by Kierkegaard in the *Fragments* leads A. H. Nielsen to suggest that Kant's *Religion* is the major stimulus for Kierkegaard's project in the *Fragments*. Nielsen speculates that Kant may be the hidden reference in some of Kierkegaard's more polemical comments in this work with respect to those who believe that a direct relationship with God in Christ can be replaced by adequate reflection on the content of Christian teachings. In any case, says Nielsen, Kant is the thinker who "comes as close as anyone" to embodying the kind of Socratic philosophical position with which Kierkegaard is wrestling.[115]

What Nielsen and others who have suspected this connection between the *Fragments* and Kant's philosophy have missed, however, is that Kierkegaard's involvement with Kant extends not just to the ideas and structure of Kant's treatment of Christ's historicity in the *Religion* but to the very wording of Kant's treatment of similar themes in *The Conflict of the Faculties*. We know Kierkegaard to have been familiar with this work because he copied out some of its humor into his journals.[116] It is striking, therefore, that in a passage we encountered earlier dealing with the role of Christ in our redemption Kant states the following:

> The biblical theologian says: "Search the Scriptures, where you think you find eternal life." But since our moral improvement is the sole condition of eternal life, the only way we can find eternal life in any Scripture whatsoever is by putting it there. For the concepts and principles required for eternal life cannot

really be learned from anyone else: *the teacher's exposition is only the occasion [Veranlassung] for him to develop them out of his own reason.*[117]

The similarity between Kant's and Kierkegaard's discussions at this point, especially the use of the cognate terms for "occasion" (Danish *Anledning* [formal: *Foranledning*]; German *Veranlassung*), indicates how closely Kierkegaard paid attention to Kant's arguments. Kierkegaard uses the term *occasion* almost forty times in the *Fragments* in conjunction with the teacher and moment of learning, but we nowhere find this joining of terms and concepts—one of the key ideas in the *Fragments*—in either the Platonic writings or in the work of any other previous philosopher in this connection, except for Kant. Although Kant is not once mentioned in the *Fragments*, this clear relationship to Kant's discussions suggests to me that he lies partly behind the "Socratic" position Kierkegaard presents and that, consciously or unconsciously, Kierkegaard often linked Socrates and Kant in his mind.

To this evidence I would add two minor observations. One is that as early as *The Concept of Irony*, Kierkegaard evidences a pattern of associating Kant with Socrates. Thus, although Socrates is the focus of this study, the chapter headings in the first three sections of the dissertation, as Stephen N. Dunning notes, are drawn from Kant's forms of modality in his "Table of Categories."[118] Second, there is the fact that in the *Religion* Kant repeatedly terms Christ "the Teacher." Since Kant expressly associates this terminology with his claim that each person has within himself (rational) resources for moral redemption, it is probable that Kant's position there became, in Kierkegaard's mind, synonymous with the Socratic point of view.

Of course, for all the similarities between Socrates and Kant, there are also important differences between the two. Socrates fashioned no "system." Like Kierkegaard he remained a gadfly to the end, whereas Kant is the grandfather of all the "systems" that came to dominate German philosophy after him. Yet this difference was not altogether in Kant's disfavor, for Kant was able to take what were only hints in Socrates' thinking and fashion them into a coherent and powerful standpoint comprising all the major questions of philosophy. To form a perspective out of the work of both Socrates and Kant, if this was what Kierke-gaard did, therefore, was to combine the viewpoint of philosophy's perpetual "outsider" with that of one of its most powerful modern spokesmen.

CHAPTER 4

Deep Engagements

Dialectics is in its truth a benevolent helper, which discovers and
assists in finding where the absolute object of faith and worship
is—there, namely, where the difference between knowledge and
ignorance collapses in absolute worship with a consciousness of
ignorance, there where the the resistance of an objective
uncertainty tortures forth the passionate certainty of faith, there
where the conflict of right and wrong collapses in absolute worship
with absolute subjection. Dialectics itself does not see the absolute,
but it leads, as it were, the individual up to it.

—Kierkegaard, *Concluding Unscientific Postscript*[1]

No sharp line separates the issues of this chapter from those of
the preceding one. A reader who wanted to do so could move
through these two chapters topically rather than sequentially,
proceeding from specific "points of contact" in epistemology or
ethics to related matters involving Kierkegaard's "deep engagement" with Kant's thought. What separates these chapters is my
judgment that we are now about to take up ideas essential to
Kierkegaard's point of view, ideas that distinguish his contribution to modern philosophy and theology, and that are usually
associated with his name. In the treatment of each matter that
follows, I hope to show the magnitude of Kierkegaard's debt to
Kant—even on those points in which his engagement with Kantian philosophy leads finally to disagreement.

EPISTEMOLOGY

Critique of the Traditional Proofs

One of the most important of Kierkegaard's unacknowledged
debts is to Kant's critique of the traditional demonstrations of
God's existence, especially the cosmological and ontological
proofs. Because of Kierkegaard's virtual lack of attribution to

121

Kant, it is easy to overlook this debt (witness the omission of mention of it by the Hongs in their lengthy footnote on Kant in the *Journals and Papers*). Yet Kierkegaard's forays into the philosophy of religion in the *Philosophical Fragments* and *Concluding Unscientific Postscript* rely heavily on Kant's arguments against the traditional rational proofs. In the *Fragments*, for example, Kant's understanding that the idea of an object with its predicates is an entirely separate matter from the question of the object's actuality is central to Kierkegaard's argument that the traditional efforts to prove God's existence do nothing more than "develop the definition of a concept" or "the ideality I have presupposed."[2] Kierkegaard's distinctions between "ideal being" and "factual being," "essence" and "being," and "concept existence" and "real existence" all parallel Kant's distinction between the logical possibility of the object and its real existence.[3] Similarly, in the *Postscript* and *Papers*, Kierkegaard bases his rejection of the ontological argument on Kant's insight that existence is not one predicate among others but "a copula of judgment" that affirms an object's presence in our experience.[4]

In both the *Fragments* and *Postscript* Kierkegaard's debt to Kant on this topic is undeniable, although it is obscured by a pattern of nearly total lack of attribution. For example, in a long footnote in the *Fragments* ostensibly directed against Spinoza's version of the ontological proof, Kierkegaard says the following:

> The intrinsically unclear use of language—speaking of more or less being, consequently of degrees of being—becomes even more confusing when that distinction is not made, when, to put it another way, Spinoza does indeed speak profoundly but does not first ask about the difficulty. With regard to factual being, to speak of more or less being is meaningless. A fly, when it is, has just as much being as the god; with regard to factual being, the stupid comment I write here has just as much being as Spinoza's profundity, for the Hamlet dialectic, to be or not to be, applies to factual being.[5]

The idea expressed here is reminiscent of Kant's famous observation in the first *Critique* that, "if we think in a thing every feature of reality except one, the missing reality is not added by my saying the defective thing exists. On the contrary, it exists with the same defect with which I have thought it, since otherwise what exists would be something different from what I thought."[6] That Kant is on Kierkegaard's mind here is made clear by a parallel journal entry where Kierkegaard openly states his preference for Kant's view that "existence brings no new predicate to a concept" over Spinoza's claim that "essence involves existence."[7]

Kierkegaard's use of the illustration of a fly here is also a variant of Kant's famous "one hundred dollars." Just as a real one hundred dollars "do not contain the least coin more than a hundred possible dollars," but affect my financial position very differently, so Kierkegaard's fly, although predicatively deficient compared with the god, has no less real existence, since existence is binary, all or nothing. Again, lest there be any doubt that Kant is the source of Kierkegaard's thinking on this point, we need only turn to a passage in the *Postscript*.[8] Here Kierkegaard ironically appears to side with Hegel, who in his *Logic*[9] had dismissed Kant's critique of the ontological proof as a "barbarism in language" because it involved an appeal to a mundane reality (one hundred dollars) to discuss being of a qualitatively superior order (God). Referring to this criticism, without naming Kant as its object, Kierkegaard initially seems to concede Hegel's point, describing the Kantian position as a "stupid attack on the identity of thought and being." Within the space of a few sentences, however, Kierkegaard rejects Hegel's view of different kinds of "being" and returns to a Kantian standpoint.

Against this background, we can see that Kierkegaard's remark in the *Fragments*, "A fly, when it is, has just as much being as the god; with regard to factual being, the stupid comment I write here has just as much being as Spinoza's profundity," is almost surely a tongue-in-cheek reference to Hegel's criticism of Kant and a position taking on Kant's side of the issue. If Kant would defeat the ontological proof by means of a "stupid" comparison of God to a hundred dollars, he (Kierkegaard-Climacus) would go one step further and compare God to a fly. He would then compound his audacity by declaring that insofar as factual being is concerned his own "stupid" comment has just as much factual being (real weight?) as Spinoza's (Hegel's?) profundity. Within the space of several sentences, in other words, Kierkegaard enters the list on Kant's side against Hegel and, like Kant, uses wit and irony to demolish his opponent.

Kierkegaard was not a "philosopher of religion" in the traditional sense. Rational proofs of God's existence hardly interested him. He regarded them as spiritually pointless, and, in any case, it was rather the ethical and psychological correlates of religious (or nonreligious) life that drew his attention. Neither was he an antirationalist, however, and for this reason it was important for him to base his own fresh and distinctive approach on a justified repudiation of the style of religious thinking that preceded him. Kant's rational dismantling of the structure of traditional theology gave Kierkegaard the chance he needed. Very shortly, we will look more closely at what Kierkegaard does with the idea that there can be no objective proof of God's existence. For now it is important to note that this point, so essential to Kierkegaard's whole position, presumes Kant's ground-clearing work in the first *Critique*.

The Contingency of Existence

Kierkegaard's Kantian understanding that the traditional proofs confuse "ideality" with "actuality" or "concept existence" with "real existence" points to another major feature of his thinking deeply linked to Kant. This is his perception of the radical contingency of existence: the fact that nothing within experience exists with necessity and that real existence and necessity are opposed to one another. For Kant, this idea follows from the understanding that necessity is not an aspect of experience but an a priori concept, a category of the understanding not found in individual objects of experience but used by the mind to link discrete experiences in a systematic unity. It also follows from his understanding that all particular objects of experience must be thought of as causally connected to one another and therefore as conditioned and dependent on events that precede them. This means that although the concept of necessity applies to the connection of events in causal sequences, no object of our experience can be thought of as itself existing with absolute necessity. In the first *Critique* Kant turns this idea against the effort made in the "cosmological proof" to prove the existence God as an "absolutely necessary being." He concludes his argument with this observation:

> If I take the concept of anything, no matter what, I find that
> the existence of this thing can never be represented by me as
> absolutely necessary, and that, whatever it may be that exists,
> nothing prevents me from thinking its nonexistence. Thus
> while I may indeed be obliged to assume something necessary
> as the condition of the existent in general, I cannot think any
> particular thing as in itself necessary.[10]

Kant goes on to argue that absolute necessity cannot be
found in things but only in our cognitive activity as we seek to
unify the world of phenomena. This activity prompts us to locate
the ground of things outside the world of causal determination
and erroneously to ascribe real existence to such a ground. The
ancients did this, says Kant, when they viewed *matter* as the sub-
stratum of phenomena and as having absolutely necessary existence. They were mistaken in doing this, Kant observes, "for
there is nothing which absolutely binds reason to accept such an
existence; on the contrary it can always annihilate it in thought
[*in Gedanken aufheben*], without contradiction; absolute necessity is a necessity that is to be found in thought alone."[11]

The ideas and terms in this passage have a remarkable reso-
nance in Kierkegaard's writings, notably in the *Fragments* and
the *Postscript*. In an important passage in the "Interlude" of the
Fragments, for example, Kierkegaard develops at length his
claim that existence is not necessary:

> Can the necessary come into existence? Coming into existence
> is a change, but since the necessary is always related to itself
> and is related to itself in the same way, it cannot be changed at
> all. All coming into existence is a *suffering* [*Liden*], and the
> necessary cannot suffer, cannot suffer the suffering of actuali-
> ty—namely, that the possible (not merely the possible that is
> excluded but even the possibility that is accepted) turns out to
> be nothing the moment it becomes actual, for possibility is
> *annihilated* [*tilintetgjort*] by actuality. Precisely by coming into
> existence, everything that comes into existence demonstrates
> that it is not necessary, for the only thing that cannot come
> into existence is the necessary, because the necessary *is*.[12]

Kierkegaard's treatment here of existence and necessity contains features not present in Kant's writings. Kant does not speak
of "coming into existence" as a suffering. Nor does he argue that

actuality annihilates possibility, although this idea follows strictly from his understanding that possible but nonnecessary things can be thought either to exist or not exist. Nevertheless, the general lines of Kant's discussion and its proximity to other matters relevant to Kierkegaard suggest its influence on his thinking. Particularly striking is Kierkegaard's repeated employment in the "Interlude" of the terms *annihilated* or *annulled* to describe what thought can do to any existing or merely possible thing as proof of that thing's contingency.[13] This is the same idea Kant employs to describe what thought can do to a contingent object to prove its nonnecessity. It is true that in the quoted passage, where the translator uses the term *annihilate*, Kant himself employs the term *aufheben* (to annul), whereas Kierkegaard's usual choice for this concept is the noncognate Danish term *tilintetgjort*. If we assume that Kant's explicit discussion in the first *Critique* directly influenced Kierkegaard's treatment of the nonnecessity of existence in the *Fragments* and *Postscript*,[14] we might try to explain this subtle change in terminology as Kierkegaard's response to the Hegelians' overuse of the term *aufheben*. However, near the end of the "Interlude" Kierkegaard more openly displays the possible debt to Kant's discussion. Repeating one last time the idea that coming into existence involves an "annulled" qualification of being, he employs the term *ophævede*, the cognate form of Kant's preferred *aufheben*.[15] If we consider that other aspects of the "Interlude" reflect a use of ideas and terminology drawn from the first *Critique*, including the important phrase μετάβασις εἰς ἄλλο γένος which we'll soon discuss, there is good reason to think that Kant's arguments in this *Critique* deeply shaped Kierkegaard's treatment of the contingency of existence.

Many commentators have regarded Kierkegaard's understanding of the contingency of existence as a foundational and defining idea of philosophical existentialism. Applied to human life, both in Kierkegaard's writings and the work of later existentialist thinkers, it leads to a sense of the sheer "givenness" of human existence and to the perception that human beings are "anxiously" caught between the mind's demands for order and necessity and the defiantly recalcitrant realm of experience, where these concepts seem to have no place. What I am suggesting is that Kierkegaard substantially owes this idea to Kant's epistemology, especially as Kant applied it to the critique of the cosmological proof. Kierkegaard's obvious interest in Kant's treatment of this theological issue led him to a full engagement with Kant's understanding of existence and then to its creative appropriation in his own thinking in theology, ethics, and psychology.

The Concept of God

Major elements of Kant's epistemology also seem to shape Kierkegaard's concept of God. The term *concept* probably puts things too strongly since, in keeping with his rejection of a traditional approach to religious matters, Kierkegaard never really develops a "theology" in the full sense. But from statements scattered throughout his writings we can piece together the outlines of his understanding of God, which turns out to be very similar to Kant's.

Overarching Kierkegaard's thinking is his statement that God is "infinite subjectivity."[16] This is a somewhat cryptic remark, but based on other views and assumptions in Kierkegaard's writings, we can attach several meanings to it, each of which evidences a debt to Kant. First, it seems to mean that we cannot reach God through the "approximation-process" of objective knowledge.[17] We cannot prove his existence either logically or empirically, our two routes to "objective" truth. The impossibility of a logical proof, of course, follows from the strict dichotomy between thought and existence taken over by Kierkegaard from Kant and employed by both thinkers in their rejection of the traditional rational proofs. The impossibility of any kind of empirical demonstration of God's existence follows from the idea that God cannot be an object of experience. For Kant, this conclusion results from his entire epistemology. All the attributes traditionally ascribed to God, among them necessity, infinity, eternity, omnipresence (as freedom from conditions of space), and omnipotence (as freedom from temporally antecedent causal determination), are what Kant calls "purely transcendental predicates" and cannot pertain to an object within the time-space domain of our cognition.[18] In the strictest sense, therefore, we cannot "know" or "experience" God, and we cannot demonstrate his existence from any facts of phenomenal experience. In his *Lectures on Philosophical Theology* Kant states flatly that, without the aid of indwelling concepts of our understanding that point us toward his nature and existence, we could not recognize God "even if [he] were to make an immediate appearance."[19]

Although Kierkegaard never exactly speaks of our "non-knowledge" of God in these terms, there is ample reason to believe he follows Kant closely here. The idea that God is not discernible through our senses, for example, partly underlies his rejection of the idea that being a contemporary eyewitness to the events of Jesus' life in any way assists faith. In the *Fragments*, Kierkegaard concedes that the contemporary "can go and observe that teacher," but he asks whether this entitles him to believe he is a follower. "Not at all," says Kierkegaard, "for if he believes his eyes, he is in fact deceived, for the god cannot be known directly."[20] As Gordon Michalson has put it, "Within Kierkegaard's scheme, the divine presence in history is protected by something like Kant's noumenal shield; indeed, Kierkegaard's position is thoroughly Kantian."[21]

Incidentally, there is solid reason to think that Kierkegaard's specific affirmation in the *Fragments* of our inability to sensorily perceive God may be directly inspired by Kant's similar observation in *The Conflict of the Faculties*. Kant raises this matter at a particularly significant moment in his discussion, at a point where, in the course of a sustained denial of any role for historical or direct revelation in our salvation, he openly criticizes Abraham for heeding God's command to sacrifice his son. Kant voices this criticism in a footnote to the following epistemological observation in the text:

> For if God should really speak to man, man could still never *know* that it was God speaking. It is quite impossible for man to apprehend the infinite by his senses, distinguish it from sensible beings, and recognize it as such. But in some cases man can be sure that the voice he hears is *not* God's; for if the voice commands him to do something contrary to the moral law, then no matter how majestic the apparition may be, and no matter how it may seem to surpass the whole of nature, he must consider it an illusion.[22]

The footnote to this observation then introduces the matter of Abraham's conduct as reported in Genesis 22. Although in the

Religion Kant had questioned whether the historical reports of this episode are to be believed,[23] here he seems to criticize Abraham directly, faulting him for not questioning the validity of the "supposedly divine voice" in view of its inducement to a serious moral violation.

This passage and footnote immediately precede Kant's introduction of the term *accessorium*, and although Kant is not openly mentioned in connection with it, we know from Kierkegaard's journals that he associated this term with Kant's idea of existence.[24] A few pages further on, Kant makes the link between Abraham and Christ by alluding to Christians' use of the sacrifice of Isaac as a "symbol of the world-savior's own sacrifice."[25] In view of the multiple links here to Kierkegaard's authorship and concerns, including Kierkegaard's own strong defense of Abraham in *Fear and Trembling*, there is good reason to think that these passages in *The Conflict* were a major stimulus for Kierkegaard's discussion of God in the *Fragments* as well.

Kierkegaard also seems to be influenced by Kant's view that God is entirely outside the realm of spatial and temporal determination. In the *Postscript* he states, "God does not think, he creates; God does not exist, He is eternal. Man thinks and exists, and existence separates thought and being, holding them apart from one another in succession."[26] This remark brings to mind Kant's understanding of the time-based nature of our cognition and his definition of the human will as the faculty that brings mental representations into reality by a temporal act of decision. Since God is not in time, it follows that his knowing and willing are very different from ours. In the first *Critique*, Kant says explicitly that since the conditions of time and space do not constrain God and his intellect is not discursive, "all his knowledge must be intuition, and not *thought*."[27] In the *Lectures on Philosophical Theology*, he adds that God's knowledge is identical to his act of creation.[28] Since for Kant time does not enter into God's intuitive cognition, he also may be thought of as "seeing" past, present, and future in a single timeless intuition.[29] In *De omnibus dubitandum est*, Johannes Climacus expresses a similar idea when he observes that "to become conscious of the eternal in the whole historical concretion, indeed, according to the standard that it did not involve only the past, this he believed was reserved for the deity."[30]

One further sign of the essential similarity of Kant and Kierkegaard's conception of God and of God's "nonpresence" to us in our phenomenal world of "becoming" is the fact that God is unchanging and therefore not subject to being influenced by us. God's changelessness is a presumption of Kant's thinking and is explicitly developed by him in his *Lectures on Philosophical Theology*.[31] It is also a major theme of Kierkegaard's religious discourses, where it serves paradoxically as an important foundation for our absolute confidence in God's unvarying love.[32] Remarkably, after having criticized Kant's doctrine of God's unchangeability in a very early journal entry (1834) because of its potential for diminishing the importance of the Christian doctrine of atonement (with its presumption that God can alter his relationship to the sinner), Kierkegaard reversed himself little more than a decade later, adopting a Kantian point of view. Now it is God's unchangeability that grounds Kierkegaard's criticisms of passive reliance on divine initiative in the process of human moral and religious change.[33] This development in Kierkegaard's thinking in relation to Kantian ideas serves as a useful warning against taking any of Kierkegaard's few youthful criticisms of Kant too seriously. These remarks precede his intense involvement with Kant's writings during the period 1837–1844, and they tend to mimic his teachers' views.

In this connection we can discern an interesting and explicit parallel between these two thinkers where the matter of prayer is concerned. In a passage in the *Religion*, Kant distinguishes between the heartfelt "wish to be well-pleasing to God" that should be "present in us 'without ceasing'" and the use of words and formulas (even inwardly). In the former "man seeks but to work upon himself," whereas in the latter he tries to work upon God. Words of prayer, Kant adds, "possess only the value of a means whereby that disposition within us may be repeatedly quickened, and can have no direct bearing upon the divine approval."[34] Similarly, in *Purity of Heart*, Kierkegaard states that "the prayer does not change God, but it changes the one who offers it."[35] This idea is not new, but its appearance in this work along with so many other parallels to Kant suggests the degree to which Kant's theological perspective informed Kierkegaard.

Finally, to say that we cannot approach God objectively

because he is "infinite subjectivity" means for Kierkegaard that we can only encounter him inwardly, in personal moral experience. Kierkegaard is explicit about this. In a journal entry he states categorically that "the medium, the only medium, through which God communicates with 'man,' the only thing he will talk about with man is: the ethical."[36] Consistent with this are Kierkegaard's repeated affirmations that human beings' awareness of the religious comes about in the encounter with sin and guilt, since these, too, belong to the inward and ethical aspects of experience.

There are many important links to Kant on this point. Kierkegaard's position brings to mind Kant's important "change of venue" in the philosophy of religion, his translation of the religious from the domain of theoretical to that of practical reason. For Kant, we encounter the divine not in the outward sphere of nature but only in the innermost realm of moral experience. We cannot prove God's existence objectively but only "postulate" it out of the most urgent requirements of the moral life. In the second chapter I reviewed Kant's arguments in this regard, but I must now emphasize the way in which Kant's thinking in this area proceeds from the concrete "experience" of moral requiredness (the "moral ought") and from the awareness of freedom this "ought" implies. For Kant, these are the only "data" that ground the religious in human life, and they also furnish the only access—and a narrow one at that—to the "intelligible" realm where God and his kingdom may be found. Kierkegaard closely follows Kant on this matter. He is keenly aware of the distinction between theoretical and practical reason,[37] he repeatedly affirms the primacy of practical over theoretical concerns, and he sees religion as rooted in ethics.[38]

There also may be some interesting terminological debts here. Kierkegaard's belief that God is "infinite subjectivity" has at least two more specific meanings. First, it associates God only with the realm of inwardness. "God is a subject and therefore exists only for subjectivity in inwardness," Kierkegaard remarks.[39] This brings to mind Kant's understanding that of the two "forms" of sensory intuition, space is the "outer" form and time is the "inner" sense. Against this Kantian background, to say that God is subjectivity is to associate him with time and with the most important temporal dimension of human life: choice and willing. For it is precisely time that separates "thought" and "being" in human life and gives willing its central place. To associate God with "subjectivity" in the sense of "inwardness" thus brings us back, circumlocutorily, to the Kantian-Kierkegaardian insistence that the ethical is the primary mode of approach to the religious.

I also would suggest that Kierkegaard's designation of God as "infinite subjectivity" brings to mind Kant's very strong understanding that God is not an object of knowledge but of "faith." For Kant, "faith" or the "pure faith" of practical reason stands in an epistemological category of its own. As a form of "moral belief" it differs from both "opinion" and "knowledge." Opinion, Kant tells us in the first *Critique*, is a judgment that is both *subjectively* and *objectively* insufficient: neither the knowing agent nor all other agents hold it with certainty. A judgment of knowledge is exactly the opposite: the holding of something to be true both subjectively and objectively. In contrast to both these cognitive forms, "if our holding of the judgment be only subjectively sufficient, and is at the same time taken as being objectively insufficient, we have what is termed believing."[40] In this category Kant places all the objects of the "moral belief" that constitute faith. Thus, the religious is subjective and God may be regarded as "infinite subjectivity" in a precise epistemological sense for Kant: religious belief belongs to the unique and somewhat paradoxical sphere of cognition where judgments are universally but only subjectively valid. They are only subjectively valid because they arise from the personal and interior experience of each moral agent and cannot be made a matter of objective knowledge. But because these judgments are required of *all* rational and moral persons (at least to the extent that they choose to be rational and moral), they are also universally valid. Hence, for Kant, religious belief occupies the sphere of subjectivity in its "purest" and most indisputable sense: the sphere where subjectivity attains a universal dimension. If we keep this in mind, we can perhaps understand the force of Kierkegaard's repeated assertions that God is subjectivity. To the extent that he is informed by Kant here, this is not an admission of religion's inferiority or even, as it is usually taken to be, a defiant assertion of the value of personal life over natural scientific knowledge (although it is also that). It is a solid affirmation of those aspects of subjective experience that have universal rational validity.

Faith versus Knowledge

This discussion of faith and knowledge points to another major epistemological parallel between Kant and Kierkegaard: their shared view that faith involves a willed acceptance of beliefs that have no support or grounding in "objective" reality and may even be opposed by it. Kant's views here are distinctive and seem deeply related to Kierkegaard's. In the second chapter we looked at several of Kant's remarks about faith that appear near the end of the *Critique of Practical Reason*. One expressed Kant's understanding that faith is not strictly required by reason, not even moral reason. It arises from the effort by someone who has already chosen morality to render that choice fully rational, and it involves the decision to accept those beliefs about reality that allow prudence and moral duty to speak in unison. Although faith is solidly based on moral reason, therefore, experience often contradicts its tenets, which always remain uncertain:

> As a voluntary decision of our judgment to assume that existence [i. e., "of a wise Author of the world"] and to make it the foundation of further employment of reason, conducing to the moral (commanded) purpose and agreeing moreover with the theoretical need of reason, it is not itself commanded. It rather springs from the moral disposition itself. It can therefore often waver even in the well disposed but can never fall into unbelief.[41]

One might suppose that Kant would regard this lack of certainty as unfortunate, but as I pointed out in the second chapter, this is not so. Precisely because Kant regards genuine moral worth as based not on actions that are outwardly good (done "in accordance with duty") but on those motivated by a genuine respect for the moral law (done "from duty"),[42] he finds the worldly disconnection between prudence and duty to be morally desirable. In a remark near the end of the second *Critique*, Kant speculates on the implications of a world of observable moral cause and effect, where the punishments and rewards of conduct are immediately present to our view. In such a world, he notes, instead of the conflict which now the moral disposition has to wage with the inclinations and in which, after some defeats, moral strength of mind may be gradually won, God and eternity in their awful majesty would stand unceasingly before our eyes...Thus most actions conforming to the law would be done from fear, few would be done from hope, none from duty.[43]

Kierkegaard's affinity to Kant on both these matters is striking. True, Kierkegaard does state on one occasion in the *Fragments* that "faith is not an act of will."[44] But his reasons for this have to do with his rejection of the claim that human beings possess within themselves "the condition" for their own redemption.[45] By the end of this chapter, we'll see that this issue is one of the sharpest points of conflict between Kant and Kierkegaard, with Kant appearing to champion a qualified human initiative in the process of moral redemption and Kierkegaard denying that human beings can redeem themselves. When Kierkegaard says that faith is "not an act of will," therefore, he is saying that the choice that faith represents has its point of departure in God, who supplies "the condition," not in the initiative of the believer. But Kierkegaard is not denying Kant's claim that faith is *experienced* as a choice. Indeed, in another passage in the *Fragments* he states, in clearly Kantian terms, that "belief is not a knowledge but an act of freedom, an expression of will."[46]

Kierkegaard also profoundly accepts Kant's view that it is desirable for faith to lack objective certainty and to be opposed by experience. In a journal entry, for example, he seems almost to borrow Kant's description of faith as something which can "waver" but never fall into "unbelief" when he describes faith as "this very dialectical suspension which is continually in fear and trembling and yet never despairs."[47] Near the end of the *Fragments*, at the close of a long argument to the effect that "immediate contemporaneity" with "the god" provides no real benefits and even poses some obstacles to faith, Kierkegaard-Climacus observes that if the disciple really understood himself, he "would have to wish that it would be terminated by the departure of the god from the earth."[48] Taunted by an imaginary interlocutor for having borrowed this idea from elsewhere, Kierkegaard-Climacus confesses his debt to the Gospel of John (16:7).[49] However, John's thought—that Christ's departure permits the advent of the

Comforter—is different from both Kierkegaard's and Kant's view that the nonpresence of God desirably places the emphasis on inner faith rather than on a reliance on empirical evidence.

Kierkegaard further develops this understanding in the *Postscript* in connection with his important definition of truth as involving *"an objective uncertainty held fast in an appropriation-process of the most passionate inwardness."*[50] The following remarks in the *Postscript* are deeply parallel to Kant's distinction between faith and knowledge and Kant's positive estimate of faith's uncertainty.

> Without risk there is no faith. Faith is precisely the contradiction between the infinite passion of the individual's inwardness and the objective uncertainty. If I am capable of grasping God objectively, I do not believe, but precisely because I cannot do this I must believe. If I wish to preserve myself in faith I must constantly be intent upon holding fast the objective uncertainty, so as to remain out upon the deep, over seventy thousand fathoms of water, still preserving my faith.[51]

> Whoever believes that there is a God and an over-ruling providence finds it easier to preserve his faith, easier to acquire something that definitely is faith and not an illusion, in an imperfect world where passion is kept alive, than in an absolutely perfect world. In such a world faith is in fact unthinkable. Hence also the teaching that faith is abolished in eternity.[52]

As we register these broad similarities, it must be said that in his employment of terms Kierkegaard's understanding of faith initially seems very different from Kant's. For example, Kierkegaard sometimes speaks of the object of faith as the "paradox" or the "absurd," and he repeatedly describes faith as an offense to the understanding and as a "leap" beyond the ordinary categories of human thought. In these respects, Kierkegaard's "faith" seems in marked defiance of reason, a celebration of irrationality that is very different from the tentative and qualified steps beyond worldly experience permitted by Kant's "moral faith."

There are undoubtedly important differences in the content of faith, as Kierkegaard understands it, and the "faith of practical reason" elaborated by Kant in the *Critique of Practical Reason* or suggested by him elsewhere. But these differences all per-

tain to the essential point of conflict between Kant and Kierkegaard: their understanding of the depth of human beings' need
for salvation and the corresponding role of Christ in the economy of redemption. Once we acknowledge this important difference, however, Kant and Kierkegaard's conceptions of faith are
much more alike than they are different. Indeed, I think we can
say that for both thinkers faith arises and takes form within the
context of what are essentially similar structures of thought.[53] On
this entire matter we find *focused disagreements within a basic
context of agreement.* For example, the "absurd" that faith
believes, according to Kierkegaard, is the reality of the God in
time, the belief that "the eternal truth has come into being in
time, that God has come into being, has been born, has grown
up…precisely like any other individual human being."[54] Kant
doesn't speak this way. As we will see, he shies away from attention to the historical Christ partly because he refuses to accept
the conclusion that human sin could require such a direct intervention by God in history. Nevertheless, even as Kierkegaard
goes beyond Kant here, he is working within a Kantian structure
of thought. Christ is the absurd, the "paradox," because he links
what Kant has told us we cannot ordinarily think of as belonging
together: God and time, the eternal and the temporal, necessity
and existence. Kierkegaard's very understanding of why Christ is
the "absurd" presupposes Kant's epistemology.

Interestingly, it is not at all clear that within Kant's frame of
thought reason really opposes the idea of the "God-Man."[55] This
may be why Kierkegaard, with some imprecision, uses the terms
paradox and *the absurd* interchangeably to designate Christ as
the object of faith. It is true that for Kant we cannot, as creatures
in time and space, "think" the "eternal," and even less, therefore, conceive of the eternal in time. But it is the whole point of
Kant's epistemology to deny that everything we cannot *think*
also cannot *be.* This distinction is central to Kant's own delimit-
ed "practical faith," which includes belief in a supreme moral
causality behind phenomenal events in the world. As Kant
repeatedly observes, moral causation of any sort, with its presupposition of freedom, appears to contradict our phenomenal experience of strict causal determination. But, as he makes clear in
the first *Critique,* we are not warranted in taking the limits of

our cognition and experience to be a description of ultimate reality, of things-in-themselves.[56] Thus, his "practical faith" involves a rationally allowable (and morally impelled) transcendence of the ordinary boundaries of human cognition. Similarly, if it were established that only the "God in time" can effect the kind of moral redemption human beings require, as Kierkegaard believes, it is not clear that Kant's epistemology rules this belief out, and it may even require it. If this is so, Kierkegaard's concept of faith is not the flight of irrationalist fancy it is sometimes taken to be, but is a philosophically informed reminder, in the spirit of Kant, of the preeminence of practical reason and of the proper limits of theoretical reason.

A paragraph in the *Fragments* sharply signals the continuities and discontinuities between Kierkegaard's and Kant's thinking on these matters and also suggests how much Kierkegaard was aware of the nuanced nature of his disagreement with Kant. In this paragraph Kierkegaard draws a contrast between faith and knowledge in a way that initially seems opposed to Kant's view:

> It is easy to see, then (if, incidentally, the implications of discharging the understanding need to be pointed out), that faith is not a knowledge, for all knowledge is either knowledge of the eternal, which excludes the temporal and historical as inconsequential, or it is purely historical knowledge, and no knowledge can have as its object this absurdity that the eternal is the historical. If I comprehend Spinoza's teaching, then in the moment I comprehend it I am not occupied with Spinoza but with his teaching, although at some other time I am historically occupied with him. The follower, however, is in faith related to that teacher in such a way that he is eternally occupied with his historical existence.[57]

Although this passage highlights, in Kantian fashion, the distinction between faith and knowledge, the actual reason offered here by Kierkegaard for this distinction, that faith has as its object the historical existence of the savior-teacher, is decidedly un-Kantian, since Kant precisely rejects such a role for the historical in religious salvation. Indeed, in a later passage of the *Fragments*, Kierkegaard goes so far as to say that a nonhistorically apprehended god is not the object of faith but of knowledge. "One does not have *faith* that the god exists [*er til*], eternally understood, even though one assumes that the god exists. That is improper use of language. Socrates did not have faith that the god existed. What he knew about the god he attained by recollection, and for him the existence of the god was by no means something historical."[58]

This view would run directly counter to Kant, who believed that any *knowledge* of God is impossible and must involve *faith* since God transcends the temporal and spatial realm to which all our knowledge pertains. Remarkably, however, in a later unused "Note" for *The Book on Adler*, Kierkegaard corrects his statement in the *Fragments*:

> Reminiscent of *Fragments*, in which I said that I do not believe that God exists [*er til* (eternally is)], but know it; whereas I believe that God has existed *[har været til* (the historical)]. At that time I simply put the two formulations together in order to make the contrast clear and did not emphasize that even from the Greek point of view the eternal truth, by being for an existing person, becomes an object of faith and paradox. But it by no means follows that this faith is the Christian faith as I have now presented it.[59]

The reference here to "the Greek point of view" is misleading. Although Socrates and Plato both assumed that religious objects pertain to a timeless realm, it is not clear that within the corpus of their writings we find anything like the very clear distinctions between faith and knowledge developed by Kant in the first *Critique* and elsewhere. As we have seen, for Kant the "timeless" quality of intelligible realities like God, freedom, and immortality necessarily locates them in a noumenal realm beyond the reach of our (temporal-spatial) knowledge and hence makes them approachable only in faith. In view of this, I think it is reasonable to suppose that in these passages in the *Fragments,* as elsewhere, Kant is very much on Kierkegaard's mind and that, once again, Socrates plays the role of stalking-horse for the Kantian position. Although Kierkegaard clearly wants to distinguish his—the Christian—view from Kant's nonhistorical perspective on faith, he is honest enough to the Kantian standpoint ultimately to acknowledge that it, too, has a faith component and is alert to the distinction between faith and knowledge.

A footnote in the *Postscript* seems to me to express the similarities and differences between Kierkegaard's and Kant's conception of faith. This note is appended to a statement concerning the "painfulness" attending any effort to find God by the route of objective knowledge. This pain is caused by the fact that for the believer in need of God, "every moment is wasted in which he does not have God." The footnote then adds:

> In this manner God certainly becomes a postulate, but not in the otiose manner in which this word is commonly understood. It becomes clear rather that the only way in which an existing individual comes into relation to God, is when the dialectical contradiction brings his passion to the point of despair, and helps him to embrace God with the "category of despair" (faith). Then the postulate is so far from being arbitrary that it is precisely a life necessity. It is then not so much that God is a postulate, as that the existing individual's postulation of God is a necessity.[60]

Kierkegaard's deliberate use here of the Kantian term *postulate* is significant. Like Kant, Kierkegaard locates faith in an epistemological zone beyond objective knowledge. Like Kant, he wants to emphasize the tension between the spheres of faith and knowledge, in terms of both their certitude and their content. However, because Kierkegaard adds a heightened perception of human sinfulness to the world's moral intractability, he widens the chasm between human moral ambitions and their fulfillment. Faith remains a postulate, as it is for Kant, but it is a postulate seized upon in the very depths of moral despair.

Faith as a "Leap"

This pattern of focused disagreement within a context of agreement is even more dramatically exhibited in Kierkegaard's use of the term *leap* to describe the movement of faith. Here I want to propose something that may, at first, strain credibility, but that has substantial evidence to support it: that Kierkegaard is most deeply informed, both in his concept of the "leap" and his use of the term itself, not, as is usually thought, by Lessing, but by Kant.

Part One of Book Two of the *Postscript* strongly suggests the importance of Lessing's influence on Kierkegaard. Throughout this section, the pseudonymous author, Johannes Climacus, repeatedly acknowledges Lessing to be a stimulus or confirmation for the views he is setting forth about the relationship between subjectivity and truth, history and faith. Chapter II of this section, entitled "Theses Possibly or Actually Attributable to Lessing," contains the important third thesis on the leap: "Lessing has said that accidental historical truths can never serve as proofs for eternal truths of the reason; and that the transition by which it is proposed to base an eternal truth upon historical testimony is a leap."[61] In the course of expounding this thesis, Climacus draws explicitly on Lessing's essay "The Proof of the Spirit and the Power" (*Über den Beweis des Geistes und der Kraft*).[62] He emphasizes and agrees with Lessing's opposition to any efforts to transform the quantitative transition represented by historical inquiry into the qualitative decision of faith. Although Climacus remains uncertain whether Lessing grasped, as he does, that even firm historical evidence (in the form of contemporaneity with some historical revelation) cannot serve as a basis for the response of faith, he nevertheless applauds Lessing's perception of the "incommensurability that subsists between a historical truth and an eternal decision." Climacus concludes this portion of his discussion with a summary statement of what he has learned from Lessing: "Understood in this manner," he says, "the transition by which something historical and the relationship to it becomes decisive for an eternal happiness, is μετάβασις εἰς ἄλλο γένος, a leap, both for a contemporary and for a member of some later generation."[63]

During this discussion, Climacus-Kierkegaard mentions other writers and thinkers who have followed Lessing in treating the "leap," including Jacobi and Mendelssohn, but he makes no mention of Kant (in fact, Kant is never mentioned in connection with any substantive point in the *Postscript*). Despite this, I want to suggest that it is Kant, not Lessing, who serves as the inspiration for Kierkegaard's treatments here of the leap of faith. I have several reasons for making this suggestion. First, Kant frequently uses the term *leap,* whether in its German form (*Sprung*), as the Latin *saltus,* or as Italian *salto mortale* (literally "death leap"), in writings with which we know Kierkegaard to have been familiar. In these writings this term is usually, but not exclusively, employed to designate impermissible flights beyond the bounds of reason. For example, in a long passage in the *Religion*, Kant emphatically rejects the idea of divine predestination. He describes this doctrine, with its teaching that God "hath mercy on whom he will, and whom he will he *hardeneth*" (Romans 9:8), as "the *salto mortale* of human reason."[64] We encounter similar uses of the term *leap* in the phrase *salto mortale*, but also by itself and sometimes in the positive sense of a daring exercise of the free use of reason, in several other essays published in the Tieftrunk edition, some of which we can be confident Kierkegaard read.[65]

In the *Critique of Pure Reason*, Kant introduces, as an extension of the idea of causality, the "principle of continuity." This principle is an extension of our understanding that all phenomenal events (events in time and space) have a cause and cannot be thought of as coming into being without an immediately preceding event in time. The principle of continuity, Kant tells us, forbids any "leap" in the series of phenomenal appearances and also forbids the conception of any "gaps or cleft between two appearances."[66] Later in the *Critique*, Kant seems to assume this principle, along with his larger conception that empirical causality cannot properly be applied to nonempirical reality, as he criticizes the cosmological proof of God's existence:

> If we begin our proof cosmologically, resting it upon the series of appearances and then regress therein according to empirical laws of causality, we must not afterwards suddenly deviate from this mode of argument, passing over to something that is not a member of the series...
>
> Nevertheless certain thinkers have allowed themselves the liberty of making such a *saltus* (μετάβασις εἰς ἄλλο γένος). From the alterations in the world they have inferred their empirical contingency, that is, their dependence on empirically determining causes, and so have obtained an ascending series of empirical conditions. And so far they were entirely in the right. But since they could not find in such a series any first beginning, or any highest member, they passed suddenly from the empirical concept of contingency, and laid hold upon the pure category, which then gave rise to a strictly intelligible series the completeness of which rested on the existence of an absolutely necessary cause.

Kant concludes his treatment by pointing out that this last move is "entirely illegitimate" since "we cannot argue from empirical contingency to intelligible contingency."[67]

These remarks by Kant are interesting because they gather together at least three important elements of Kierkegaard's treatments of the leap. First, and most obviously, they contain an explicit reference to the "leap." Second, they present this leap as a movement of thought from the realm of worldly or temporal determination and reasoning to a realm of metaphysical or religious ("intelligible") causality. Whereas the traditional metaphysician tries to make this movement through a regressive argument in which causality is pushed quantitatively backward to origins, what Kierkegaard might call a process of "infinite approximation," Kant perceives that this movement involves a decisive (and here illegitimate) qualitative transition. It not only violates the "law of continuity" as it applies to phenomenal appearances, but, more seriously, it seeks to apply the phenomenally grounded law of causality to a realm beyond time and space. Finally, in describing this transition, Kant uses an expression drawn from Aristotle's *Posterior Analytics*[68] that Kierkegaard also employs to describe the leap; he calls it a μετάβασις εἰς ἄλλο γένος (a transition from one genus to another).

Some of these elements are also present in Lessing's "On the Proof of the Spirit and the Power." Not only does Lessing use the term *leap* (*Sprung*), but he also employs the Aristotelian phrase μετάβασις εἰς ἄλλο γένος in this connection. (Since Lessing's essay precedes the first *Critique* by four years, Kant may be indebted to him for this terminological conjuncture.) Even more important, Lessing directly connects these terms with the idea of the transition from historical knowledge to faith, the central theme of Kierkegaard's discussion in this section of the *Postscript*. Like Kierkegaard, Lessing denies that historical facts can ground faith, and like Kierkegaard, he insists on the prior movement of faith that allows one to regard a historical event as revelation. In view of these parallels, it seems reasonable to take Kierkegaard-Climacus at his word and assume that Kierkegaard's primary debt for his conception and Greek phrasing of the leap is to Lessing's discussion. Niels Thulstrup does just this in his *Commentary on Kierkegaard's Concluding Unscientific Postscript*.[69] There, speaking of the phrase μετάβασις εἰς ἄλλο γένος, he states flatly that Kierkegaard "has taken the expression from Lessing," who picked it up from Aristotle.[70] Typically, Thulstrup makes no mention of Kant's related use of the phrase in the first *Critique*.

Nevertheless, Lessing's treatment of the leap in "On the Proof of the Spirit and the Power" lacks one important element, perhaps the most important one, found in Kierkegaard's fuller understanding of the leap: the idea that the leap stands in tense or "paradoxical" relationship to the accustomed domain of human knowledge, that the leap goes beyond knowledge and defies knowledge. Kierkegaard seems aware of a difference between his employment of the leap and Lessing's. In an entry in his *Papers*, he questions whether Lessing grasped, as he did himself, the "thought" of the leap or whether he merely used it as an "expression."[71] In the *Postscript* itself, Climacus-Kierkegaard asks whether Lessing really appreciated the fact that even the direct proximity to revelation afforded by historical contemporaneity is not of the "slightest assistance" in matters of faith but only provides the "occasion" for faith.[72] It is noteworthy that in putting this question Climacus-Kierkegaard again uses the term *occasion* (*Anledning*) that he employed in the *Fragments* to describe the Socratic teacher, a term probably borrowed from Kant's directly analogous discussion in *The Conflict of the Faculties*.[73]

The possible oblique reference to Kant here is important because, in contrast to Lessing, there can be no doubt that Kant clearly grasped the "thought" of the leap. Kant perceives the leap as a sharp transition from the domain of reason and experience to the religious. We know that, for Kant, all religious matters belong to a separate cognitive realm, the sphere of faith, where the ordinary categories of our cognition do not obtain and that cannot be reached by any process of approximation through reason or knowledge but only through an act of will. Strictly speaking, Kant does not oppose a movement from one genus of thinking to another; indeed, his philosophy of religion requires it. What he opposes is an illegitimate leap, a leap that deceives itself and converts quantitative change into a qualitative transition. In all these ways, therefore, Kant's insight that the religious involves a leap beyond knowledge is far closer to Kierkegaard's thinking than anything found in Lessing. It is noteworthy, as well, that

Kierkegaard's earlier use of the term *leap* in the third chapter of the *Fragments* occurs in a context unmistakably connected with Kant's treatment of "existence" in the first *Critique*. Kierkegaard introduces the term in the heart of a discussion about the proof of God's existence and just a few passages away from his employment of the Kantian term *accessorium*. Somewhat further on, in the "Interlude," Kierkegaard uses the phrase μετάβασις εἰς ἄλλο γένος. This series of conjunctions suggests to me that Kierkegaard's concept of the leap, including his employment of the term, is most directly traceable to Kant's use of this term in the first *Critique* and elsewhere.

I would support this claim with several additional items of evidence. First, there is the fact that the concept of the leap in its broader and nonhistorical sense is already well developed by Kierkegaard in *Fear and Trembling* and *The Concept of Anxiety*, works I believe to be intensely involved with Kant's writings, including the *Religion* and *The Conflict of the Faculties*. Interestingly, in the *Postscript* Climacus confesses that he had read *Fear and Trembling*, with its discussion of the leap, before he had read Lessing's essay.[74] Then, almost as though he were signalling Lessing's secondary importance in this regard, Climacus ends his treatment of the third thesis with the observation "Whether Johannes *de silentio* [the pseudonymous author of *Fear and Trembling*] has had his attention called to the leap by reading Lessing, I shall not attempt to say."[75] Clearly, Climacus-Kierkegaard is playing a strange and involuted game here, directly raising questions of influence but coyly leaving them unanswered. This forces us to ask who, if anyone, is the stimulus for Johannes *de silentio*'s, Climacus's, or Kierkegaard's conception of the leap. If it is not Lessing, is it perhaps Kant? Is Kierkegaard trying here to hint at his unacknowledged involvement with Kant in these pseudonymous writings?

A second item of evidence for the claim that Kant is the immediate source of these ideas is the fact, noted in the previous chapter, that Kierkegaard sometimes explicitly used the term *leap* and the phrase μετάβασις εἰς ἄλλο γένος in connection with the qualitative transition from prudence to duty, a deeply Kantian point.[76] Third, there is the fact that sections of the *Postscript* dealing with the leap and Lessing also display Kierkegaard's attention to the first *Critique* and to the very portions of the *Critique* dealing with the cosmological proof. For example, in a footnote on the same page where he introduces the terms *leap* and μετάβασις εἰς ἄλλο γένος, Kierkegaard also recalls his discussion in the *Fragments* of the point that "nothing comes into being by necessity," a point similarly made by Kant in connection with the cosmological proof.[77]

Fourth, I draw a small bit of evidence for Kierkegaard's primary dependence here on Kant from a peculiarity of Kierkegaard's employment of the phrase μετάβασις εἰς ἄλλο γένος in *The Book on Adler*. Kierkegaard uses this phrase several times in his writings and *Papers*, usually to identify the kind of qualitative transition a leap represents.[78] In one of its uses in *The Book on Adler*, Kierkegaard employs the expression pejoratively to accuse Adler and the disordered orthodoxies and heterodoxies of the era of confusing everything, of being "guilty of delusions each one madder than the other, of paralogisms each one worse than the other, of μετάβασις εἰς ἄλλο γένος each time more confusing than the other."[79] Noteworthy both here and in the earlier use of this phrase in *The Book on Adler* is Kierkegaard's employment of the term *paralogisms* (*Paralogisme*) to describe the delusions and logical fallacies of all these speculative thinkers. This, of course, is the term Kant uses as a title for the section of the first *Critique* immediately preceding the discussion of the antinomies, a section where he begins his criticism of "dialectical illusion." This linking of terms and ideas in Kierkegaard's mind— μετάβασις εἰς ἄλλο γένος, paralogisms, speculative delusion— suggests that Kant's discussion of the leap in the fourth antinomy of the *Critique* exerted a powerful and permanent impression on Kierkegaard's thinking about this matter.

A final item of evidence that Kant is the most important source for Kierkegaard's thinking here comes from a lengthy footnote in the *Religion*. The topic of this footnote is a theme, as we shall soon see, that is absolutely central to Kierkegaard's tense relationship to Kant: the theme of the historicity of Jesus Christ. Although both Kierkegaard and Kant understand that religious faith involves a qualitative and volitional movement beyond the sphere of knowledge, Kant, as we'll see, does not allow this transition to encompass belief in the historical savior, whereas for Kierkegaard, such a belief, the presence of the eternal in time, is a key component of the leap in faith. In view of the importance of this issue I think we can suppose that Kierkegaard read this footnote with care. The note itself concerns the question of whether it is legitimate to schematize religious objects in sensory terms, and specifically whether it is allowable actually to attribute sensory, human qualities to God or to the conceptual archetype of perfected human morality associated with God (what Kant terms God's "only begotten Son"[80]). In this note, Kant acknowledges that schematization generally serves as a useful aid to our thinking about intelligible objects, but he vehemently rejects the inference that these religious objects really possess the sensory qualities attributed to them. "On the contrary," Kant concludes, "between the relation of a schema to its concept and the relation of this same schema of a concept to the objective fact itself there is no analogy, but rather a mighty leap [*ein gewaltiger Sprung*], (μετάβασις εἰς ἄλλο γένος), which leads at once to anthropomorphism."[81]

Here, then, we find a treatment of the leap almost exactly parallel to Kierkegaard's discussion in the *Postscript*. All the features of that discussion are present in this note: the term *leap,* the phrase μετάβασις εἰς ἄλλο γένος, the sense that the leap involves a sharp transition in our mode of thinking (in this case from the intelligible realm of concepts to the historical realm of time and space), and the specific concern with the historicity of Jesus Christ. It remains true, of course, that Kant disallows the "leap" involved here (although even Kierkegaard denounces irresponsible leaps and Kant has leaps of which he approves[82]). As far as the content of the leap of faith is concerned, specifically whether it permits or requires belief in a historical savior, therefore, Kant and Kierkegaard disagree. But this difference occurs within a remarkably similar framework of thought. What is striking is not that Kierkegaard differs with Kant on this specific point, but that, for both thinkers, Kant seems to have established the terms of the debate.

ETHICS

In the previous chapter we looked at the many ways Kierkegaard seems to have appropriated important insights from Kant's ethics.

I could easily have classified some of these borrowings as "deep engagements" with Kant's thinking. It is a measure of how significant are the two borrowings I want now to consider that they merit separate treatment. The first of these, the assertion of human freedom, represents another central idea of existentialism; the second, the conception of the "ideality of ethics," forms the basis for Kierkegaard's understanding of the transition from morality to religion, from the "ethical" to the "religious" sphere of life.

Freedom

No one can doubt the importance of freedom in Kierkegaard's thinking. One of his earliest journal entries expresses a passion for human freedom,[83] and freedom remains a central theme of his mature thought, where, with the constraints of finitude, it comes to be seen as a defining feature of human existence.[84]

This centrality of freedom in Kierkegaard's thought itself constitutes a sign of influence by Kant, since freedom is a major element of Kant's theoretical and practical philosophy. Kant is by no means the "inventor" of the idea of human freedom. But for many persons his writings have had the effect of converting a preferred belief into a matter of rational conviction. Kant accomplished this through a powerful new set of arguments, some of which appear to have had an impact on Kierkegaard.

One of these arguments has already occupied much of our attention: Kant's rejection of "dogmatic" empiricism and its claim that we must explain all phenomena, including human choices and actions, in terms of natural causes. If this kind of empiricism were absolutely true, human freedom could not exist because we would have to regard people as subject to nothing more than impulse and desire and incapable of respecting the constraints the moral law imposes. But it is just Kant's contention in the first *Critique* that what is true for our cognition, rooted as it is in the world of "appearances," may not also be true of ultimate reality. By denying the absoluteness of natural causation, Kant opens the possibility of the kind of nontemporal, conceptual (or "intelligible") causality freedom represents.

If the first *Critique* aims at establishing the "possibility" of freedom, the *Foundations* and the second *Critique* seek to estab-

lish its reality for us as rational beings. Kant advances several
different arguments to this end. One, appearing near the beginning of the third section of the *Foundations* under the heading
"Freedom Must Be Presupposed as a Property of the Will of All
Rational Beings," is derived from an examination of the logical
presuppositions of any exercise of reason, whether theoretical or
practical. Kant argues that rational thought itself presupposes
the judgment that we are determined by nothing more than concepts. A reason that denied this, Kant observes, would undermine the conceptual authority of its very denial since it would
then "attribute the determination of its power of judgment not
to reason but to an impulse."[85]

Elsewhere in the *Foundations*, the second *Critique,* and the
Religion, Kant tends to construct his argument for freedom on
moral ("pure practical") rather than theoretical grounds. For
example, he maintains that the "moral ought" represents an interior confirmation of freedom, since this "ought" could not logically impose its demands if we lacked the ability to comply. But
since this "ought" is a firm and inescapable part of our experience, we must assume we have the freedom needed to obey it.
This argument lies at the base of Kant's famous statement in the
second *Critique* that "freedom and unconditional practical law
reciprocally imply each other" and his often quoted remark that
whereas freedom is the "*ratio essendi*" of the moral law, the
moral law is the "*ratio cognoscendi*" of freedom.[86] In some passages of the second *Critique* and the *Religion*, Kant also points
to common sense and ordinary experience to support the reality
of freedom. Anyone who denied his rational ability to resist
impulses, says Kant, could easily be persuaded by sufficient
threats of punishment to exhibit the required self-restraint.[87]

Within the structure of Kant's thought, morality and freedom
not only "reciprocally imply one another," but they constitute
the firmest evidence for the reality of that "intelligible" world
toward which human religious belief points. In the second *Critique*, Kant observes that the three "postulates" of practical reason—immortality, God, and freedom—differ in their cognitive
status. God and immortality, as postulates of pure practical reason, receive no support from theoretical reason. Freedom, however, is an idea of reason known a priori. "We do not understand

it," says Kant, "but we know it as the condition of the moral law which we do know." As a result, "freedom...is the keystone of the whole architecture of the system of pure reason, and even of speculative reason. All other concepts (those of God and immortality)...attach themselves to the concept of freedom and gain, with it and through it, stability and objective reality."[88]

Apart from his shared enthusiasm for human freedom, Kierkegaard seems directly influenced by Kant on several of these matters. In *Either/Or*, for example, Judge William frequently emphasizes that we are not tied to the world of causal determination but that we can transcend natural causation and "choose ourselves" in free resolve. My history achieves continuity and becomes my own, the judge observes, "not when it is a summary of what has taken place or has happened to me, but only when it is my personal deed in such a way that even that which has happened to me is transformed and transferred from necessity to freedom."[89] The judge recognizes that, for a variety of reasons, the choice of oneself can be both alarming and difficult. Yet it is stimulated, he says, by the "passion of freedom." In terms deeply reminiscent of Kant, he adds that this passion "is aroused in the choice just as it presupposes itself in the choice."[90] In the *Postscript* Johannes Climacus suggests the centrality of freedom for Kierkegaard's religious position in a remark that recalls Kant's understanding of freedom as our unique access to the realm of intelligible reality. "Freedom," says Climacus, "is the true wonderful lamp; when a man rubs it with ethical passion, God comes into being for him."[91]

Many themes in Kierkegaard's developed religious philosophy appear to militate against this conception of human freedom. We will soon see that, like other Christian thinkers, he views sin as so complete that, in terms borrowed from the theological tradition, human beings can be said to be "captive" to it.[92] Correspondingly, Kierkegaard is prepared to give God a primary role in human redemption and perhaps to reduce human beings' autonomy and initiative in this respect. Nevertheless, freedom always runs like a red thread through Kierkegaard's thinking. Human sin, even in its most inescapable forms, results from the exercise of freedom, never from divine determination or predestination. In a journal entry in the last year of his life,

Kierkegaard observes that although God may be present in all a person's inward transformations, "God can give help for what only freedom can do."[93] It is fair to say that Kierkegaard's odyssey from ethics to religion, like Kant's, begins and ends in the certainty of freedom.

The Ideality of Ethics

To appreciate the importance of this next area of possible influence by Kant, it helps to keep in mind two of Kierkegaard's important convictions. One is his belief, often stated in the *Postscript*, that the "ethical and the religious stages have an essential relationship to one another," since it is "an essential requirement" for the religious "that it should have passed through the ethical."[94] The second is his belief that we make the transition to the Christian-religious through the awareness of moral failure, guilt, and sin. "The consciousness of sin," he states in a journal entry for 1844, "is and continues to be the *conditio sine qua non* for all Christianity, and if one could somehow be released from this, he could not be a Christian."[95]

Although Kierkegaard's concept of sin involves more than moral failure, our inability to comply with the demands of morality and conscience is a major part of what sin means to him. Hence, Kierkegaard's understanding of the rigor of the moral demand is crucial to his thinking. Because he regards morality as stern and unyielding in its requirements, he highlights the repeated fact of human moral failure, and this points the way, through the understanding of our need for forgiveness, to the decisive movement from ethics to religion.

Kierkegaard's sense of the rigor of ethics' demands is a fixed star of his moral and religious firmament. "The Christian requirement is infinite," he asserts.[96] "The ethical begins straightaway with this requirement to every person: you *shall* be perfect; if you are not, it is immediately charged to you as guilt."[97] Kierkegaard also opposes any relaxation of the demand: "To pare down the requirement in order to fulfill it better (as if this were earnestness, that now it can all the more easily *appear* that one is earnest about wanting to fulfill the requirement)—to this Christianity in its deepest essence is opposed."[98] Nor is Kierkegaard's view confined to Christian ethics, with its admittedly demanding standard of internal purity and selflessness. He believes that ethics in its universally human sense is just as exigent. A long passage in *The Concept of Anxiety* shows that he has in mind philosophical ethics when he speaks of this demand. This passage, which appears at the beginning of Kierkegaard's development of the idea of hereditary sin, also shows the importance of ethics' ideality for Kierkegaard's whole religious viewpoint:

> Corresponding to the concept of sin is earnestness. Now ethics should be a science in which sin might be expected to find a place. But here there is a great difficulty. Ethics is still an ideal science, and not only in the sense that every science is ideal. Ethics proposes to bring ideality into actuality. On the other hand, it is not the nature of its movement to raise actuality up into ideality. Ethics points to ideality as a task and assumes that every man possesses the requisite conditions. Thus ethics develops a contradiction, inasmuch as it makes clear both the difficulty and the impossibility. What is said of the law is also true of ethics: it is a disciplinarian that demands, and by its demands only judges but does not bring forth life. Only Greek ethics made an exception, and that was because it was not ethics in the proper sense but retained an esthetic factor. This appears clearly in its definition of virtue and in what Aristotle frequently, also in *Ethica Nicomachea*, states with amiable Greek naiveté, namely, that virtue alone does not make a man happy and content, but he must have health, friends, and earthly goods and be happy in his family. The more ideal ethics is, the better. It must not permit itself to be distracted by the babble that it is useless to require the impossible. For even to listen to such talk is unethical.[99]

If we pause a moment to reflect, we might note that Kierkegaard's point here is not obvious. It may be true that a special religious ethic is utterly demanding, but it is less clear that a universal rational ethic, a "science" of ethics, should demand the impossible. Why does Kierkegaard believe this to be so? Where does he get the idea that ethics demands the ideal? As this passage suggests, he seems to have in mind a tradition of ethical reflection different from the Greek, a tradition that is anti-eudaimonistic in nature and that conceives of ethics in terms of "law" rather than happiness. We find all these features, of course, in Kant's ethics. Not only does Kant's idea of the categorical imperative meet this description, but Kant, in an important section of the *Religion*, offers a penetrating discussion of the rigor of the moral demand that corresponds to Kierkegaard's view of ethics' ideality.

Although I outlined Kant's argument in the second chapter, I want now briefly to reiterate and focus on some of his most important points. At the heart of Kant's thinking is the understanding that the categorical imperative is universal, not only in all the previous senses we have explored, but also because it applies at *every* moment in an individual's life. To be a *rational* person, in Kant's view, is not to be subject to ever changing directions of choice and resolve, but to make the choice that brings all one's choices under a comprehensive policy of choice, or what Kant calls a "maxim."[100] If a person is to be *moral,* this maxim must involve unconditional obedience to the dictates of the categorical imperative. A morally good person, therefore, is one who agrees to live up to this standard, who never allows merely private willing to govern conduct, and who always submits each specific choice to the test of universal acceptability as law.

That rationality requires a coherent policy of choice seems clear. But why must moral willing be so unconditional? If we must develop a single, governing policy of choice, why not allow ourselves *within the scope of a single maxim* occasional departures from the moral law? Or why can't we choose to be *generally* good? Kant considers this question in a long passage of the *Religion* where the ostensible focus is on the related question of whether we are to judge human beings as good or evil by nature. Observing that these are two opposite and exclusive evaluations, Kant adds: "It might easily occur to anyone, however, to ask whether this disjunction is valid, and whether some might not assert that man is by nature neither of the two, others, that man is at once both, in some respects good, in other respects evil. Experience actually seems to substantiate the middle ground between the two extremes." But Kant hastens to add that a middle ground here is as untenable in the estimate of human nature as it is in judgments of moral worth:

It is, however, of great consequence to ethics in general to avoid admitting, so long as it is possible, of anything morally intermediate, whether in actions (*adiophora*) [*sic*] or in human characters; for with such ambiguity all maxims are in danger of forfeiting their precision and stability. Those who are partial to this strict mode of thinking are usually called *rigorists* (a name which is intended to carry reproach, but which actually praises)...

According to the rigoristic diagnosis, the answer to the question at issue rests on the observation, of great importance to morality, that freedom of the will is of a wholly unique nature in that an incentive can determine the will to an action *only so far as the individual has incorporated it into his maxim* (has made it the general rule in accordance with which he will conduct himself); only thus can an incentive, whatever it may be, co-exist with the absolute spontaneity of the will (*i.e.*, freedom). But the moral law, in the judgment of reason, is in itself an incentive, and whoever makes it his maxim is *morally* good. If, now, this law does not determine a person's will in the case of an action which has reference to the law, an incentive contrary to it must influence his choice; and since, by hypothesis, this can only happen when a man adopts this incentive (and thereby the deviation from the moral law) into his maxim (in which case he is an evil man) it follows that his disposition in respect to the moral law is never indifferent, never neither good nor evil. Neither can a man be morally good in some ways and at the same time morally evil in others. His being good in one way means that he has incorporated the moral law into his maxim; were he, therefore, at the same time evil in another way, while his maxim would be universal as based on the moral law of obedience to duty, which is essentially single and universal, it would at the same time be only particular; but this is a contradiction.[101]

Kant's argument here is a penetrating analysis of the meaning of human rationality in its application to a life of moral willing. Kant perceives that our understanding of rationality does not permit us to escape blamelessly into rationally unguided moments of choice. He also perceives that there is no intermediate position between moral and immoral willing. Such an intermediate position would presumably involve a commitment to respecting the moral law but would reserve the right *on occasion* to pursue otherwise unpermitted objects of personal interest. But Kant sees that this position, despite its bid to morality, makes something other than the moral law the final arbiter of choice and is therefore another form of "private" willing conceptually indistinguishable from crasser forms of "self-love." Put simply, since morality allows of no "condition" higher than itself, a conditional commitment to duty is no commitment at all. For Kant, morality is an *either/or*: either one chooses *always* to be guided by the moral law or one does not and is then properly regarded as immoral.

We find here, therefore, just the ideality of which Kierkegaard speaks. Ethics brooks no compromise. It requires a commitment to lifelong, unerring rectitude, and it refuses in advance to permit indulgent concessions to occasional episodes of weakness. If this is true prospectively, in the definition of standards of moral worth, we'll see that it is also true retrospectively: Kantian ethics cannot excuse a single moral lapse over one's previous course of life.

For several reasons it seems to me certain that Kierkegaard is deeply indebted to Kant's perceptive development of the full rigor of the moral demand in this passage of the *Religion*. One is the fact, already mentioned, that the "science of ethics" Kierkegaard has in mind displays Kantian overtones, especially in its sharp difference from eudaimonistic Greek ethics. Second, there is independent evidence in several remarks by Kierkegaard in his *Papers* that he associated this distinction between ideality and actuality with Kant and saw it as one of the stronger aspects of Kant's ethics.[102] Third, there is the fact that Kierkegaard introduces this matter of the ideality of ethics during a discussion in *The Concept of Anxiety* that displays striking similarities to Kant's discussion in the *Religion*. Both treatments start with this observation of ethics' rigorous demand; both proceed to the problem of human sin, and both deal with Adam's sin and the problem of hereditary sin. These textual parallels suggest to me that Kierkegaard read these pages in the first book of the *Religion* with great care. Finally, elsewhere in his writings, Kierkegaard shows his clear understanding of Kant's point in this defense of moral rigorism. I could cite several passages, but two in particular stand out. The first is from *Purity of Heart*, a work we know to be permeated with Kantian ethical ideas; the second is from the *Postscript*.

> The double-minded one stands at a parting of the ways...He believes he has found that there is a third way and that it is in this third way along which he is going. This third way has no name. For it does not really exist, and so it is obvious that he, if he is sincere, cannot say which way he is taking...And how does he go along this third way which is narrower than any rope-dancer's rope, for it simply does not exist? Does he go steadily and firmly like one who has a definite goal before his eyes...? No, only a person upon the path of the Good walks in this fashion with only the Good before his eyes.
>
> Does he, then, go like one that is hunting for every sensation along the broad way of pleasure? No, that he does not do...He walks so slowly...He feels his way forward with his foot and as he finally plants his foot and takes a step, he immediately looks about at the clouds, notes the way the wind blows, and whether the smoke goes straight up from the chimney. It is, namely, the reward—earth's reward—that he is looking for. And that reward is like the clouds and like the wind and like the smoke of the chimney.[103]

This passage displays Kierkegaard's literary genius. In his hands Kant's complex and dense prose becomes a compelling image. The second passage, from the *Postscript*, returns us to Kierkegaard's own particular philosophical vocabulary:

> It is possible to *be both* good and bad, as we say quite simply, that a man has tendencies to both good and evil. But it is impossible *at one and the same time to become both good and bad*. Aesthetically the requirement has been imposed on the poet not to present these abstract patterns of virtue, or satanic incarnations of evil, but to follow Goethe's example and to give us characters which are both good and bad. And why is this a legitimate demand? Because the poet is supposed to describe human beings as they *are*, and every human being is *both good and bad*; and because the medium of the poet is imagination, is *being* but not *becoming*, or at most becoming in a very much foreshortened perspective. But take the individual out of the medium of imagination, the medium of being, and place him in existence: Ethics will at once demand that he be pleased to become, and then he becomes—either good or bad. In the seri-

ous moment of self-examination, and in the sacred moment of the confessional, the individual takes himself out of the medium of becoming, and inquires into the medium of being, how it is with him; and, alas! the unfortunate result of this inquiry is that he *is both* good and bad. But as soon as he again enters the medium of becoming he becomes either good or bad. This *summa summarum*, that all men *are* both good and bad, does not concern Ethics in the least. For ethics does not have the medium of *being*, but the medium of *becoming*. [104]

I might add that this last passage has a further intriguing connection to Kant. In the *Postscript* it is immediately followed by a brief but ethically oriented criticism of Hegel's disparaging treatment of "reflection," a concept Hegel elsewhere explicitly associated with Kant's philosophical methodology.[105] In essence, therefore, Kierkegaard is again in the position of "going back" to Kant to defend his ethical seriousness against the Hegelians' efforts to "mediate" all life's conflicts and challenges. Despite the absence in the *Postscript* of any reference to Kant in connection with this important assertion of the ideality of ethics, we can suppose that Kierkegaard was well aware of the extent to which he was appropriating Kant's thinking.

Radical Evil

The concept of radical human evil, iniquity at the very *root* of human willing, seems to me another major area in which Kierkegaard is deeply indebted to Kant. Strictly speaking, in developing this idea we remain in the realm of ethics, since its components derive wholly from aspects of moral reason and moral experience. Only the response to this problem takes us out of ethics into religion, and it is there, we'll see, that Kant and Kierkegaard begin to part ways. Although I briefly outlined Kant's views on this matter in the second chapter, I want to review them here in a more focused way in connection with Kierkegaard's views.

Kant develops the idea of "radical evil" in the first book of the *Religion*. He presents it as emerging from two compelling aspects of the moral life that work together, like jaws of a vise, to crush our moral pride. We have just examined one: ethics' rigorous and unyielding demand that we commit ourselves to a life of moral obedience, a demand that, in Kierkegaard's terms, constitutes the "ideality of ethics." The other aspect is our awareness that we *have not* shown this commitment in the past and therefore have good reason to believe (or, as Kant says, "to postulate"[106]) that we *will not* sustain it in the future. The virtual certitude, based on past experience and honest present self-assessment, that we will not maintain a commitment to morality almost amounts to the conclusion that we cannot do so, and, in one sense of the term *cannot,* as a statement of what we can reasonably find within our power, we know in good faith that we "cannot" be moral. Since this "cannot" does not arise from any natural constraint on our willing but from a virtual certitude regarding the shape of our future course of free willing, we must regard it as a morally responsible failure and imputable to us as evil.

Several distinct considerations underlie Kant's claim that we know ourselves to be unable to make the kind of unwavering commitment to duty the moral law demands. One is the fact that human beings, as finite creatures with natural "inclinations" and needs, have an ever present incentive to disobey the moral law. Unlike God, whose will is "holy" because his every personal desire accords with the interests of "all," our private interests can conflict with the common good, and we experience the moral law as an imperative that constrains the will.

Our natural desires do not, in themselves, mean we must do wrong. Kant is clear to insist that although these desires or "inclinations" play a role in our wrongwilling, they are not the *cause* of it. This is so because, as he says, "natural inclinations, *considered in themselves, are good.*"[107] They form the substance of moral choice and become evil only through their misuse. Furthermore, the idea that natural desires *cause* wrongful choice runs directly counter to the certitude associated with our sense of freedom that we can always resist the force of impulse. If wrongful choice takes place, therefore, it is not because desire overpowers reason, but because we choose to give the satisfaction of desire priority over the dictates of the moral law.

Why should we do this? In the second chapter, I pointed to Kant's mature understanding of the degree of human freedom with respect to morality—the fact that we are not even compelled

by impartial reasoning to accept morality's primacy in our decisions. Rational willing can encompass both moral and immoral
choice. To say we are rationally free to choose immorality does
not explain why we should do so, but it is just Kant's point that
there can be no explaining this choice. Since immorality rests on
the exercise of freedom and cannot be traced to any natural event
preceding it or determining it, it utterly defies our accustomed
efforts at "causal" explanation. In an important footnote in the
Religion, Kant insists that any attempt to "explain" either human
good or evil ultimately ends in the fact of freedom:

> That the ultimate subjective ground of the adoption of moral
> maxims is inscrutable is indeed already evident from this, that
> since this adoption is free, its ground (why, for example, I have
> chosen an evil and not a good maxim) must not be sought in
> any natural impulse, but always again in a maxim. Now since
> this maxim also must have its ground, and since apart from
> maxims no *determining ground* of free choice can or ought to
> be adduced, we are referred back endlessly in the series of sub-
> jective determining grounds, without ever being able to reach
> the ultimate ground.[108]

Taken by itself, the knowledge that we are radically free to be
moral or immoral may seem to support a confidence in our future
choices. But, in Kant's view, several other considerations intervene
to erode this confidence and, indeed, lead us to the opposite conclusion: to "postulate" that we are virtually incapable of sustained moral willing.[109] One factor is the opacity of our innermost
wills, even to ourselves. At the heart of all our lifelong willing, in
Kant's view, is a single "maxim" of choice that shapes and directs
all our phenomenal choices. But we are time-space beings, and
our knowledge of ourselves is no less "phenomenal" than our
knowledge of outer reality. Thus, our innermost guiding maxim
remains "inscrutable" to us and can only be guessed at on the
basis of the continual process of willing we have exhibited to ourselves and others. By itself, this inscrutability weakens our confidence in the goodness of our will, since even an impeccable record
might conceal wrongful motives. But, in conjunction with even a
single past act of moral defection, it becomes a nearly fatal argument against the moral reliability of our future willing.

The reason for this has to do with Kant's acute understanding of human freedom. If I did not know myself to possess the ability always to subordinate impulse to reason, I might be able to put an isolated past act of immoral choice behind me. I could argue, for example, that I was "overcome" by passion or desire, or I might plead ignorance, that I was not aware that what I was doing was wrong. But the latter excuse usually runs counter to the indwelling sense of my ability to make moral judgments (and my knowledge that I am responsible for trying to make them correctly), and the former runs flat up against the fact of freedom. To the extent, therefore, that any act in the past was made knowingly and freely, it was strictly speaking *unconditioned* and not necessary. But if I have once knowingly done wrong without being constrained to do so in any way, what makes me think I will not do so again? In other words, even a single past act of deliberate wrongwilling on my part casts a pall on all my future free choices. It suggests that some of these choices will similarly, and freely, go astray, and it deprives me of the kind of certitude about the stability and goodness of my underlying maxim of choice that I need for any valid judgment of moral worth. Furthermore, if it is the case, as Kant believes, that anything less than unwavering obedience to the moral law is equivalent to complete nonobedience, then, in the mind of a conscientious and honest moral person, a single free, wrongful choice, of which each of us can find many examples in our past, amounts to a judgment of total self-condemnation and total moral guilt.[110]

This is a dark view, but one that follows inevitably from Kant's understanding of the moral law and the nature of human freedom. In view of this pessimistic conclusion, it is understandable that, near the end of the first book of the *Religion*, Kant reflects on the rational significance of the biblical doctrine of original sin. Certain aspects of the Genesis story strike him as obviously unacceptable. He rejects as "inept" the explanation of human moral evil that describes it as "descending to us as an *inheritance* from our first parents."[111] But he finds a demythologized and experiential meaning in the biblical story's representation that Adam's sin, like each of our wrongful choices, represents a free and uncoerced "original" use of the will. In this sense, Adam is every person. Quoting a phrase from Horace, "*Mutato nomine de te fabula narratur*" ("Change but the name, of you the tale is told."—*Satires*, I, 1), Kant believes this interpretation makes sense of Paul's statement (Roman 5:12) that "in Adam all have sinned."[112]

This has been a quick review of a complex argument, but I hope it provides some sense of the brilliance of Kant's deduction of the concept of radical evil and his rationalist rediscovery of a form of "original sin." I emphasize the brilliance of this deduction because it seems to me that a thinker like Kierkegaard, interested as he was in this issue, could not fail to be impressed by Kant's argument. There is also no doubt in my mind that Kant's discussion directly influenced Kierkegaard. In at least five places in his writings and *Papers* he makes reference to Kant's doctrine of "radical evil." His lecture and reading notes also frequently allude to it.[113] Many aspects of Kierkegaard's understanding of sin seem identical to Kant's, and in several important places in his writings Kierkegaard displays some very specific conceptual and terminological debts to Kant's discussion in the *Religion*. Let me review the most important of these.

Kierkegaard's indebtedness to the *Religion* involves three major ideas found there and several smaller conceptual or terminological borrowings related to the biblical episode of the Fall. The three major ideas include an understanding of the *inexplicability* of sin, its *continuity,* and its *totality.*

The first of these, sin's *inexplicability*, has its foundation in Kierkegaard's shared perception with Kant that sin has its roots in human freedom. Like Kant, and the orthodox tradition which both thinkers presume, Kierkegaard refuses to attribute wrongdoing to human desires and to the natural limitations of the human condition. "Sin," he remarks in a journal entry for 1841, "is not simply finitude, but in sin there is an element of freedom and free finitude."[114] In *The Concept of Anxiety* he states that sin arises "not by necessity...but by freedom."[115]

But if sin, for Kierkegaard as for Kant, primarily involves neither impulse nor ignorance but the deliberate misuse of freedom, why do human beings choose to exercise their wills this way? Kierkegaard's answer is the same as Kant's. He insists that we cannot "explain" actions based on freedom because, by definition, they are neither logically nor causally necessary. "To want to give a logical explanation of the coming of sin into the

world," Kierkegaard says in *The Concept of Anxiety,* "is a stupidity that can only occur to people who are comically worried
about finding an explanation."[116] Sin must be thought of as
entering the world in a qualitative leap with the "suddenness of
the enigmatic."[117] In a remark that brings to mind Kant's argument that any effort to seek a "ground" for moral or immoral
choice involves an infinite regress that always ends in freedom,
Kierkegaard states, "We have nowhere been guilty of the foolish-
ness that holds that man *must* sin...We have said what we again
repeat, that sin presupposes itself, just as freedom presupposes
itself, and sin cannot be explained by anything antecedent to it,
anymore than can freedom."[118]

Interestingly, Kierkegaard's familiarity with Kant's position
on this matter is not only conceptually apparent; he makes it
explicit in his writings. Over the course of a decade of reflecting
on the problem of sin, Kierkegaard comes to an ever deeper
appreciation of the manner in which Kant handles the issue. In a
passage in *The Concept of Irony,* for example, he disparagingly
likens Kant's treatment of radical evil to Plato's use of "myth," in
that for Kant "the evil, namely, with which thought cannot cope
is placed outside thought and is handed over to imagination."[119]
By 1847 Kierkegaard focuses his disagreement with Kant on a
narrow issue. In a journal entry for that year, he states, "Kant's
theory of radical evil has only one fault: he does not definitely
establish that the inexplicable is a category, that the paradox is a
category." Kierkegaard adds that "it is specifically the task of
human knowledge to understand that there is something it cannot understand and to understand what that is."[120] Kierkegaard
fully credits Kant with perceiving this—Kant's "nonknowledge"
(*ikke-Viden*) is already a firm part of Kierkegaard's understanding of the philosopher's contributions[121]—but he faults him for
not including the "inexplicable" among the "categories" of
thought.[122] Finally, by 1851, in a journal entry comparing Kant's
treatment of sin with Julius Müller's handling of the problem in
his quasi-Hegelian *Die christliche Lehre von der Sünde,*[123]
Kierkegaard treats Kant's approach favorably. "Kant with his
radical evil," says Kierkegaard "was essentially more honest, for
he never pretends that his theory is supposed to be a speculative
comprehension of the Christian problem."[124]

A second major area of conceptual indebtedness to Kant concerns the *continuity* of sin. We saw that, for Kant, all our choices in time rest on a single "universal" maxim, a choice for or against morality. This maxim is never evident to us since it pertains to our intelligible selves, but it accounts for the importance of even a single instance of "phenomenal" willing because this instance may reveal the underlying directionality of our will. Any number of passages could be cited from Kierkegaard's writings to suggest his agreement with this point, which leads in his thinking to what he calls the "unfathomable continuity" of sin,[125] but a long passage from *The Sickness unto Death* strikes me as most expressive of his agreement with Kant's philosophical insight:

> In the deepest sense, the state of sin is the sin; the particular sins are not the continuance of sin but the expression for the continuance of sin; in the specific new sin the impetus of sin merely becomes more perceptible to the eye.
>
> The state of sin is a worse sin than the particular sins; it is the sin...In other words, deep within itself sin has a consistency, and in this consistency in evil itself it also has a certain strength. But such an observation is never arrived at by merely looking at the particular sins.
>
> Most men probably live with too little consciousness of themselves to have any idea of what consistency is; that is, they do not exist *qua* spirit...They play along in life, so to speak, but they never experience putting everything together on one thing, never achieve the idea of an infinite self-consistency. That is why they are always talking among themselves about the particular, particular good deeds, particular sins.[126]

It is this consistency/continuity of sin, of course, that, in Kant's view, renders even a single free act of wrongwilling morally fatal, and here again, Kierkegaard is in agreement. Continuing his treatment of this matter in *The Sickness unto Death*, he remarks, "The believer, one who rests in and has his life in the consistency of the good, has an infinite fear of even the slightest sin, for he faces an infinite loss."[127] Speaking in the *Postscript* of the consequences of a single wrongful choice, he states:

> So here there can be no question of the childish thing of making a fresh start, of being a good child again, but neither is there any question of the universal indulgence that all men are

like that. One guilt is enough, as I have said, and with that the exister who along with this is related to an eternal happiness, is forever caught. For human justice pronounces a life sentence only for the third offense, but eternity pronounces sentence the first time forever.[128]

Two other essentially Kantian ideas combine to lead to the third major point of agreement between Kant and Kierkegaard: their perception of the *totality* of human sin and of human beings' infinite guilt. The first is the idea, developed in connection with the ideality of ethics, that there is no middle way between good and evil. The individual who reserves the right, however infrequently, to turn from duty is qualitatively identical to the individual who persistently makes immoral choices. The second is the idea, just discussed, that even a single instance of wrongful choice, with which all our experience abounds, can bespeak this kind of fundamental disposition to immorality. For both Kierkegaard and Kant, these insights lead to the conclusion that if we are morally honest we must regard ourselves as totally lacking in moral worth or, what is the same thing, as absolutely guilty. Two remarkably similar passages in the *Religion* and *The Concept of Anxiety* bring out their agreement on this matter. Indeed, if we strike from Kant's statement the parenthetical remarks he uses to translate the religiously expressed point into his own rationalist terms, these passages are so alike they can almost be superimposed on one another. To make this clear, I present the full passage by Kant, an edited version of this passage eliminating Kant's rationalist clarifications, and then Kierkegaard's treatment of the issue. First the full passage by Kant:

This debt which is original, or prior to all the good a man may do—this, and no more, is what we referred to in Book One as the *radical* evil in man—this debt can never be discharged by another person, so far as we can judge according to the justice of our human reason...Now this moral evil (transgression of the moral law, called SIN when the law is regarded *as a divine command*) brings with it endless violations of the law and so *infinite* guilt. The extent of this guilt is due not so much to the *infinitude* of the Supreme Lawgiver whose authority is thereby violated...as to the fact that this moral evil lies in the *disposition* and maxims in general, in *universal basic principles* rather than in particular transgressions. (The case is different before a human court of justice, for such a court merely attends to single offenses and therefore to the deed itself and what is relative thereto, and not to the general disposition.) It would seem to follow, then, that because of this infinite guilt all mankind must look forward to *endless punishment* and exclusion from the kingdom of God.[129]

Now the edited version of this passage:

This debt which is original, or prior to all the good a man may do...can never be discharged by another person...Now this moral evil...brings with it endless violations of the law and so *infinite* guilt. (The case is different before a human court of justice, for such a court merely attends to single offenses and therefore to the deed itself and what is relative thereto, and not to the general disposition.) It would seem to follow, then, that because of the infinite guilt all mankind must look forward to *endless punishment* and exclusion from the kingdom of God.

Finally, Kierkegaard's treatment of the issue:

Whoever learns to know his guilt only from the finite is lost in the finite, and finitely the question of whether a man is guilty cannot be determined except in an external, juridical, and most imperfect sense. Whoever learns to know his guilt only by analogy to judgments of the police court and supreme court never really understands that he is guilty, for if a man is guilty, he is infinitely guilty.[130]

The ideas expressed in these two passages are not unique to Kierkegaard or Kant. They form part of the Christian religious heritage. But if we consider the many other textual signs that Kierkegaard closely modeled *The Concept of Anxiety* on Kant's discussions in the early portions of the *Religion*, the precise parallels in expression between these two passages suggest direct, unacknowledged borrowing by Kierkegaard from Kant. More, these parallels provide a measure of how closely Kierkegaard followed Kant's text.

Beyond his debt to Kant for the understanding of sin's inexplicability, continuity, and totality, Kierkegaard also displays a series of important agreements on the meaning of the biblical episode of the Fall in its connection with human sin. This becomes apparent if we compare Kant's treatment of Adam in the first book of the *Religion* with Kierkegaard's discussion of him in *The Concept of Anxiety*. We saw that Kant rejects as "inept" any effort to explain sin as an inheritance from Adam. In Kant's view, this kind of explanation runs counter to the fact that we must regard ourselves as accountable for wrongwilling, which could not be true if it were traceable to some inherited feature of our nature. Kierkegaard, too, refuses to regard Adam's sin as merely the first in a series that causes all the others that follow. To explain hereditary sin through every man's relationship to Adam and not through the individual's "primitive" relationship to sin, he says, is to place Adam fantastically outside history and outside the human race.[131] Hereditary sin would then be a reality, but Adam would be "the only one in whom it was not found."

For Kant, Adam's significance for us lies in his being a prototypical human being. He is like us in all essential respects, and he uses his freedom to move, without any compulsion, from a state of innocence to guilt. "In Adam all have sinned," says Kant, quoting Romans 5:12, because what was true for him also occurs to each of us in our moral experience. We, too, plunge into sin without necessitation. By tracing evil back to an uncoerced first choice, Kant adds, the biblical story also shows how any free choice, because it is undetermined by antecedent outer or inner constraints, represents an essentially "original" use of our will. Thus, the biblical episode instructs us that "in the search for the rational origin of evil actions, every such action must be regarded as though the individual had fallen into it directly from a state of innocence."[132]

Kierkegaard follows Kant closely here. If Adam's sin has any meaning at all, if human beings participate in that sin, a different explanation must be sought than in causal connection to us through inheritance. It is to be found, he says, in the fact that Adam's sin, the first sin, is "something different from *one* sin (i.e. no. 1 in relation to no. 2)."[133] It is the first sin because it "constitutes the nature of the quality: the first sin is the sin."[134] Adam is "himself and the race," and "that which explains Adam also explains the race and vice versa." Furthermore, the biblical story traces the appearance of sin to the only thing that can "explain"

it: sin. "Sin presupposes itself." If Adam's sin brought sin into
the world, "precisely in the same way it is true of every subsequent man's first sin, that through it sin comes into the world."[135]

Earlier, we saw that in seeking to convey succinctly the
meaning of Adam for us, Kant, near the conclusion of his discussion, reaches for a Latin phrase, Horace's "*Mutato nomine de te
fabula narratur.*"[136] Kierkegaard, too, uses a Latinism, his well-
known *unum noris, omnes.*[137] A further bit of evidence that
Kierkegaard paid rapt attention to Kant's argument in the *Religion* and was deeply influenced by it, especially in these sections
of *The Concept of Anxiety* dealing with the nature of human sin,
is the fact that he copied out Horace's phrase into his notes on
Marheinecke's Berlin lectures dealing with Kant's *Religion.*[138]

I might close this section by saying that I don't wish to argue
that Kierkegaard's view in *The Concept of Anxiety* is merely a
recapitulation of Kant's position in the *Religion* or his other
writings. It is true that other matters elsewhere in this book evidence possible debts to Kant. For example, the long treatment of
sexuality and sinfulness strikes me as reflecting important aspects
of Kant's treatment of sexuality in *The Metaphysics of Morals.*[139]
There is also the striking parallel I noted in the first chapter
between Kant's treatment of anxiety in his essay *Conjectural
Beginning of Human History* and Kierkegaard's own development of the relationship between freedom and anxiety.[140] Nevertheless, major features of Kierkegaard's discussion, especially his
elaborate development of the psychology of anxiety and sin,
have no parallel in Kant. Here as elsewhere my point is not that
Kierkegaard merely repeats Kant, but that he uses key Kantian
insights as a springboard for his own thinking.

Possibly nowhere do we see this process of creative borrowing more thoroughly displayed than in this appropriation from
the *Religion* of Kant's perceptive analysis of radical human evil.
Here, in strict connection with Kant's rationalist doctrine of
ethics and freedom, Kierkegaard perceived a dramatic rediscovery and redevelopment of major aspects of the Christian doctrine
of original sin, a doctrine that had long been a source of tension
between orthodox theology and rationalist philosophy. Kierkegaard did not need Kant to persuade him of the truth of this doctrine. He was a Christian, and his life was an active encounter

with the reality of sin in himself and others. Nevertheless, Kant's treatment of this matter in the *Religion* must have given Kierkegaard enormous confidence that he was on the right track in stressing Christianity's uniqueness and importance in a world that was ready to "go beyond" both sin and Christianity. If the consciousness of sin is the door that leads to Christian faith, Kant, in his doctrine of radical human evil, had given Kierkegaard a key to that door.

SIN AND REDEMPTION

The expert diagnosis of a problem does not amount to its solution. Kant may have developed the Western philosophical tradition's most penetrating understanding of human beings' moral failure, and may have even helped rationally validate the biblical idea of original sin, but when it came to developing a conceptual response to this problem, his efforts were halting and incomplete. Kierkegaard seems to have realized this. His treatments of human sinfulness reveal an active engagement with Kant's handling of the problem, but in the end he rejects Kant's rationalistic solutions and even turns Kant's insights about the depth and intractability of sin against him. Nevertheless, this does not mean that Kierkegaard's and Kant's views on this matter are neatly distinguishable, with Kant championing an Enlightenment emphasis on unaided human moral self-renewal and Kierkegaard favoring a Christian "orthodox" reliance on grace. As we'll see, the lines are more blurred than that, and in their full understanding of the workings of grace and human moral effort, Kant and Kierkegaard are probably closer to one another than either was to their philosophical or religious contemporaries.

In the second chapter we saw that Kant offered a multifaceted response to the problem of "radical evil" he had identified. Above all, he emphasized the primacy of personal moral renewal, of a "revolution" or "rebirth" of our disposition accompanied by penitent suffering for wrongs done in the past. Because previous experience gives us ample reason to doubt the worth of our intentions, however, Kant also believed that to undertake and sustain this renewal rationally we must entertain certain transcendent religious ideas. These include the belief that divine grace, evident to us in our abiding "predisposition to good," would assist us in this course of willing, and the belief that the suffering we voluntarily undertake in repentance would, in the eyes of God, the supreme judge, be sufficient to render satisfaction for our previous wrongs. Kant was also willing to make use of some "revealed" Christian conceptions to the extent that they were compatible with our "natural" moral experience. For example, he accepted the idea of Christ as a symbol for a perfected human nature and as an ideal toward which we must strive despite our sin. He also accepted the theological idea of Christ's vicarious sacrifice, not in the sense of the God-Man's atonement for our sins, but as a way of expressing the penitent suffering each person undergoes for the deeds of a former self. Despite these modest concessions to biblical faith, however, Kant saw no moral value in the idea of a historical divine savior. Each of us, he insists, is responsible for undertaking his or her own moral reform. The idea of a superhuman God-Man entering history can only frustrate this effort because it provides no nourishing moral example on which those who are merely human can draw.[141]

It does not take an acute philosophical sense to see the difficulties in Kant's religious solutions to the problem of sin. On the one hand, he maintains that each of us must confess that the root maxim that guides all our moral decisions may be corrupt. On the other hand, he says that we must nevertheless heed the inner voice that bids us reform and that sustains our confidence that we can accomplish this goal. But if, as Kant observes, "a man is corrupt in the very ground of his maxims," how can he trust any judgment on his part? Why must he not regard his impulse to reform as inadequate or, worse, as a self-deceptive evasion of the very depth and intractability of his sin? "Man is never more easily deceived than in what promotes his good opinion of himself," Kant tells us in the *Religion*.[142] Yet his whole account of human moral renewal rests on a confidence that what the inner voice of conscience bids us to do offers insight into the uncorrupted possibilities of our will. Would not the more consistent and morally honest conclusion of a Kantian analysis of human sin be the confession that the best we dare look forward to is our total and deserved condemnation?

Kant's logic, in other words, seems to lead to what we would today call a "catch-22" of human sinfulness. Those who fail to appreciate the absolute depth and intractability of sin by believing they can overcome it by renewed efforts further convict themselves of sin, and those who fully accept their sin cannot rationally justify any hope of moral renewal but can only expect their own deserved destruction. In the *Postscript* Kierkegaard seems keenly aware of this general conceptual dynamic:

> But to will essentially to throw off guilt from oneself, i.e. guilt as the total determinant, in order thereby to become innocent, is a contradiction, since this procedure is precisely self-denunciation. It is true of guilt, if it is of any other determinant, that there is a catch to it; its dialectic is so crafty that he who justifies himself totally, denounces himself, and he who justifies himself partially denounces himself totally.[143]

The Problem of Repentance

This general problem exhibits its seriousness in connection with Kant's discussion in the *Religion* of how we are to overcome past sins. Kant acknowledges that our past misdeeds present the "greatest difficulty" facing anyone striving for moral renewal. This is so for at least two reasons. First, even a single past misdeed points to a corrupt universal maxim of choice and hence to the deserved receipt of *"endless punishment* and exclusion from the kingdom of God."[144] Second, even if I manage to reorient my will, how I can I pay for my past wrongs? Where do I get that "surplus" of good conduct needed to render satisfaction to justice? The morally reformed person, Kant, observes, "cannot regard the fact that he incurs no new debts subsequent to his change of heart as equivalent to having discharged his old ones. Neither can he, through future good conduct, produce a surplus over and above what he is under obligation to perform at every instant, for it is always his duty to do all the good that lies in his power."[145]

Kant attempts to solve the second of these problems by emphasizing the cleansing function of the penitent suffering experienced during the act of moral reform and subsequently in the natural vicissitudes of life. Viewed as voluntarily accepted punishment that makes up for prior wrongs, however, this suffering poses another problem, since it is not really due the "new man" we have become. As we know, Kant handles this difficulty by demythologizing and individualizing the idea of vicarious satisfaction. In all these ideas taken together, Kant believes he has found an appropriate and even biblically inspired remedy for past wrongs:

> The coming forth from the corrupted into the new disposition is, in itself (as "the death of the old man," "the crucifying of the flesh"), a sacrifice and an entrance on a long train of life's ills. These the new man undertakes in the disposition of the Son of God, that is, merely for the sake of good, though really they are due as *punishments* to another, namely to the old man (for the old man is indeed morally another)...So far as he is a new man, consequently, these sufferings are not ascribed to him as punishments at all. The use of the term "punishment" signifies merely that, in his quality of new man, he now willingly takes upon himself, as so many opportunities for the testing and exercising of his disposition to goodness, all the ills and miseries that assail him, which the old man would have had to regard as punishments.[146]

Readers of Kierkegaard will find in this remark some familiar ideas. They include Kierkegaard's repeated affirmation that "suffering in this world belongs to being a Christian"[147] and his belief that the redeemed Christian does not have to regard these sufferings as punishment. Nevertheless, despite these similarities, Kierkegaard's attitude toward the possibility of overcoming past misdeeds through repentance is diametrically opposed to Kant's. Repeatedly, Kierkegaard tells us that repentance is unable to attain its goal of spiritual renewal. As an infinitely "negative" movement, repentance can deepen our conviction of sin but cannot effect the positive atonement we require. In *The Concept of Anxiety* Kierkegaard puts the problem succinctly: "Repentance cannot cancel sin; it can only sorrow over it."[148] Characteristically, the Kantian ethicist Judge William in *Either/Or* pins his highest hopes on repentance.[149] But in Kierkegaard's view these hopes are illusory, and repentance, like the ethical-religious stage to which it belongs, must finally give way to the reliance on divinely initiated forgiveness and atonement that characterize the highest, or Christian-religious, stage of life.

Although Kierkegaard is explicit in his criticism of repentance, he offers relatively little explanation of why he views it as such a limited instrument of spiritual renewal. The main problem seems to be ethical. In *Fear and Trembling*, for example, he says that repentance "is the highest ethical expression, but also precisely as such it is the deepest ethical self-contradiction."[150] In *The Concept of Anxiety* he repeats this statement and expands on it. The problem, he says, is that although ethics "requires ideality," it must "be content to receive repentance."[151] Repentance is also "dialectically ambiguous" about what it is to remove, an ambiguity that only dogmatics eliminates with the idea of atonement and hereditary sin.[152] Finally, repentance is ethically unacceptable because it "delays action." Approvingly mentioning J. G. Fichte's remark that within a proper understanding of the ethical "there was no time for repentance,"[153] Kierkegaard concludes that if these difficulties were dialectically developed they would lead repentance to "annul itself by new repentance and then collapse."[154]

As the sum of Kierkegaard's criticisms of repentance—and of the ethical-religious stage of which it is the culmination—these remarks are somewhat cryptic. They rest on an understanding of the ethical and its relation to repentance that Kierkegaard assumes but nowhere develops. Nevertheless, if we keep in mind Kant's lengthy discussion of moral reform and penitent suffering in the *Religion*, and regard this as the principal source of Kierkegaard's thinking, we can begin to understand why he boldly characterizes repentance as an "ethical self-contradiction." For although Kant seeks to defend self-initiated repentance as a solution to the problem of sin, his discussion has the opposite effect of heightening the ethical difficulties associated with this response to sin.

One problem explicitly mentioned by Kant concerns where the "surplus" of moral energy needed to repay past deeds is to come from, since it is always our duty to do all the good in our power.[155] We saw that Kant "solves" this problem by pointing to the value of penitent suffering, even though this solution forces him to strain moral reasoning to the limit by invoking a notion of vicarious sacrifice. To the extent that our ethical sensibilities bridle at this solution and we find it morally unjust that a "new" person suffer for the deeds of the old, justice itself resists repentance and we encounter a form of ethical self-contradiction in the effort to repent.

Kant's discussion also may be the stimulus for Kierkegaard's claim that ethics allows no time for repentance. (Kierkegaard makes a similar point in a journal entry for 1842 in which he tells the reader, "You shall do the ethical at every moment, and you are ethically responsible for every moment you waste."[156]) Although in *The Concept of Anxiety* Kierkegaard alludes, without citation, to the elder Fichte as a source for this view, Fichte's treatments of this issue are not exactly relevant. In a letter to Jacobi in 1807 Fichte criticizes morbid preoccupation with the state of one's soul as a form of "laziness" in view of the many tasks and deeds awaiting us in the world,[157] but in *The Vocation of Man* he describes repentance as a firm requirement of the moral life, and he adds that only morally ignoble natures lack the time or energy to repent.[158] In contrast to these uncertain remarks, Kant explicitly develops this problem in the *Religion* in connection with his question of where the surplus of good conduct can come from since we are always obligated to do "all the good in our power." That this insistence on the unremitting nature of the moral demand stems from Kant's understanding of the "ideality" of ethics, an idea that also deeply impressed Kierkegaard, suggests that the *Religion* is the principal source for all of Kierkegaard's views here.

By far the deepest "ethical contradiction" in repentance is not explicitly mentioned by Kant. It appears when we juxtapose the premises of Kant's discussion in the *Religion* to his conclusions. On one page—in a remark quoted above that Kierkegaard elsewhere seems to paraphrase[159]—Kant tells us that our awareness of sin must result in a judgment of *endless punishment* and total exclusion from the kingdom of God, but on the very next page he allows us to regard the suffering experienced in repentance and whatever later misfortunes we encounter in life as adequate payment for our violations of morality. But how can any finite and self-accepted suffering make up for an infinite wrong? Does this not amount to a consummate injustice, a merely partial payment for a total sin? If so, our ethical sensibilities must rebel against this idea and we must regard our repentance as morally inadequate. Alternatively, we may forswear this self-serving partial penalty and take the punishment due a penitent person to its logical extreme. Then, the proper conclusion of Kant's analysis would be that only our total spiritual and physical annihilation constitutes a satisfaction appropriate to our total sinfulness. But, if so, repentance ethically contradicts itself in the most dramatic way by eliminating the "selves" at whose moral regeneration repentance aims.

In *The Concept of Anxiety* Kierkegaard develops the idea of a "crazed repentance." This begins when we take sin with the utmost seriousness but without the "courage" and faith needed to accept unmerited forgiveness. Because this kind of repentance conceives of the consequence of sin only as suffering penalty, it ends in complete perdition. "Its judgment," he tells us, "is pronounced, its condemnation is certain, and the augmented judgment is that the individual shall be dragged through life to the place of execution."[160] We might easily apply this same description to the kind of repentance invoked by Kant's conception of sin. If Kant does not carry repentance to this insane conclusion, it is only because he attenuates the ethical requirement he previously developed. The repentance depicted in the *Religion* avoids becoming crazed by ignoring ethics' stern requirements and by "finitizing" guilt.[161] We can easily imagine Kierkegaard saying that this form of repentance must ultimately "annul itself by a new repentance," perhaps even proceeding to the point where it becomes crazed and then collapses despairingly in upon itself.

In view of these ethical complexities, it is easy to see how informative for Kierkegaard Kant's lengthy treatment in the *Religion* of the problem of past sins must have been. What Kant tried to do there was offer a solution to the problem of radical evil that retained an emphasis on human initiative and that minimally employed transcendent religious ideas, especially those drawn from orthodox Christian faith—this despite the fact that the whole tendency of his discussion was to highlight the pervasiveness and seeming inescapability of our moral situation. Kant's discussion was not irreligious. He relied on a concept of divine grace to interpret and validate the abiding presence of a human predisposition to good amidst all our wrongdoing, and he was also prepared to admit a measure of divine assistance in the process of steady moral development that followed one's change of heart.[162] But Kant was not willing to criticize the integrity of our moral self-judgment. He was also definitely unwilling to admit our powerlessness before the fact of sin or our need for an infusion of divine grace as the cause of our initial awareness of sin and of our subsequent turn toward good, since he believed these admissions would undermine moral autonomy and imputability and thereby remove our responsibility for moral reform. Above all, he was reluctant to yield to the morally dangerous allure of what he called "historical" or "ecclesiastical faith" by admitting any role for a historical savior whose initiative and suffering we require both to recognize and to make up for our deficiencies. For Kant, Jesus remained merely an indwelling rational archetype of what we might be and should become.

The inconsistencies in Kant's treatment of repentance opened the way for Kierkegaard to the orthodox ideas he would defend. Above all, Kant's treatment showed the essential powerlessness of human beings in the face of sin. "Even if repentance is defined at its outermost boundary as a suffering," says Kierkegaard, it cannot solve the problem of sin. It can only accentuate it and make reliance on a divinely initiated atonement more necessary:

> Repentance is no paradox, but when it lets go, the paradox begins; therefore he who trusts in the atonement is greater than the most profound penitent. Repentance always entraps itself, for if it is to be the highest, the ultimate in a man, the saving factor, then it enters into a dialectic once more—whether it is now deep enough, etc.[163]

> No, the Atonement and grace are and remain definitive. All striving toward imitation, when the moment of death brings it to an end and when one stands before God, will be sheer paltriness—therefore atonement and grace are needed. Furthermore, as long as there is striving, the Atonement will constantly be needed to prevent this striving from being transformed into agonizing anxiety in which a man is burned up, so to speak, and less than ever begins to strive. Finally, while there is striving, every other second a mistake is made, something is neglected, there is sin—therefore the Atonement is unconditionally needed.[164]

In a peculiar way, Kant's treatment of repentance also must have reinforced Kierkegaard's orthodox conviction that the situation of human beings is not merely that they are unenlightened and "outside the truth," but that they are "polemical against the truth."[165] They remain defiantly unaware of the depths of their sin and thus lack the "condition" needed for their correction and redemption, a condition that only God can provide. For here was Kant, the philosopher who had plumbed the depths of sin more profoundly than almost any thinker before him, departing from the conclusions of his own analysis and accepting, in the end, an attenuated understanding of sin in order to avoid entertaining Christianity's deepest and most basic claims. If Kant's rigorous analysis of sin was a positive sign of the importance of reason in human beings' spiritual development, Kant's failure to follow through on this analysis showed that reason, like the moral law to which it gives rise, leads in every way to judgment and condemnation, not life. Referring briefly to Kierkegaard at the close of his study of Kant's philosophy of religion, Gordon Michalson sums up the differences and relations between the two thinkers on the matter of grace:

> In Kierkegaard's hands, the muted Kantian appeal to grace is transformed into a full-blown "project of thought" in which a transcendent act alone is the only antidote to our willed "error," or sin. Contrary to our usual view of these matters, it is in fact Kierkegaard and not Kant who has the more "rational" position here. For where Kant attempts to offset a willed error with another act of will and ends up on the borders of incoherence, Kierkegaard openly shows that the only way to offset a willed error is through a reconciling act coming from the "outside," producing the "new creature" that even Kant admits each of us must become.[166]

Faith and History

So far I have maintained that Kant's powerful series of arguments in the *Religion* furnished Kierkegaard with much of the intellectual ammunition he needed for his project of defending Christian orthodoxy. My stress on the importance of Kant's failed treatment of repentance may make it appear that Kierkegaard followed Kant up to this point but thereafter abandoned

Kant in order to elaborate his own specifically Christian viewpoint. But the truth is more complex, for Kierkegaard's Christian theology is also significantly permeated by Kantian assumptions, and this is sometimes true even when Kierkegaard's thinking seems most distant from Kant.

We find an important illustration of this—perhaps the most important—in Kierkegaard's understanding of the significance of the historical Christ. On the surface, Kant and Kierkegaard seem worlds apart on this matter, since Kant repeatedly downplays Christ's historicity. As early as the *Foundations*, while making specific reference to "the Holy One of the Gospel," he denies that we can draw moral or religious nourishment from historical "examples" since these attain their power and must always be tested against the indwelling moral concepts of our own reason.[167] In a passage in *The Conflict of the Faculties* on which I have argued Kierkegaard drew in developing the "Socratic" standpoint in the *Fragments*,[168] Kant carries this idea further. Rejecting the "biblical theologian's" admonition to "search the Scriptures for eternal life," Kant states, "Since our moral improvement is the sole condition of eternal life the only way we can find eternal life in any Scripture whatsoever is by putting it there. For the concepts and principles required for eternal life cannot really be learned from anyone else: the teacher's exposition is only the occasion for him to develop them out of his own reason." Kant concludes his discussion of history and faith in *The Conflict* by calling it "superstition" (*Aberglaube*) "to hold that historical belief is a duty and essential to salvation."[169]

Kierkegaard, of course, directly rejects this view. Christianity's "teacher" is no midwife who draws out our a priori knowledge. As the argument in the *Fragments* makes clear, this "teacher" is "the god himself," the judge and savior who in a "decisive" moment in time redeems the learner from his captivity to sin and error.[170] It follows that belief in a historical redeemer is not *Aberglaube*, as Kant maintained, but its opposite: faith (*Glaube*; Danish: *Tro*) that has as its focus the "eternalizing of the historical and the historicizing of the eternal."[171]

Despite this strong contrast, however, Kierkegaard's redeemer turns out to be no more a historical personage than Kant's "Holy One of the Gospel." As Josiah Thompson observes, in Kierkegaard's later writings "the historical Jesus fades into the background leaving the reader of these works alone with the single fact of his historicity."[172] Kierkegaard also displays this extreme disinterest in the historical Jesus in his diatribe against scientific biblical scholarship and in his belief that "contemporaneity" with Christ offers the believer no spiritual advantage.[173]

How can we explain this disinterest in historical fact combined with the repeated affirmation of the savior's historicity? The answer, I believe, is that like Kant (and Lessing before him) Kierkegaard believed that we must view the events of revelation through the eyes of faith. Like Kant, he believed that sacred truth is not a matter of empirical evidence of any sort, whether natural or historical, but rests on an internal conviction of that truth. Where Kant and Kierkegaard differ is their understanding of how we arrive at this conviction. For Kant, we do so through the operations of our moral reason, which leads us to the acknowledgement that Jesus conforms to our indwelling moral archetype. In contrast, precisely because he has taken Kant's discussion of radical evil to the conclusion that we are impotent in sin, Kierkegaard must assume that we lack the condition for proper moral knowledge or conduct. From this assumption, the deductive argument of the *Fragments* follows. Since we do not eternally possess knowledge of the good, we can arrive at it only temporally through the decisive initiative of another, the God who enters history to redeem and who provides us with "the condition" for learning. On this point Kierkegaard deeply agrees with Kant's imaginary orthodox interlocutor in *The Conflict of the Faculties* who says that "to believe that God, by an act of kindness, will in some unknown way fill what is lacking to our justification is...to commit a *petitio principii*; for when we expect something by the grace of a superior, we cannot assume that we must get it as a matter of course; we can expect it only if it was actually promised to us...[and] has actually been pledged through divine *revelation*."[174] But although this savior for Kierkegaard acts in time, he is no more encountered in history than is Kant's archetype. All his qualities, including his historical reality and initiative in grace, are conceptually validated within the realm of our subjective moral experience, although the logic of this position requires Kierkegaard to attribute this validation to

God's initiative, not to the agency of our unaided moral reason. In an important sense, therefore, Kierkegaard's Christ is Kant's eternal moral archetype logically transformed into a decisive historical redeemer as the result of Kierkegaard's fuller appreciation of the Kantian problem of sin. Gordon Michalson is undoubtedly right in seeing that Kierkegaard owes this devaluation of the religious importance of actual historical knowledge to a line of thinkers beginning with Lessing and including Kant.[175] But he misses the decisive role played in Kierkegaard's thinking by Kant's treatments of radical evil. By so brilliantly developing this doctrine within the context of two prolonged diatribes against "positive" or revealed religion (the *Religion* and *The Conflict of the Faculties*), Kant extended an invitation to Kierkegaard (or any other discerning Christian reader) to repudiate the naive faith in human self-improvement that Kant was unable to relinquish. Working within Kant's otherwise nonhistorical structure of thought, it would then be a simple matter to affirm its necessary completion in a historical act of redemption, whose truth requires faithful "inner" appropriation and is indifferent or inimical to historical demonstration.

The Moral Meaning of Redemption

Another illustration of the affinity between Kierkegaard and Kant, despite their obvious theological differences, concerns their shared sense that moral striving takes *practical* primacy in the structure of the redeemed life. We saw that Kant concedes a role to divine grace in the economy of redemption. The assumption of grace as a "supernatural supplement" to our moral efforts answers important "speculative" questions without which we would be "wholly unable to reconcile with divine justice man's hope of absolution from guilt."[176] Kant is even aware that without some prior assumption of grace human beings cannot rationally embark on what otherwise seems a hopeless project of moral reform. Nevertheless, in the end he chooses to bypass the question of whether God's grace or our works initiate the process of redemption. This question, he says, belongs to the realm of intelligible causality. It "cannot be resolved theoretically" because it transcends the speculative capacity of our reason.

"But practically, the question arises: What in the use of our free will, comes first, (not physically [in time] but morally)? Where shall we start, *i.e.*, with a faith in what God has done on our behalf, or with what we are to do to become worthy of God's assistance (whatever this may be)? In answering this question we cannot hesitate in deciding for the second alternative."[177]

Kierkegaard, of course, is unwilling to subordinate this "speculative" or theoretical question. He insists that it must be addressed and then answered in terms of the traditional confidences of Christian faith if the human moral project is to find its proper course. But, just like Kant, Kierkegaard also affirms that, on the practical and human side, redemption shows itself above all in the most strenuous moral striving. A journal entry for 1852 makes this point in terms deeply reminiscent of Kant's emphasis on the primacy of practical over theoretical or "speculative" reason:

> The highest is not to understand the highest but to do it and, please note, with all the weights laid on.
> Only then did I properly understand that "grace" had to be introduced; otherwise a person is shattered the minute he is supposed to begin.
> But, the "grace" is not to be introduced in order to prevent striving, no, here it comes again: the highest is not to understand the highest but to do it.[178]

Readers of Kierkegaard know how often he repeats these sentiments in his writings. They form the substance of his bitter "attack on Christendom" and of his persistent criticism of bourgeois Christianity for its interpretation of grace as involving nothing more than a life of material comfort and tepid moral commitment. The same sentiments underlie Kierkegaard's idea of "imitation" (*Efterfølgelse*), according to which the Christian disciple is called to follow the master's path of suffering service. A journal entry for 1850 captures Kierkegaard's understanding of the relationship between grace and Christian discipleship in terms that sound almost as though they are drawn from Kant's criticism of "ecclesiastical faith" in the *Religion*. "Nothing," says Kierkegaard, "can be taken in vain as easily as grace; and as soon as imitation is completely omitted, grace is taken in vain. But that is the kind of preaching men like."[179]

A final illustration of the deep affinity between Kierkegaard and Kant on the matters of sin, grace, and moral works is their mutual rejection of the traditional doctrine of predestination. We saw that Kant is very outspoken on this matter. In his little essay "The End of All Things" he points to the difficulties that beset the nonuniversalist view of salvation. He is particularly troubled by the moral presumption implicit in this idea and asks whether it is not perhaps an "absurd conceit" to try to establish one's own preeminent position over others in the divine regard.[180] In the *Religion* he calls the teaching of predestination "the *salto mortale* of reason" and offers as a preferable solution the alternative of divine foreknowledge or "prevision."[181] In *The Conflict of the Faculties*, Kant explicitly states the basis of his objection: "Reason," he says, "finds that predestination cannot be reconciled with its own teachings on freedom and the imputation of action, and so with the whole of morality."[182]

Remarkably, despite his clear advocacy of a Pauline position on grace and his corresponding absolute stress on God's initiative in our redemption, Kierkegaard holds the same opinion of predestination as Kant. In several places he suggests that the doctrine is morally offensive because of the way it fosters a cruel discrimination among human beings. In the *Postscript* he speaks of the "desperate presumption of predestination,"[183] and in *The Book on Adler* he blames this "despairing election by grace" for positing "the most dreadful discord" among human beings. "To be saved, to be happy—and to know that all others are not and cannot be saved," he exclaims, "...what human heart can endure such blessedness!"[184] Elsewhere, it is the way predestination contradicts freedom that draws his criticism. Like Kant, he appears to favor a view based on God's foreknowledge as the only one consistent with human freedom.[185] Deeply in Kant's spirit is the observation in a late journal entry that although God is present in all a person's inward transformations, "God can give help for what only freedom can do."[186] Also Kantian is Kierkegaard's characterization of predestination, in a related journal entry from this late period, as "the dogma of sedentary piety."[187]

These deep affinities between Kierkegaard and Kant, beyond their obvious difference on the matters of grace and atonement, are a sign of the extent to which Kant's thinking serves as a stimulus for Kierkegaard's whole religious position. Freedom, the rigor of the moral law, human beings' inevitable failures before its ideality and their corresponding need for divine assistance in fulfillment of the human moral project—these were Kant's great insights that Kierkegaard took over and made the foundation of his vigorous modern assertion of Christian orthodoxy. Kierkegaard was not unwilling to capitalize on Kant's hesitations and equivocations. In Kant's uncertain handling of issues of repentance, grace, and atonement Kierkegaard saw an opportunity for an even more strenuous assertion of the truths of Christian faith. But since Kierkegaard built his position on key Kantian ethical assumptions like the reality of freedom and moral accountability, he could no more abandon these ideas than Kant. The landmarks of Kierkegaard's own intellectual journey, his rediscovery of ethics in the face of Hegelian moral indifference, his development of ethics to the point where it must internally collapse and give rise to a fully religious state of being, and his insistence on moral striving as the hallmark of the Christian way of life, are abiding signs of Kant's unique impact on Kierkegaard's life and thought.

CHAPTER 5

A Kantian Rereading

Abraham should have replied to this supposedly divine voice:
"That I ought not to kill my good son is quite certain. But that
you, this apparition, are God—of that I am not certain, and never
can be, not even if this voice rings down to me from (visible)
heaven."
—Kant, *The Conflict of the Faculties*[1]

Recognizing the extent of Kierkegaard's debt to Kant enhances
our appreciation of the philosophical subtlety and precision of
his thinking. Several major premises of Kierkegaard's work, especially his understanding of the nature and problems of the ethical
stage of life, are only fragmentarily developed in his writings.
Although Kierkegaard's views on ethics can be and have been
interpreted without reference to Kant—criticisms of the "law,"
for example, are a staple of Christian theology—seeing the presence of Kant behind these views deepens our sense of the power
of Kierkegaard's arguments. Perceiving the extent to which he
was involved with Kant's philosophy also reinforces our view of
Kierkegaard as a sophisticated modern "apologist" for Christianity, and it presents a picture of him more consistent with his
own substantial estimate of his philosophical competence.

In at least one major instance, seeing Kierkegaard's debt to
Kant also significantly—even dramatically—alters our understanding of what Kierkegaard has to say. The instance I have in
mind concerns *Fear and Trembling*, whose argument for a fearful
"teleological suspension of the ethical" has often been read as a
pointed attack on the rational ethics and stress on human ethical
autonomy of the Kantian (and Hegelian) tradition.[2] This understanding of *Fear and Trembling* is very prevalent, and it reinforces the view that Kierkegaard lumped Hegel and Kant together in his religious attack on philosophical rationalism or that he
took over aspects of Kant's ethics only to reject Kantianism as a
whole. However, once we realize that in all his writings, especial-

ly the earliest pseudonymous works, Kierkegaard is deeply engaged with Kant's mature philosophy of religion as it is found in works like the *Religion within the Limits of Reason Alone* and *The Conflict of the Faculties*, then our reading of *Fear and Trembling* is transformed and the nature of the book's central concerns becomes a further sign of the degree of Kierkegaard's involvement with Kant. In what follows, I propose to "reread" *Fear and Trembling* against the background of the Kantian ideas we've explored in previous chapters.

A problem in understanding *Fear and Trembling* is that it is a deliberately enigmatic book. It has long been recognized, for example, that *Fear and Trembling* is a cryptogram. Encoded within its series of reflections and commentaries on Genesis 22 is a hidden message directed at a reader or readers presumably capable of deciphering the hidden meaning. That this is true is suggested by the book's epigraph: "What Tarquinius Superbus said in the garden by means of the poppies, the son understood but the messenger did not."[3] This epigraph is a quotation from the German literary critic Johan Georg Hamann, who drew it from an episode in Roman history involving Tarquinius Superbus and his son.[4] After seizing control of the city of Gabii, the son sent a messenger to his father asking how power might be secured. Since Tarquinius was not sure of the loyalties of the envoy, he gave no reply but took him for a walk through the garden. As they strolled, he used his cane to cut off the heads of the tallest poppies. When the perplexed messenger reported this behavior, the son understood that he was to eliminate the leaders of the city.

Because of this epigraph, it is easy to conclude that the reader of *Fear and Trembling* is possibly in the position of the envoy: the recipient of a message not meant for him and one whose deepest meaning is not apparent. But if this is so, what is this hidden message, and to whom is it directed? Usually these questions are answered with reference to Kierkegaard's relationship with Regine Olsen. The episode of Genesis 22, with God's fearful command to Abraham to sacrifice his son, is seen as having its parallel in Kierkegaard's breaking of his engagement to Regine under the conviction that "divine Governance" had issued a fateful "no" to the marriage.[5] Some, by extrapolating from this reltionship between Søren and Regine, also read *Fear and Trembling* as a secret message from its author to any reader willing to understand its terrible portrayal of radical religious obedience.

In what follows I want to offer an alternative "decipherment" of *Fear and Trembling*'s secret message. In doing so, I do not wish to contest the relevance of this book to Kierkegaard's relationship with Regine. Allusions to romantic love are everywhere present in Kierkegaard's discussion, from a first mention of the impossible love of a young lad for a princess to the story of Agnes and the merman in the third problema.⁶ Nor do I want to deny that *Fear and Trembling* anticipates the demanding conception of Christian discipleship that Kierkegaard ultimately develops out of these painful events in his life, a conception that involves the possibility of consummate personal sacrifice and suffering. Nevertheless, although these ideas represent possible levels of hidden meaning, I wish to show that they are not the only nor even the most important ones. It is helpful to remember here that Kierkegaard was a master of irony. *Fear and Trembling* itself is subtitled a "dialectical lyric," something of a contradiction in terms: a work at once both philosophical and poetic. Furthermore, the outspoken and very wordy author of this argumentative lyric is given the name "Johannes *de silentio*." All signs, therefore, suggest that from the outset Kierkegaard approached this creation ironically. Since the breaking of his engagement to Regine was known publicly, it hardly evidenced much of an ironic sense to make this event or any related meaning the secret message of this volume. How much more ironic if the easily discerned "secret message" of a broken engagement contained an even more secret message known only to Kierkegaard and its recipient.

There are at least three clues to the coded message I have in mind. We find one in the epigraph itself. A second is derived from some familiar but important details of Kierkegaard's biography. The third arises in connection with a close conceptual analysis of the structure of Kierkegaard's argument in the book as a whole and a reading of this with the understanding that Kierkegaard was informed by Kant's writings. Since the third of these "clues" affords the most solid and direct evidence for this reading of *Fear and Trembling*, I want to begin with it. Only after developing an alternative understanding of the intent of Kierkegaard's argument will I turn to biographical and other textual details that support the decipherment of Kierkegaard's message I have in mind.

STRUCTURE AND ARGUMENT

The overarching aim of Kierkegaard's argument in *Fear and Trembling* is to comprehend the religious implications of Genesis 22. To this end, Kierkegaard develops two distinct but deeply related ideas: the idea of a "teleological suspension of the ethical" and the idea of faith as involving a "double movement" of the spirit.[7] God's command to Abraham to sacrifice his son represents the first of these concepts. What Abraham is called to do, Kierkegaard tells us, fully defies moral obligation and amounts to murder. Agamemnon, Jeptha, or Brutus also offer up their children, but they do so for the sake of the common good and for the welfare of others in their society. They are thus "tragic heroes" who suspend one expression of the ethical for a still "higher expression of the ethical."[8] But Abraham "is at no time a tragic hero."[9] As a single individual he steps entirely outside the ethical, the universal, to enter into a private and particular relationship with God. If we are to comprehend Abraham, therefore, this step must be possible. Only if the individual is in some way "higher than the universal," only if a "teleological suspension of the ethical" is a religious possibility so that the single individual can stand in an "absolute relation to the absolute,"[10] can we regard Abraham as the father of faith and not a common criminal.[11]

If God's command illustrates the first of the concepts Kierkegaard wishes to develop, Abraham's response to this command illustrates the second, the double movement of faith. Faced with such a command, says Kierkegaard, it would be fully understandable if Abraham proved obedient but succumbed to despair. This might take several forms: hesitancy and doubt in complying with the command, a loss of enthusiasm for life itself, or the inability to sustain a sense of happiness in the presence of his child.[12] Then Abraham would be a "knight of infinite resignation," one who is willing to put aside the joys and possibilities of finite existence. But he would not be what he is: a "knight of faith." Abraham's special distinctiveness—and even Johannes (Kierkegaard?) confesses himself unable to make this double movement of the spirit—is that "by virtue of the absurd" he believes that what he sacrifices he will regain. He is able and willing to relinquish everything, but he never loses his hold on finitude and his hope for fulfillment within its domain.

This is an admittedly brief sketch of what in *Fear and Trembling* are several complex, reiterated, and expanding treatments of these themes. But the major points in Kierkegaard's argument should now be clear enough to take us beyond their important surface meaning (here, the defense of religious possibilities that Kierkegaard believed his contemporaries had neglected) to the additional "encoded" message of the text. If we keep in mind Kierkegaard's biography, it is reasonable to suppose, as many readers have done, that these two concepts interest him because of their relationship to the recent crisis in his life. Thus, the possibility of a "teleological suspension of the ethical" becomes a way of justifying (religiously if not morally) his decision to break off his engagement to Regine. As God had called Abraham to violate his deepest personal wish and highest ethical ideals, so had he summoned Kierkegaard to a religious vocation in a way that meant injuring his beloved. The "two movements" of resignation followed by faith represent precisely the stance to which Kierkegaard believed himself called but which (as Johannes proclaims of himself) he was unable fully to achieve. Although able to renounce Regine, he proved unable to make the movements of spirit that might bring her back to him. In a journal entry Kierkegaard remarks, "If I had had faith, I would have stayed with Regine."[13] What precisely this double movement may have meant in Kierkegaard's case is not clear. It might have involved his seeking to surmount those "faithless" obstacles within him that made his religious calling seem inimical to a married life. Had he truly followed Abraham, Kierkegaard might have been able to marry *and* comply with the divine command.[14] In any case, these remarks by Kierkegaard suggest that he did come to see his personal experience in these religious terms.

The substantial parallelism between these details of Kierkegaard's life and the surface meaning of the text supports the view

that this romantic crisis constitutes the hidden message of the
book, a message directed perhaps to Regine herself or to others
close to the events.[15] Nevertheless, in several respects, the parallelism between Kierkegaard's surface argument and this decoded
meaning is not altogether complete. In at least two different
ways, Kierkegaard suggests that the issues raised by Abraham's
trial are not entirely analogous to the personal romantic struggle
of a single individual. Thus, he tells us more than once that the
stakes for Abraham are fateful: in Kierkegaard's words, unless
we admit the possibility of a suspension of the ethical, then
"Abraham is lost."[16] He also suggests that the issues raised by
Abraham's trial, especially the possibility of a teleological suspension of the ethical, are of great significance for us all. Several
times he states his belief that if the single individual cannot, like
Abraham, enter into an "absolute relation to the absolute" then
faith itself does not exist.[17]

It is, of course, possible to make both these extreme evaluations of the episode fit the romantic crisis through which Kierkegaard had recently passed. We might sympathize with Kierkegaard if, having wronged a young woman and possibly forsaken
his personal happiness, he compared his situation to that which
Abraham would face as the unwarranted killer of his son. The
estranged suitor would then regard himself as "lost" just as Abraham might be lost. But surely it does Abraham an injustice to
compare his trial and possible abandonment to the emotional for-
sakenness of a heartbroken young lover, and it appears excessive
to use this kind of rhetoric of perdition in relation to a romantic
episode. Can it be that Kierkegaard had such a self-indulgent perception of himself in writing this book? Similarly, although it is
possible to do so, it is hard to find any general religious significance for us all in the episode of Kierkegaard's broken engagement. Few of us are called, as Kierkegaard was, to renounce our
worldly lives and careers in the name of a religious vocation.
Must we assume that Kierkegaard perceived the fundamental
outlines of "faith" in his very personal romantic and religious
biography? If not, then the analogy between surface text and the
encoded private experience to which it refers is not complete.

These difficulties are not decisive, of course. To the extent
that Kierkegaard perceived his experience as modeling the kind

of radical discipleship to which all Christians are called, there is a more reasonable parallelism between Abraham's sacrifice, Kierkegaard's romantic biography, and the course that each Christian must follow to attain salvation. Nevertheless, Kierkegaard's conception of Christian discipleship matured over his lifetime, assuming its most demanding form only after the bitter events of the Corsair affair. It is not clear that Kierkegaard fully understood the life to which all Christians are called in these terms as early as *Fear and Trembling* and, therefore, that his special romantic sacrifice was relevant to the universal message he believed Genesis 22 contained.

These considerations throw open to question the claim that it is the experience with Regine that Kierkegaard had in mind in understanding the meaning of Abraham. They also point to the *kind* of personal experience that might make the parallel between Kierkegaard's life and Abraham's trial more complete. This experience would have to be one of ultimate significance, involving the stakes of redemption or perdition. If the religious possibility he sketches is a chimera, then Kierkegaard, no less than Abraham, would be "lost." This private experience also would have to involve issues of religious faith that are relevant to us all. But what experience in Kierkegaard's life might contain something in which anyone might discern a matter of pressing, immediate, and universal spiritual significance?

If we keep these questions in mind and turn again to Kierkegaard's biography, some answers are forthcoming. All have to do with the burden of sinfulness that Kierkegaard bore and that he apparently believed himself to share with his (equally sinful) father, Michael Pedersen Kierkegaard. This problem of personal and familial sin is not altogether separable, of course, from the events of Kierkegaard's relationship with Regine. It was partly because of this burden of sin, what Kierkegaard called "the eternal night brooding within me,"[18] that he believed himself unable to carry through with the marriage: fearful, perhaps, that his melancholy disposition, one consequence of this tradition of familial sin, would ruin young Regine's life and make a happy union impossible.[19] But the issue of sin in Kierkegaard's thought and life transcended this one relationship and constituted a major focus and preoccupation in his writing. It is this issue, I believe, that forms the "hidden message" of this book. Here we find the experience on whose resolution literally depends Kierkegaard's spiritual salvation. Here we find an issue which, however personal and related to Kierkegaard's life it may have been, also has immediate spiritual significance for us all.

Shortly, I will return to some of the biographical and other details that point to this "hidden message." But first, I must justify the claim that *Fear and Trembling* deals in any significant way with the problem of sin. We know that this issue preoccupies Kierkegaard in other writings, notably *The Concept of Anxiety* and *The Sickness unto Death*. But ordinarily, this problem is not seen to be to the fore in *Fear and Trembling*, which appears to deal instead with the separate problem of divine command morality, with whether it is possible for there to be a command of God calling us beyond the domain of the ethical. At issue, in other words, is the fundamental normative basis of human existence—and its accompanying spiritual attitudes—rather than the question of how we are to understand or deal with human imperfection and sin.

Careful attention to Kierkegaard's discussion, however, suggests that the problem of sin, in some of its classical Christian formulations, is far more central to this text than it seems to be. For one thing, the issue of sin inhabits that of divine command morality. As Kierkegaard repeatedly says, we require the possibility of a command of God that can suspend the ethical and take priority over it not only to understand Abraham's conduct but also to "justify" it. Without the possibility of such a divine command, Kierkegaard tells us, "judgment has fallen on Abraham,"[20] and the patriarch stands in sin.

Apart from this important theme, however, the issue of sin and redemption from sin receives independent treatment in *Fear and Trembling*. This issue arises, moreover, almost as a climax to the book's development—in connection with the story of Agnes and the merman that occupies most of the third problema. Well into the treatment of the tale, Kierkegaard asks how the merman can extricate himself from the terrible dilemma created by his having fallen in love with Agnes after having first intended to seduce her. If he refuses to return to his "demonic" former existence, Kierkegaard tells us, the merman can be saved only by repentance. This can take two forms. Either the merman can renounce Agnes and hope that she will be saved by God (in which case he would follow the path of infinite resignation earlier charted by medieval monasticism), or he can marry Agnes. But to do the latter requires faith.

So far we are on familiar ground. Kierkegaard is partly reiterating his understanding of the double movement of faith that involves not only renunciation but the trust, however incredible and paradoxical, that one who has relinquished finitude may get it back. Suddenly, Kierkegaard's discussion takes a peculiar turn: the merman's expectations are momentarily put aside and we enter into a brief disquisition on the problems of sin and repentance. Kierkegaard's remarks here are so significant that they merit being quoted at length. Developing his statement that the merman can marry Agnes, Kierkegaard adds,

> He must, however, take refuge in the paradox. In other words, when the single individual by his guilt has come outside the universal, he can return only by virtue of having come as the single individual into an absolute relation to the absolute. *Now here I would like to make a comment that says more than has been said at any point previously.* Sin is not the first immediacy; sin is a later immediacy. In sin, the single individual is already higher (in the direction of the demonic paradox) than the universal, because it is a contradiction on the part of the universal to want to demand itself from a person who lacks the *conditio sine qua non.* If, along with other things, philosophy were also to think that it just might enter a man's head to want to act according to its teaching, we would get a strange kind of comedy out of it. An ethics that ignores sin is a completely futile discipline, but if it affirms sin, then it has *eo ipso* exceeded itself.[21]

These comments bring forth a complex set of issues, none of which Kierkegaard's previous discussion has prepared us for. Kierkegaard seems aware of this because he hastens to add that "nothing" of what he has just said explains Abraham, "for Abraham did not become a single individual by way of sin—on the contrary, he was a righteous man."[22] He drives the same point home in a complex footnote appended to the already quoted remark, "Now here I would like to make a comment that says

more than has been said at any point previously." This note
states,

> Up until now I have assiduously avoided any reference to the
> question of sin and its reality. The whole work is centered on
> Abraham, and I can still encompass him in immediate cate-
> gories—that is, insofar as I can understand him. As soon as sin
> emerges, ethics founders precisely on repentance; for repen-
> tance is the highest ethical expression, but precisely as such it is
> the deepest ethical self-contradiction.[23]

We have here, then, a series of reflections that Kierkegaard
acknowledges to be something of an interruption in his course of
argument. Yet he is nevertheless compelled to introduce them at
this point, and he is even willing to signal them as saying "more
than has been said at any point previously."

What is going on here? What precisely is the meaning of
Kierkegaard's remarks? Why is he compelled to introduce these
complex themes as an aside in the middle of a romantic tale? My
reply is that at this point Kierkegaard has allowed the hidden
message of *Fear and Trembling* to break through the surface.
Like a stony outcropping that pushes up through shallow layers
of vegetation and reveals the underlying rocky foundation of a
plain, Kierkegaard's brief interruption of his discussion of Agnes,
the merman, and Abraham signals a deeper preoccupation animating the book.[24] To understand this fully, we must look more
closely at what he tells us here about sin and repentance.

This interruption makes several important, but somewhat
abstruse points. First, we are told that sin is not the "first"
immediacy but a "later immediacy." Second, we learn that if philosophy and philosophers were to take their own moral teaching
seriously and expect people to obey the moral law, then a
"strange kind of comedy" would ensue, presumably because the
result would be an awareness of sin and the reality of sinning.
Third, and finally, with sin, philosophical ethics comes to grief.
In neglecting sin philosophy becomes a futile discipline. But if it
takes sin seriously, then it has outstripped its own categories or
abilities. Very specifically, philosophical ethics shipwrecks on the
matter of repentance. Moral and philosophical analysis leads to
repentance as the "highest ethical expression," but founders on

this idea because repentance is also "the deepest ethical self-contradiction."

The first of these points is probably directed against Hegel and his followers. In various discussions of original sin, Hegel had suggested that the very particularity of the person, and the fact that each one of us is a creature of nature, thrusts us up against the requirements of morality and constitutes the "original sin."[25] Sin is a "first immediacy" because it manifests itself with the fact of individuality ("isolated subjectivity") and is only remedied in an encounter with the ethical requirement. This viewpoint, Kierkegaard knew, had been adopted by some important followers of Hegel.[26] This is not Kierkegaard's position. Sin, he believes, is more complex and is not to be identified merely with the fact of individuality. Rather, as the "second immediacy," sin *follows* the moral law and presumes a full understanding of and engagement with it. Sin arises in and through the moral law and represents a reassertion of the self precisely in defiance and rebellion against it.

Although Kierkegaard does not develop this view in *Fear and Trembling*, he does so in both *The Concept of Anxiety* and in *The Sickness unto Death*. In the first of these works, for example, he introduces the idea of "anxiety about evil" as a form of response to one's previous sins. Unassuaged, this anxiety can lead to "crazed repentance," sensual debauchery, spiritual pride, and defiance.[27] In *The Sickness unto Death*, Kierkegaard describes the genuinely demonic in sin as a replunging into sin after an encounter with one's own potential for sin. He tells us that the pharisaic and the demonic mentalities represent alternate but equally despairing flights from the encounter with one's sinfulness.[28] In these respects, Kierkegaard belongs to the Pauline, Augustinian, and Lutheran tradition with its rejection of the view that sin represents a pardonable early phase in human development. He also stands with this tradition in its understanding of the seriousness of sin and in its perception of sin as arising in a conscious rebellion against the law.

Kant, of course, does not develop this kind of "psychology" of sin, nor does he explore the way in which anxiety about sin can deepen one's alienation from morality. Nevertheless, in his understanding of sin, Kierkegaard stands closer to Kant than to

Hegel. Kant nowhere associates sin with individuality and particularity, as Hegel does. We know that Kant deliberately refuses to "explain" sin in any way or to attribute its appearance to the facts of our individuality or finitude. These may furnish an occasion for sin, but finally, he believes, any decision to violate the moral law rests on a freely chosen maxim of self-love that defies further explanation.

The Kantian background of these almost parenthetical comments in *Fear and Trembling* becomes even more apparent when we look at Kierkegaard's other observations in this passage. The second is the observation that if philosophy and philosophical ethics were to take their task seriously and ask that people act on their teachings, we would have a "comedy" because the only result would be an awareness of sin. We might paraphrase this by saying that a rigorous understanding of the principles of morality only serves to highlight the enormous difficulty and perhaps the impossibility of an individual's ever fully acting on these principles. But we know this is precisely the point of Kant's lengthy development of the idea of "radical evil" in the *Religion*. A rigorous analysis of moral concepts, Kant tells us there, shows that the committed moral agent is caught in a terrible dilemma. One horn of the dilemma is created by the moral law, which in its full "ideality" permits the individual not a single instance of defection from its mandate and allows of no intermediate position between a will *always* oriented to morality and one *not* oriented to it. The other horn of the dilemma is created by responsible agents' perception that they cannot vouchsafe to themselves or others abiding, unexceptional commitment to the priority of the moral law. The resulting judgment of one's possible moral unworthiness is further sharpened by the fact that even a single instance of past wrongdoing strongly evidences an underlying evil maxim and creates, in addition, a burden of moral debt that the unaided person cannot discharge. Together, we know, these considerations lead Kant to his own version of a doctrine of original sin and to the assertion that each of us must regard ourselves as totally guilty and as forever excluded from the ideal ethical commonwealth of righteous persons he calls "the kingdom of God." Kant's rigorous—and rigoristic—analysis, therefore, leads to the conclusion that a sensitive understanding of the moral law must lead to an awareness of the persistent sinfulness of human willing. This is precisely the point of Kierkegaard's observation that if philosophy and philosophers were to take seriously their own moral teaching and expect people to obey the moral law, then a "strange kind of comedy" would ensue because the reality of sin would become even more apparent.[29]

We need hardly spend much time developing the Kantian background of Kierkegaard's third point, his observation that repentance is "the highest ethical expression" but also "the deepest ethical self-contradiction." In the previous chapter, we saw that this point, reiterated and developed in *The Concept of Anxiety*, makes deepest sense when interpreted against the background of Kant's lengthy and anguished treatment of the problem of past sin in the *Religion*. Kierkegaard's mention of this matter is another sign that Kant's discussion in the *Religion* is very much on his mind as he raises these issues at this point in *Fear and Trembling*.

Why, then, does Kierkegaard introduce this complex topic as an apparent aside during a treatment of what seem to be other matters? I believe we are now able to see that these remarks are not an aside at all: they pertain to the hidden message of *Fear and Trembling* and have been animating Kierkegaard's discussion from the start. To understand this we need only ask a question raised by the preceding analysis of sin and repentance: how is the problem of sin to be overcome? How can individuals, in bondage to sin and experiencing repentance as only an accentuation of their dilemma, find relief from moral despair and self-condemnation? As long as they stay *within* the domain of ethics, of course their fate is sealed, for they have already "suspended" the ethical by their conduct in an utterly final way. The very requirements of the moral law convict them. Repentance, in turn, at least if it is taken seriously, must lead to total self-annihilation. So long as the moral law is the final and supreme arbiter of our spiritual destiny, the result for each of us must be spiritual perdition.

As we state the problem its solution appears. If there is to be an escape from sin and from our own freely undertaken suspension of moral commitment, then ethics itself must not have the last word on our personal destiny. Ethics must not be the highest possibility of human existence. It must be transcended by a more ultimate possibility in which forgiveness and the suspension of our merited punishment by a source of moral judgment more authoritative than our own become realities. In short, it must be possible for there to be a divine "teleological suspension of the ethical." But this is precisely the main theme of *Fear and Trembling*. True, this theme is developed in an altogether different way and in separation from the problem of sin and forgiveness. God "suspends the ethical" by asking Abraham to go beyond the moral law. It is whether this is possible and whether Abraham is justified in obeying a divine command violative of conscience, not the question of whether God can suspend the ethical to forgive a sinner, that seem to be the main subject of the book. Nevertheless, we already know that *Fear and Trembling* has a deliberately hidden meaning. We also know that this meaning involves a problem of ultimate consequence for us all: we have been told that unless what Johannes *de silentio* argues for in this book is possible, unless there is such a thing as a "teleological suspension of the ethical," then faith is naught and we are all in a sense "lost." What problem has these consequences more directly than the problem of sin? If the ethical cannot be transcended and we must remain under its judgments, then not only Abraham but all of us as moral agents are lost.

Speaking of *Fear and Trembling* in the *Postscript* and restating the core of his argument there, Kierkegaard makes these connections more explicit than they are in *Fear and Trembling* itself. He admits, for example, that *Fear and Trembling* is something of a "noble lie" (*eine erhabene Lüge*), since the problem animating it has been given the "deceptive form" of an outward shriek,[30] whereas the problem's real fearsomeness lies in the "abyss of inwardness." Kierkegaard then briefly sketches the essential content of this fearful inner meaning and the response to it that *Fear and Trembling* has offered: "*The ethical constitutes the temptation*; the God-relationship has come into being; the immanence of ethical despair has been broken through; *the leap is posited; the absurd constitutes the notification*."[31]

Several pages later, Kierkegaard offers a redescription of *Fear and Trembling*'s central theme:

> The teleological suspension of the ethical must be given a more distinctively religious expression. The ethical will then be present every moment with its infinite requirement, but the indi-

vidual is not capable of realizing this requirement. This impotence of the individual must not be understood as the imperfection of a persistent striving toward the attainment of an ideal; for in that case no suspension is posited; just as an official is not suspended from his office if he performs his duties only moderately well. The suspension in question consists in the individual's finding himself in a state precisely the opposite of what the ethical requires, so that far from being able to begin, each moment he remains in this state he is more and more prevented from beginning. He is not related to the task as possibility to actuality, but as impossibility. Thus the individual is suspended from the requirements of the ethical in the most terrible manner, being in suspension heterogeneous with the ethical, which nevertheless has an infinite claim upon him.[32]

These remarks are freighted with ideas and issues closely associated with Kant's developed philosophy of religion. The infinite requirement of the ethical, the idea of "persistent striving" toward virtue (a theme developed by Kant in the second *Critique* as a response to the problem of our moral inadequacy but replaced by him in the *Religion*, following his analysis of radical evil, with a greater stress on the need for divine grace)—these suggest that Kant was very much on Kierkegaard's mind as he wrote *Fear and Trembling*. Beyond this, Kierkegaard's willingness to present the central problem of *Fear and Trembling* in terms of the "infinite claim" of ethics and the resulting problems of sin and moral despair tells us that the seemingly parenthetical remarks in the midst of the merman narrative are at the center of his attention. It is as though at this moment in *Fear and Trembling* Kierkegaard availed himself of a natural opportunity (treatment of the merman's spiritual dilemma) to expose this deeper preoccupation. The structure of *Fear and Trembling* and Kierkegaard's comments on it, therefore, reveal that sin and redemption form an important hidden message of the text.

BIOGRAPHICAL EVIDENCE

There are other clues to this message as well. To understand these it helps to recall some familiar features of Kierkegaard's biography. One is the very deep spiritual connection between

Søren and his father Michael Pedersen Kierkegaard. Not only
was Søren his father's "favorite" son, but he was also his father's
spiritual heir. Kierkegaard's biographers report the intensity of
philosophical and religious communication between them.
Unfortunately for Kierkegaard, this inheritance was a mixed
blessing. The elder Kierkegaard was a melancholy and tormented
individual. As a young shepherd on the Jutland heath he was led
by the misery of his existence to climb a hillock and raise his fist
against God.[33] Later he compounded his sins by becoming sexu-
ally involved with his housemaid Ane Lund while still in mourn-
ing for his first wife. Though this woman was to become his wife
(and Kierkegaard's mother), the first child of the union was conceived out of wedlock.[34]

There is no doubt that Søren believed a curse lay on his family because of these and other deeds of his father.[35] Apparently
believing in some connection between sexuality, procreation, and
the transmission of sinfulness (an entire section of *The Concept
of Anxiety* deals with the relationship between sexuality and sinfulness[36]), Kierkegaard attributed his own melancholy, and perhaps his own perceived tendency toward lust, to this family
curse.[37] Thus, the problem of sin and its forgiveness was an
urgent one for Kierkegaard. As I suggested earlier, it may even
have played a role in his break with Regine: one of the reasons
he felt that a divine "no" had been pronounced against the
union. Kierkegaard says as much in more than one entry in his
journals. Thus, in an entry for May 17, 1843, already partly
alluded to, he states,

> If I had not honored her higher than myself as my future wife,
> if I had not been prouder of her honor than my own—then I
> would have married her...But if I were to have explained
> myself, I would have had to initiate her into terrible things, my
> relationship to my father, his melancholy, the eternal night
> brooding within me, my going astray, my lusts and debauch-
> ery, which, however, in the eyes of God are perhaps not so
> glaring.[38]

In this sense, the problem of sin was even more basic to
Kierkegaard's romantic crisis than the call to a religious vocation. This is further suggested by the fact that the "interruption"

in the argument of *Fear and Trembling* appears in the middle of the narrative dealing with Agnes and the merman. Like Kierkegaard, the merman had fallen in love with an innocent young woman, but he can never complete his union with her because he began it from a standpoint of sin and is powerless, through any effort of his own, especially repentance, to restore his lost integrity. If we perceive the merman's dilemma to be the same as Kierkegaard's and the underlying cause of the romantic crisis that constitutes an obvious surface occasion for this book, we can now more fully understand Kierkegaard's remark about Abraham in a journal entry of 1843: "He who has explained this riddle has explained my life."[39]

In view of these biographical details, several additional aspects of *Fear and Trembling* assume much greater importance than they are usually given. One is the fact that the book deals essentially with the relationship of a father to a son, and even more specifically, with a father whose conduct imperils the son's survival. Gregor Malantschuk, in the only previous treatment of *Fear and Trembling* I know of focusing essentially on this father-son relationship, observes that it is mistaken to believe that Kierkegaard means in *Fear and Trembling* to place himself in the role of Abraham (one who commits a dreadful deed that endangers another). Instead, says Malantschuk, Kierkegaard must be thought of as comparing himself to Isaac, the imperiled object of his father's life of sin. This, Malantschuk concludes, forces us to regard the problem of sin and its overcoming as the principal "hidden meaning" of the book.[40] It is a small additional item of evidence supporting Malantschuk's view that Kierkegaard often referred to himself, in Abrahamic terms, as the child of his father's old age.[41]

It remains true, of course, that Abraham is no sinner, and in this respect, the analogy to the lives of the elder and younger Kierkegaard is not complete. Yet Kierkegaard acknowledged the "deceptive form" of *Fear and Trembling* in this regard.[42] The analogy is also precise enough for Kierkegaard's purposes. God does intervene to spare Isaac. Although his initial command imperils the youngster, his suspension of that same command allows the son to live. All this suggests that Kierkegaard saw in this aspect of the story a relationship between father, son, and

God that addressed the most urgent question of his life: can God intervene to put an end once and for all to the familial inheritance of sin?[43]

THE EPIGRAPH

Besides all this there is the epigraph. Although the recipient of the secret message is often thought to be Regine, what is striking is that the epigraph deals with a communication between a father and a son. From the very beginning, therefore, Kierkegaard may be signalling the deeper concerns of this book. If we assume that Kierkegaard was aware that others might rely on the epigraph to read *Fear and Trembling* primarily as a private communication to Regine, what could be more ironic than for him to have concealed within it a clue to the even more deeply hidden message of the book?

Of course the epigraph has matters turned around: here it is the father who, remaining silent, sends a secret message to the son, whereas the message of *Fear and Trembling* proceeds from the "silent" son to the father. The reversal is ironical: a son who is a teacher, not a learner; a son through whom God makes possible the salvation of the father. At the risk of carrying these reversals to the furthest extreme, I would point out that the text possibly contains one other. Genesis 22 identifies Isaac as the beloved son of Abraham. Omitted from mention is Ishmael, the rejected first son of Sarah's handmaid, Hagar. Yet *Fear and Trembling* was authored by an individual who was the beloved son of a first wife's handmaid. In *Fear and Trembling* the child of sin praises the father and child of faith.[44]

Whether these very specific relationships and reversals were consciously in Kierkegaard's mind, mention of them serves to return us to the main point of my discussion. For the sins that preoccupied Kierkegaard were very much related to the sexual and marital transgressions of his father. That he should choose a biblical text in which these same themes play a role and in which the tense relationship between father and son is central only reinforces my claim that this familial inheritance of sin constitutes the main hidden message of the book. To whom, then, is this message directed? Possibly to the spirit of Michael Pedersen Kierkegaard. Søren clearly accepted the traditional Christian doctrine of the immortality of the soul, and it would not be unreasonable to see this book as a very private communication between Søren and the spirit of his recently deceased father: a reflection, as it were, on the possibility of both their spiritual redemptions.[45] Then, too, it might be directed to others in the Kierkegaard family who could be expected to understand and share the concerns that beset Søren. Finally, the message may even be thought of as directed to Regine. The message of *Fear and Trembling* that she might then be expected to receive is not simply that Kierkegaard was summoned by God to break their engagement, but that he complied because of his own profound involvement with and complicity in a familial tradition of sin that it was beyond his power to overcome.

All this is speculation. Far less speculative, I believe, is the fact that the problem of sin and grace is central to this book. Nor should this be surprising, since the works immediately following this one in Kierkegaard's pseudonymous authorship and several of the religious discourses that accompanied its publication also deal centrally with the problem of sin.[46]

THE RELATIONSHIP TO KANT

Apart from matters of internal evidence or the book's relationship to Kierkegaard's authorship as a whole, this reading of *Fear and Trembling* is significantly reinforced by the understanding that, at the time he was preparing this and the other early pseudonymous works, Kierkegaard was deeply involved with Kant's mature philosophy of religion, particularly as it was developed in the *Religion within the Limits of Reason Alone* and *The Conflict of the Faculties*. If we fail to recognize this, and accept the standard view that Kierkegaard was either not interested in or was hostile to Kant's rationalistic philosophy, then it becomes reasonable to see *Fear and Trembling* primarily as an effort to use the Genesis episode to defend a distinctly un-Kantian, heteronomous (or "theonomous") ethic of divine command. As Abraham set God's will above all reasoned moral duty, so must we. The analogous secret message becomes a religious justification of Kierkegaard's hurtful break with Regine. Typically, students of Kierkegaard who see him as essentially opposed to Kant have tended to read *Fear and Trembling* this way and have also tended to use this book as evidence for Kierkegaard's essential opposition to Kantian ethics.

However, we saw in Chapter 3 that Kierkegaard owes much more to Kant's approach to ethics than he rejects, and although he makes some infrequent remarks in his journals about the need for an ethics based on divine command rather than autonomous human reason, he never develops this point of view (unless we regard *Fear and Trembling* as his effort to do so). If we also see *Fear and Trembling* as deeply in conversation with Kant's later writings in the philosophy of religion, not his ethics, then we must shift the focus of the book. In the *Religion* and related writings, the issue of ethical autonomy is merely presumed and Kant is overwhelmingly concerned with the problem of sin and how it is to be overcome.[47] Here he stakes out a rationalist view and one that in its entirety Kierkegaard will not accept. But the position that Kant develops and Kierkegaard's orthodox alternative to it are far closer to one another than any simple positing of Kierkegaard's "rejection" of Kant suggests.

The focus on Abraham is a further important sign, although one requiring some interpretation, that Kant's later writings in the philosophy of religion were very much on Kierkegaard's mind as he prepared *Fear and Trembling*. In both the *Religion* and *The Conflict of the Faculties*, in a series of comments virtually without precedent in the entire preceding philosophical-theological tradition, Kant voices criticisms of Abraham's conduct in the Genesis episode. In the *Religion* the criticism is muted and indirect. One comment occurs during his discussion of an "inquisitor" who, on the basis of the commands of "a supernaturally revealed Divine Will," insists on persecuting heretics. In Kant's view, this inquisitor is caught in a conflict between ordinary human duty, which prohibits killing persons because of their religious beliefs, and obedience to the divine command. Kant concedes (somewhat oddly) that an explicit command from God "made known in extraordinary fashion" could override human duty here, but, he states, "that God has ever uttered this terrible injunction can be asserted only on the basis of historical documents and is never apodictically certain." He then adds,

> And even did it appear to have come to him from God himself (like the command delivered to Abraham to slaughter his own son like a sheep) it is at least possible that in this instance a mistake has prevailed. But if this is so, the inquisitor would risk doing what would be wrong in the highest degree; and in this very act he is behaving unconscientiously. This is the case with respect to all historical and visionary faith; that is, the *possibility* ever remains that an error may be discovered in it. Hence it is unconscientious to follow such a faith with the possibility that perhaps what it commands or permits may be wrong, *i.e.*, with the danger of disobedience to a human duty which is certain in and of itself.[48]

Earlier in the *Religion*, we encounter a second, less direct, but in some ways more sharply critical reference to Genesis 22. During a discussion of miracles, Kant remarks: "Even though something is represented as commanded by God, through a direct manifestation of Him, yet, if it flatly contradicts morality, it cannot, despite all appearances, be of God (for example, were a father ordered to kill his son who is, so far as he knows, perfectly innocent)."[49] Finally, in *The Conflict of the Faculties*, Kant's defense of the priority of reasoned duty over supernatural revelations is impassioned, and his criticism of Abraham takes the form of the explicit denunciation of Abraham quoted at the beginning of this chapter.

These criticisms of Abraham are not found in the writings of any other previous philosopher[50], and they must have caught Kierkegaard's eye. If they had appeared in the course of Kant's treatment of heteronomy in the *Foundations*, they might have furnished an important item of evidence that *Fear and Trembling* is particularly directed against Kant's autonomous rational ethics. *But this is not their context.* Instead, they appear in Kant's later writings where his essential concern, in the wake of his evolved discovery of the ideality of ethics and the radicality of human evil, is the issue of how sin is to be overcome and how this is related to belief in a historical redeemer. In the previous chapter we saw that Kant always remained uncomfortable with the solution to this problem offered by "historical faith," with its emphasis on the atoning death of the God-Man. He repeatedly brings this solution under criticism in the *Religion* and *The Conflict of the Faculties*. Not only is this God-Man an intimidating rather than uplifting moral example, Kant tells us, but the idea of another person rendering satisfaction for our sins can only weaken our moral effort. In place of these alternatives, Kant favored a dehistoricized and demythologized Christ, the archetype within us of an abiding disposition to good that is "well pleasing to God."

In the previous chapter we also saw that Kierkegaard rejected these views. He appears to have believed that the problem of sin identified by Kant was so serious that no self-initiated repentance or reform could satisfactorily resolve it. Salvation, he maintained, could only be effected by God's decisive intervention in history to prove his willingness to forgive. If we now examine Kant's criticisms of Abraham, however, we can see that behind the issue of divine command versus duty lurks the more basic issue of the reliability of historical faith. Indeed, this issue is the principal theme of the sections of the *Religion* and *The Conflict of the Faculties* where Kant's criticism of Abraham occurs. *The point of Kant's treatment of Abraham in these important passages is precisely to stress the sufficiency of reason and to dismiss the need for a historical faith as the basis for our moral redemption from sin.*

This indicates that, for Kierkegaard, Abraham is the symbol for the larger question of whether we can rely on the teachings and confidences of a historically revealed religion, especially when these run counter to the dictates of autonomous reason. In the relevant sections of the *Religion* and *The Conflict of the Faculties* Kant shows how reluctant he is to allow matters of moral importance to rest on questionable and perhaps morally dangerous historical assumptions. What Kierkegaard seems to be saying in response to this is that Kant has matters upside down. The foremost moral danger we face, as Kant's own discussions make clear, is our bitter involvement in sin, and the most questionable matter is our ability to escape from this on our own. If the only way to move beyond sin is via the uncertain faith in a God who has decisively entered history, so be it. Anything less is to accept spiritual self-destruction. Putting matters this way amounts to turning Kant's own brilliant analysis of the priority of practical over theoretical reason against him.

That Abraham and Isaac serve as symbols for historical faith in general, and for Christian redemption in particular, should not surprise us. There is a long tradition of Christian interpretation of Genesis 22, a tradition with which Kierkegaard was familiar, in which countless texts present Abraham's sacrifice of Isaac as a "type" of God's sacrificial offering up of his son for the salvation of humanity.[51] Remarkably, Kant draws attention to this typological use of Genesis 22 in *The Conflict of the Faculties* when he characterizes Abraham's offering "as the symbol of the world-savior's own sacrifice."[52] On the basis of this symbolism alone, Louis Mackey has concluded that the problem of sin must be far more central to *Fear and Trembling* than it appears to be.[53] We can see that Mackey's hunch about this matter is amply reinforced by a perception of how much Kant's treatments of sin and grace were on Kierkegaard's mind when he wrote this book.

If Abraham symbolizes central issues in Christian theology, then in its way *Fear and Trembling* symbolizes Kierkegaard's whole relationship to Kant. Interpreted superficially as a criticism of Kantian ethics, it reinforces the impression that Kierkegaard was indifferent or hostile to Kant's thought. The absence of even one reference to Kant in this work reinforces this impression. Read, however, as a penetrating exploration of the problems of sin and the possibility of grace as these were raised by Kant in the *Religion* and *The Conflict*, it brings the full complexity of Kierkegaard's relationship to Kant into high relief. That Kierkegaard resisted Kant's rationalistic solutions to the problem of sin is certain. Equally certain, however, is that Kant played a major role in helping Kierkegaard identify and respond to this very problem. *Fear and Trembling* is an argument with Kant, but one evidencing not simple rejection of Kant on Kierkegaard's part but also enormous indebtedness and respect.

CONCLUSION

Weaker talents idealize; figures of capable imagination appropriate
for themselves. But nothing is got for nothing, and self-
appropriation involves the immense anxieties of indebtedness, for
what strong maker desires the realization that he has failed to
create himself?

—Harold Bloom, The Anxiety of Influence[1]

In the Introduction, I tried to convey my surprise and excitement
when, on reapproaching *The Concept of Anxiety* after many
years and in the wake of intervening study of Kant, I encountered theme after theme, idea after idea that seemed drawn from
Kant's work. I hope the reader of the preceding chapters now
shares some of this excitement. The parallels in Kierkegaard's
and Kant's writings and the pattern of Kierkegaard's extensive
engagement with problems or issues identified by Kant point to
substantial involvement by Kierkegaard with Kant's philosophy.

In view of the extent of this pattern of involvement and borrowing, it is surprising that no one has previously identified
Kierkegaard's debt to Kant. One reason for this, as I've observed,
has to do with the sociology of knowledge and the relative sepa-
ration of the communities of Kant and Kierkegaard scholarship.
Also important are the scant number of references to Kant in
Kierkegaard's writings. The *Postscript* and the *Fragments* illus-
trate the problem. The index of Swenson's translation of the
Postscript lists more than twenty references to Hegel, eight to
Grundtvig, at least twenty-three to Lessing, and over thirty to
Socrates—but only two to Kant.[2] *Fear and Trembling*, with its
impassioned defense of Abraham, was certainly influenced by
Kant's sharp criticisms of the patriarch in the *Religion* and *The
Conflict of the Faculties*, yet Kant is not once mentioned in
Kierkegaard's work. We've seen that the *Fragments* resonates
from beginning to end with Kantian ideas and terms, but despite
many references to a host of lesser and greater philosophers,

Kant is not mentioned in either the text or notes. Indeed, an explicit reference to Kant that appears in the *Papers* in connection with Kierkegaard's use there of the term *accessorium* is expunged from the related passage in the *Fragments* where Kierkegaard employs this term. Similarly, the *Postscript*'s unstated but clear reference to Kant in connection with Hegel's criticism of a "barbaric" critique of the ontological proof makes its debut in the *Fragments* as an ironical footnote remark about an unspecified "stupid attack" on the proof. If it is true, as I have tried to show, that Kant is a major influence on Kierkegaard's religious-ethical thinking, how can we account for this systematic pattern of nonattribution?

One possibility is that Kierkegaard merely took Kant for granted. In the first chapter we saw that elements of a popularized Kantian philosophy were probably in the air that Kierkegaard breathed—as Freudianism or Marxism would be for a young writer earlier in this century. This suggests that Kierkegaard may have been so deeply informed by a Kantian perspective that he rarely felt the need to distinguish his own views from those borrowed from the German philosopher. This also may partly explain why Kierkegaard never cites Kant in those places where he is obviously drawing heavily on the philosopher's better-known insights, as, for example, in the several instances where he repeats almost verbatim Kant's critique of the ontological proof. But relatively few of Kierkegaard's borrowings from Kant involve matters so generally known. This is especially true of explicit borrowings from the *Religion* and *The Conflict of the Faculties*, works by Kant that have never been widely read. Yet even here the pattern of nonattribution prevails.

Another way of understanding this pattern of nonattribution has to do with the allegedly nonscholarly nature of Kierkegaard's authorship. It is well known that Kierkegaard did not regard himself as a technical scholar. Over the course of his career he voiced bitter criticism of writers for whom erudition was a substitute for independent thought or personal involvement with the subject of their work. For example, Anti-Climacus, the author of *The Sickness unto Death*, echoes Kierkegaard's own views when he criticizes and calls "unchristian" the "kind of scholarliness and scienticity that ultimately does not build up."[3] In a journal entry for the same year Kierkegaard denounces Martensen for his "perpetual talking about Kant, Hegel, Schelling, etc." This kind of scholarship, says Kierkegaard, "provides a guarantee that there must be something in what he says. It is similar to the journalistic practice of writing in the name of the public."[4] If we recall how thoroughly Kierkegaard opposed the role the "public" had come to play in the culture of his day,[5] we can see how much he disliked a purely scholarly approach to religious or ethical matters.

The positive side of this position was Kierkegaard's wish to be a "primitive" author, one who employs whatever materials he draws on to develop universal truths in a personal and original way. In *The Concept of Anxiety* Kierkegaard provides a vivid description of his understanding of the writer's task and of the writer's relation to his sources:

> In my opinion, one who intends to write a book ought to consider carefully the subject about which he wishes to write. Nor would it be inappropriate for him to acquaint himself as far as possible with what has already been written on the subject. If on his way he should meet an individual who has dealt exhaustively and satisfactorily with one or another aspect of that subject, he would do well to rejoice as does the bridegroom's friend who stands by and rejoices greatly as he hears the bridegroom's voice. When he has done this in complete silence and with the enthusiasm of a love that ever seeks solitude, nothing more is needed; then he will carefully write his book as spontaneously as a bird sings its song.[6]

Kierkegaard's systematic failure to cite Kant may thus be seen to reflect his creative appropriation of Kant's work. But this interpretation has the serious drawback that Kierkegaard usually does not fail to cite other writers whose work he used extensively. I have mentioned the many other thinkers cited in the *Fragments* and the *Postscript*. *The Concept of Anxiety* furnishes a good example itself of this attention to attribution. The book as a whole is dedicated to Kierkegaard's friend and teacher Poul Martin Møller, who had died just a few years before. Many themes in the book directly traceable to Møller are clearly signalled in the dedication,[7] and Kierkegaard openly cites in the text other writers on whose work he draws, such as Franz Baader or

Karl Rosenkranz.[8] *The Concept of Anxiety* is also profoundly penetrated by Kant's thought, especially as he developed it in the opening sections of the *Religion*. Yet Kierkegaard's entire discussion makes only one reference to Kant, a brief but somewhat favorable remark about him in the context of a criticism of Hegel.[9] If we assume that Kant's work was at least as influential for Kierkegaard in this book as Møller's, how can we account for the disparate treatment of these two sources?

A further sign that it is not enough to blame this absence of references on Kierkegaard's alleged disdain for the scholarly process is the fact that Kierkegaard sometimes presents himself as zealously committed to using the apparatus of scholarship. Consider, for example, this journal entry for 1854: "In one respect I almost resent having begun to read Schopenhauer. I have such an indescribably scrupulous anxiety about using someone else's expressions without acknowledgement. But his expressions are sometimes so closely akin to mine that in my exaggerated diffidence I perhaps end by ascribing to him what is my very own."[10] Consider, too, the following passage that appears in a draft of the Preface to the *Fragments*. We can speculate on why Kierkegaard omitted this passage from the published version of the *Fragments*, a work absolutely permeated by Kantian thought and centrally employing terms introduced by Kant. In any case, this passage shows that Kierkegaard was not unaware of or unconcerned about the attributional requirements of scholarship:

> I really do not credit myself with scientific scholarship; I do not fraternize with its devotees; I do not force myself on anyone. My thought and its fate are not of the slightest importance to anyone, with the exception of myself. What I do, I do *proprio marte, propriis auspiciis, proprio stipendo* [by one's own hand, on one's own behalf, at one's own expense]—in short, I do it as a *proprietarius* [independent owner], insofar as one can be that without owning something, without coveting something. I do it candidly, not sophistically...I do it honestly, for it is not my intention to deceive anyone. If to the best of my poor ability I take note of some individual thinker, I shall conscientiously quote him as well as I can. As for stray remarks, I follow my old custom of placing in quotation marks everything I know is not my own and everything of which I do not know the source.[11]

This remark becomes particularly odd when we recall that in the *Fragments* Kierkegaard takes from Kant's *The Conflict of the Faculties* the expression and idea of the "teacher as occasion" and makes it a central leitmotif of his book, without once mentioning Kant's little treatise or the many other ideas he draws from it. It becomes even odder if we consider the many other unacknowledged borrowings from Kant in this work, including, perhaps, one quoted but unattributed remark arguably drawn from Kant's first *Critique*.[12]

Finally, it might be thought that Kierkegaard's failure to cite Kant results from his sense of sharp disagreement with Kant's views. We saw in Chapter 4, for example, that Kierkegaard ultimately takes a position directly opposed to Kant on the role of revealed faith—and a historical savior—in the economy of salvation. In the *Fragments*, Kierkegaard concludes that belief in God in history defines Christian faith (Danish *Tro;* German *Glaube*), whereas Kant, in *The Conflict of the Faculties*, brands such belief the opposite of faith, superstition (*Aberglaube*). In Kierkegaard's mind, these differences may have justified his failure to cite a thinker whose final position he regarded as mistaken and profoundly opposed to his own. But we have also seen that Kierkegaard's repudiation of Kant rests on a platform of ethical-religious insight constructed by Kant. Kierkegaard was well aware of how much his own conception of ethics and his understanding of moral failure drew on Kant's work. He also had to be aware of how much some of his writings (especially his treatment of Abraham in *Fear and Trembling*) were direct rejoinders to Kant's positions in the *Religion* and *The Conflict of the Faculties.* Yet Kierkegaard never discusses or acknowledges the degree of his involvement with Kant. Even if Kierkegaard perceived himself to be in disagreement with Kant, what must be explained is why he so seldom openly argues with Kant about the matters that divide them.

Although each of these efforts to account for the paucity of Kierkegaard's references to Kant has a grain of truth, therefore, none adequately explains the massive pattern of unacknowledged borrowing from Kant we have seen. To understand this, I think, we must look elsewhere. In my view this requires us to suppose a more active effort on Kierkegaard's part to obscure the lines of his relationship to Kant. *Kierkegaard's debt to Kant has remained hidden, I believe, because he wanted it to be.* I am convinced that, for a complex set of reasons about which we can only speculate, Kierkegaard went out of his way to erase the lines that connected his work back to Kant's. Before speculating about why he might have done this, I want briefly to recall some of the evidence we have encountered supporting the claim that Kierkegaard deliberately sought to conceal his debt to Kant.

The most important sign that Kierkegaard deliberately tried to conceal his use of Kant is the pattern of misleading attribution where borrowings from Kant are concerned. More than once, we've seen, Kierkegaard suggests that he owes a point he is making to a thinker other than Kant, when Kant is arguably the most immediate stimulus for Kierkegaard's discussion. The most important illustration of this is Kierkegaard's repeated references to Lessing in his lengthy treatment of the "leap" in the *Postscript*, when Kant's treatments of the "leap" in the first *Critique* and the *Religion* are more relevant. Since the *Postscript* is permeated by Kantian themes—from the treatments of proofs of God's existence early in the discussion to the handling of sin and repentance later—the deliberate attribution of the idea of the leap to Lessing and the total neglect of Kant suggest a deliberate effort at concealment.

In previous chapters I pointed out other instances of this pattern of misleading attribution. They include the repeated references to Socrates, when Kant's positions and terms are equally or more applicable, and mention of the elder Fichte in *The Concept of Anxiety* in connection with the claim that ethics allows no time for repentance, a claim whose substance, if not phrasing, is much informed by Kant's treatment of the problem of past wrongdoing. My point is not that Kierkegaard's other references are inappropriate but that it is odd that, throughout his whole discussion of sin in *The Concept of Anxiety*, Kierkegaard makes no mention of Kant's strikingly similar treatment of these themes in the *Religion*.[13]

We find a small example of this same pattern of misleading attribution in Kierkegaard's treatment of the theme of the irreversibility of sin in the *Fragments*. In a lengthy footnote on this matter, Kierkegaard (Johannes Climacus), after stating that he intends to "discuss this somewhat in Greek fashion," employs a series of illustrations to develop the point that once we make the choice of sin we cannot then renounce it and choose good. His examples—the spending of money on a nonreturnable purchase or siding with one contending party rather than another in a war—illustrate the weightiness and irreversibility of certain free decisions. Kierkegaard concludes this note by quoting Aristotle: "The depraved person and the virtuous person presumably do not have the power over their moral condition, but in the beginning they did have the power to become the one or the other, just as the person who throws a stone has power over it before he throws it but not when he has thrown it."[14]

References like this to Aristotle are common in Kierkegaard's writings. They have led commentators like George Stack to argue that Aristotle's ethics had a powerful, possibly predominant, influence on Kierkegaard.[15] Yet the point Aristotle is making in this quotation, drawn from the *Nicomachean Ethics*, is far different from Kierkegaard's. For Aristotle, individual acts are important to the extent that over time they habituate us to good or to evil. Aristotle believed that we lose the power to shape our moral disposition only after a sustained course of immoral conduct, just as gluttons or alcoholics may eventually lose their powers of self-control. But since there is no question for Aristotle, or any of the Greek ethical teachers, of measuring one's moral worth in relation to a demanding moral law, there is no reason within this tradition to believe (as Kierkegaard wants to suggest) that a single wrongful act fatally binds us to sin. The assumed correspondence between virtue and happiness within the Greek eudaimonistic tradition and the confidence that to know the good is to do it also exert a strong counterpressure against the development of a vicious character and render a single act even less determinative of our life course.

Kierkegaard was aware of these and other essential differences between Greek and Christian ethics. In an important passage in *The Concept of Anxiety* concerning the ideality of ethics, a matter partly underlying his remarks in the *Fragments* on the irreversibility of sin, Kierkegaard explicitly rejects Aristotle's Greek eudaimonism and, without naming Kant, expresses his preference for a "science of ethics" that emphasizes a demanding

moral law leading to a knowledge of sin. Not only is Kierkegaard's general attitude toward ethics far closer to Kant's than to
Aristotle's, therefore, but Kant's insight that a single wrongful
choice may be irreversible because it reveals the supreme maxim
(*die oberste Maxime*) or general rule of all our choices is also far
closer to the point Kierkegaard is trying to make in this footnote
in the *Fragments*. We can assume that Kierkegaard was familiar
with Kant's view, since he alludes to it in other discussions of the
"continuity of sin." Yet in this footnote he does not mention
Kant at all.

This pattern is repeated time and again in the *Fragments*.
Ideas or terms recognizably associated with Kant—the "teacher
as occasion," the nonnecessity of existence, the location of perceptual error in judgment rather than in the senses, and the non-
perceptibility of God—are attributed to ancient thinkers or
philosophers preceding Kant, while Kant goes unmentioned. In
the end, I believe, we must explain this use of classical or early
modern sources (the Skeptics, Socrates, Aristotle, Descartes) as
part of a deliberate effort by Kierkegaard to camouflage the
degree of his involvement with Kant's philosophy. The substantial literature on Kierkegaard's debt to Socrates, Aristotle, Lessing, and others and the paucity of studies of his relation to Kant
show how well this effort succeeded.

But why would Kierkegaard do this? If we grant for the
moment that Kierkegaard sought deliberately to efface his ties to
Kant, why did he go to all this trouble? In answering this question I can only speculate. At least two different explanations suggest themselves. One traces Kierkegaard's reluctance to mention
Kant to the difficulties that revealing this debt would have created for the success and acceptance of his authorship. A second
explanation moves in a different direction and sees Kierkegaard's
effacement of Kant as part of an ironical and only half-concealed
trick played on his smug Hegelian contemporaries.

A link to Kant would have impeded the acceptance of
Kierkegaard's authorship by either of Kierkegaard's two main
readerships: orthodox Christians or adherents of the regnant
Hegelian philosophy (whether in its religious or secular forms).
Revealing a debt to Kant would surely not have impressed
Kierkegaard's more traditionally religious readers. Kant, after all,

was the archrationalist, the "world-destroyer" (*Weltzermal-mender*), as Heinrich Heine had called him,[16] whose ethical objections to traditional piety and whose criticism of traditional theology amounted, in many minds, to an atheistic assault on orthodox faith. True, in his later writings Kant developed a creative and penetrating reassessment of key elements of biblical faith. But even if Kierkegaard was deeply instructed by Kant, how could this tireless religious polemicist, this "sworn enemy of philosophical systems,"[17] let it be known that some of his most creative insights were drawn from Kant?

The problem was even more acute where the Hegelians were concerned. Among them, Kantian philosophy was widely regarded as passé. The rage of the era was to "go further" (*gaa videre*) and transcend all previous philosophy. Although Kierkegaard often ridiculed this mania for novelty and intellectual progress at the expense of serious attention to the wisdom of the past,[18] he knew very well that Kant's work had not yet reached the stage of veneration where reliance on it could avoid the contempt directed at the unfashionable. It might be possible to "go back" to Socrates or Paul, but it was not possible for a Danish writer of the 1840s and 1850s to "go back" to Kant. To be labeled a Kantian was thus to risk being dismissed as naive by the philosophically avant garde of the day. From the perspective of a budding writer, this was an even more dangerous categorization than being regarded as a religious eccentric. Kierkegaard may have believed that Kant's work required the deepest study before it was "gone beyond." In one journal entry he describes "the critical period" as "related to the present as a hydraulic gold mine is to the bank which mints the gold nuggets and puts them into circulation."[19] But he would not force this view of Kant's creativity on his arrogant Hegelian contemporaries. Whereas the Kierkegaard of the post-Attack period might be willing to suffer the scorn of the Hegelian "coterie" dominated by Martensen and the Heibergs, there is reason to believe that the younger Kierkegaard, as Henning Fenger has argued, was keenly interested in retaining the favor of the Heiberg circle.[20]

None of this, of course, explains Kierkegaard's effort also to shape the posthumous record. Here, it seems to me, we have to probe more deeply into the psychology and personal biography of a young writer working in the atmosphere of post-Enlightenment, romantic culture. Speaking of the poetic writers of this period, Harold Bloom has argued that they characteristically exhibit a compulsion toward priority in intellectual and artistic creation and a fear of being regarded as derivative. Bloom terms this state of mind "the anxiety of influence." In his study with this same title, Bloom observes that "all quest-romances of the post-Enlightenment, meaning all Romanticisms whatsoever, are quests to re-beget one's own self, to become one's own Great Original."[21] Surprisingly, in this study Bloom repeatedly draws on Kierkegaard's statements about artistic and intellectual creativity to illustrate his own points about the poet's efforts at self-creation, the poet's demand for priority and for freedom from the influence of his precursors.[22]

Although Bloom is entirely unaware of Kierkegaard's relationship to Kant, it is not accidental that he draws on Kierkegaard's preoccupation with originality of authorship in describing this "anxiety of influence." As Kierkegaard reminds us from virtually the first to the last words of his published work, he was always a poet, and a poet writing and thinking in an era when originality—the secure possession of one's own *daimon*, one's genius—was the mark of greatness. Even a cursory reading of Kierkegaard's *Papers* tell us how much he was concerned with the singularity of his religious-literary effort. From *Either/Or* and *Fear and Trembling* onward the poetic Kierkegaard always remained concerned with his place in literary and intellectual history. Furthermore, as Christoph Schrempf reminds us in his exhaustive biography, Kierkegaard's strong sense of sacrificial destiny—his wish to offer up his life as the vehicle for a unique and redemptive idea—exhibits a turn of mind characteristic of many other "poetic" writers of this period.[23]

In view of this, we might suppose that Kierkegaard also suffered from "the anxiety of influence," that he, too, sought to cut the ties to his predecessors and, above all, to that predecessor on whose originality and genius his own novel creation so depended. In the course of his discussion, Bloom repeatedly quotes a remark by Kierkegaard that Bloom presents as a virtual synopsis of the poet's effort to creatively appropriate the work of his predecessor: "He who is willing to work gives birth to his own father."[24] If the pattern of borrowing we've seen is indicative, Kant is, in a sense, Kierkegaard's intellectual "father." Understood in terms of Bloom's analysis, therefore, Kierkegaard's authorship becomes an impassioned effort to "re-create" Kant's philosophy in a way that makes it fully the product of Kierkegaard's own creative genius. The absence of any tradition of scholarship relating Kierkegaard to Kant and the difficulty many Kierkegaard biographers have had in tracing the lines of his descent show how well Kierkegaard was able to obscure his own intellectual paternity.

This first explanation of Kierkegaard's deliberate effort to erase the lines leading back to Kant assumes a measure of concealment and intellectual ambition. A second explanation moves in a different direction and relates Kierkegaard's handling of Kant to the central intellectual concerns of his authorship and to his ongoing employment of irony as a philosophical tool. Simply stated, it sees Kierkegaard's covert use of Kant as a subtle, necessary, and deserved trick played by Kierkegaard on his arrogant Hegelian foes.

To understand this second effort at explanation, it helps to keep in mind Louis Mackey's point that Kierkegaard faced a daunting task in taking on Hegelianism from an orthodox Christian-religious point of view.[25] The challenge before Kierkegaard, Mackey observes, was to call into question a philosophy that regarded itself as the dialectical fulfillment of human thought and as thus able to comprehend all possible philosophical and religious positions. To accomplish this seemingly impossible task, Kierkegaard chose to avoid philosophical argumentation and to employ the method of Socratic irony, arraying its "infinite negativity" against Hegelian pretensions.

I would deepen Mackey's observations by adding that part of this ironic strategy for Kierkegaard may have involved a decision to employ Kantian philosophy in his struggle against the Hegelians: to use a thinker who had been "transcended" (*aufgehoben*) and fully assimilated into the dialectic against the discipline's now reigning giant. Philosophy could thus be turned against its own methodological and substantive pretensions. To prevent this from becoming just another page in this history of philosophical debates, however, and to avoid the Hegelians' premature dismissal of his position, Kierkegaard would have had to conceal Kant's presence in his own reformulated statements of Christianity. In this way Kierkegaard could appropriate and use Kant's brilliant destruction of the tradition of rationalism while ironically exposing the hollowness of the Hegelians' claims to have mastered all preceding thought.

There are hints in Kierkegaard's writings that he was aware of the joke he was playing on the smug but philosophically less-than-well-trained Danish Hegelians. Kierkegaard knew that Martensen and his acolytes, for the very reason that they did not take the past seriously, were often ill-versed in the writings of philosophers whose work they purported to have transcended. In a remark to his brother in 1841 he caustically dismisses possible criticisms of his doctoral dissertation by what he calls "one or another half-educated Hegelian robber."[26] Having endured Martensen's and others' lectures on Kant, and knowing how little the Hegelians really understood Kant's profound ethics and philosophical theology, Kierkegaard may well have enjoyed the one-upmanship involved in surreptitiously turning Kant against his teachers.

I have already mentioned one possible instance of this kind of playfulness on Kierkegaard's part: his handling in the *Postscript* of the matter of the philosophical pedigree of the idea of the "leap." Although Johannes Climacus, the *Postscript's* pseudonymous author, repeatedly confesses his debt to Lessing for this idea, even giving the title "Attributable to Lessing" to the section where he discusses the leap, the section itself ends with mention of the fact that Johannes *de silentio*, author of *Fear and Trembling*, had previously discussed a similar idea. Climacus adds that he had read Johannes *de silentio*'s book before encountering Lessing's essay, and he closes his discussion with the remark "Whether Johannes *de silentio* has had his attention called to the leap by reading Lessing, I shall not attempt to say."[27] This comment invites the discerning reader to ask, who, if not Lessing, might be Climacus's/Kierkegaard's primary philosophical source for this idea? Since *Fear and Trembling* centrally addresses Kant's repudiation of the leap of faith as this was symbolized for both Kant and Kierkegaard by the episode of Genesis 22, there can be little doubt that this remark about influence points toward Kant. Almost as though he were unwilling to totally obscure his debt to Kant, in other words, Kierkegaard gives the informed reader a glimpse into the game he is playing with the Hegelians.

The *Fragments* offers another sign of this playfulness. On at least six occasions, the author, Johannes Climacus, raises questions of scholarly attribution and openly acknowledges the unoriginality of his ideas and his susceptibility to the charge of plagiarism.[28] In almost all these instances, Climacus is able ironically to defend himself against such accusations because the intellectual property he is appropriating derives from the very public domain of biblical teaching. At the same time, many other elements in this volume are borrowed from Kant, possibly including at least one idea attributed by Climacus to the Bible.[29] The project itself is stimulated, in part, by Kant's position on historical revelation in *The Conflict of the Faculties*, a work we might suppose relatively few Hegelians had read. Hence, concealed within Climacus's openly confessed plagiarism lies a deeper level of unacknowledged borrowing. Kierkegaard's irony and sense of humor seem to me to be at work here. Openly signalling the derivative quality of this work, he leaves it to the Hegelians to detect his employment of Kant against them, while remaining confident that, despite their vaunted philosophical erudition, the Danish Hegelians will surely fail to see or understand the presence of the philosopher they had "gone beyond."

Was it, then, authorial ambition or a only half-veiled playfulness and irony that led Kierkegaard to obscure his debt to Kant? In the complex world of human motives, which Kierkegaard himself so masterfully explored, these two explanations may be less opposed than they appear. Perhaps both motives were at work, a youthful author's passionate quest for originality tempered by conscientious self-disclosure and a willingness to reveal his philosophical legerdemain to those able to appreciate it.

Whatever Kierkegaard's motives, there can be no doubt that Kant played a major role in Kierkegaard's intellectual formation. From the pattern of borrowing we've seen, I am led to conclude that as early as his student years Kierkegaard was deeply intrigued by what he had read in Kant's mature works on religion. This interest shaped the course of his writing and thinking in the period immediately following. We saw that as early as

1835 Kierkegaard expressed the wish that he might find "the idea" to which he could give his life.[30] Over the course of the next five years, reading Kant in preparation for his degree examination, Kierkegaard found this idea. Although his best teachers treated Kantianism as merely a way station en route to Hegel, Kierkegaard perceived that Kant's contributions to religious thought had not even begun to be assimilated. If Kant's ethics were taken seriously—and despite many criticisms, including Hegel's, Kant's ethical writings everywhere commanded respect—then his contentions in the *Religion* also had to be taken seriously. They had to be viewed neither as the work of a great philosopher in his dotage (the opinion of some philosophers) nor as a wooden and perhaps dangerous effort to translate biblical truth into philosophical terms (the orthodox view). Instead, they had to be seen as a rigorous exposition of ideas that pointed inevitably to their limits and to the requirement that they be transcended by faith. Over the next five years, during the intensely creative period of the major pseudonymous writings, Kierkegaard sought to develop a new form for the communication of these ideas, and he tried to carry Kant's beginning to the thoroughly religious or "faithful" conclusions Kant resisted.

A journal entry for 1836–1837 written at the time Kierkegaard was beginning his formal study of Kant provides an early hint of the importance Kierkegaard attached to Kant's philosophy.[31] Kierkegaard here presents Kant, along with Goethe and Holberg, as belonging to the "royal procession" of thinkers whose work represents a fundamental breakthrough in thought and who, because of this, are resisted by their contemporaries. These thinkers, Kierkegaard suggests, play a decisive a role in conveying the "password which God whispered in Adam's ear, which one generation is supposed to deliver to the next and which shall be demanded of them on judgment day." Since Kierkegaard's own sense of personal mission was very much in formation at this time, it is reasonable to conclude that he regarded himself as a recipient, in his generation, of the "password" uttered by Kant. Remarkably, in an omission characteristic of the whole tradition of Kierkegaard scholarship on this matter, the Hongs fail to include Kierkegaard's mention of Kant in their otherwise meticulous translation of this entry.

Either/Or offers a further hint that carrying on and fulfilling Kant's initiative is an accurate depiction of Kierkegaard's project in the pseudonymous works. In Chapter 3 we saw that the ethical stage of life sketched there by Judge William is broadly Kantian in nature. Kierkegaard himself shows his sympathy for this position when he states that in every way the ethics which Judge William champions "is quite the opposite of the Hegelian."[32] Yet *Either/Or* also seeks to point to the possibility of a religious stage of existence where the ethical is dialectically transcended and fulfilled. This stage is suggested in the position presented by the unnamed country pastor whose view is developed in the "Ultimatum" of the book, a view that moves toward faith via a recognition of the unavoidability of sin. The ethical must be transcended (but not eliminated), the pastor tells us, because if ethics alone were to shape our destiny, we would all succumb to moral despair.

Significantly, as Judge William concludes the exposition of his own moral doctrine, he states emphatically that he does not believe in "radical evil."[33] The phrase is Kant's. What Kierkegaard (Victor Eremita) seems to be telling us, therefore, is that the ethical stage of life reaches its apogee in a Kantian position like Judge William's *just before Kant's own discovery of the doctrine of radical evil*. With this discovery, however, this stage collapses in upon itself and remains one of despair until it is properly completed by the qualitative transition that Christianity alone makes possible. Thus Kant's work in the *Religion* and *The Conflict of the Faculties* is here clearly suggested as representing the transition from the ethical to the religious stages of life. We know that Kant himself never fully made this transition. Despite his clear delineation of the limits of his own ethical position through his doctrine of radical evil, he could never accept the promise of historically mediated redemption to which his own thinking so clearly pointed. Half Judge William, half the country pastor, Kant hesitated to make the qualitative leap that would complete his work. Kierkegaard had no such hesitation. From *Either/Or* onward, he sought to fulfill the promise of Kant's philosophy.

If this is an accurate depiction of what Kierkegaard did, his instincts were good. He was right to perceive that Kant had effected a dramatic transformation in the philosophical approach to Christian faith. For nearly two millennia, Christian philosophers had tried to combine the powerful ethical and religious heritage of the Bible with the equally powerful tools of analysis provided by the classical Greek and Roman philosophical tradition. Always, however, this effort was made on the terrain of Greek metaphysics, through the exercise of "theoretical" or scientific reason, as the famous traditional proofs of God's existence show. Kant severely damaged this tradition by his critique of these proofs and, more deeply, by his perception that no employment of theoretical reason would yield the traditional God of Jewish and Christian faith. Only an approach rooted firmly in ethics could do that. Kant's great achievement was to show that a rigorous development of the concepts of practical reason led directly to the main religious ideas of biblical faith, including those that criticized or set limits to reason's pretensions. Although Kant in some ways broke with the tradition of thought that preceded him, in other, more important ways he was in direct continuity with that tradition: seeking to employ reason to vindicate the central ethical and theological truths of biblical faith.

In the deepest sense, my work in this book serves to show that what is true for Kant is also true for Kierkegaard. Superficially regarded, his authorship seems a sharp break with the preceding philosophical tradition. Although Kierkegaard is adept at picking up bits and pieces from the writings of the philosophers and employing them to his advantage, the general character of his writing appears antiphilosophical and even antirational. Key ideas, including the importance of passion and subjectivity, the concept of faith as a leap, and the idea of a "teleological suspension of the ethical," all contribute to the impression that Kierkegaard located ethical and religious life in a nonrational domain of experience.

I realize that the question of Kierkegaard's relationship to philosophy and rational analysis is not reducible to a matter of first impressions. Many commentators have noted the depth of Kierkegaard's philosophical involvement.[34] Kierkegaard also repeatedly expressed the view that precisely because reason leads to its own collapse, it is an irreplaceable instrument for discovering the truths of faith.[35] But this philosophical and rationalist side of Kierkegaard's work is easily eclipsed by the strong emphasis on the seemingly nonrational aspects of religious life, and even those who would defend Kierkegaard's rationalism are hampered if they are unaware of the less obvious philosophical issues or concerns motivating Kierkegaard's work, especially those raised by Kant.

This is why an understanding of Kierkegaard's relationship to Kant is important. What it allows us to see is that he was actively informed by the style of philosophy of religion pioneered by Kant. Like Kant, he believed that we must approach religion through the sphere of practical, not theoretical reason. Like Kant, he saw that the highest task of reason is to identify and probe its own limits. And like Kant, he saw that these two ideas together lead inevitably to a comprehension of the depth of human freedom and the ethical limits of human life—to the recognition of human sin and our dependence for moral fulfillment on a realm approached only in faith.

Uncovering the link between Kant and Kierkegaard, therefore, enhances our appreciation of the essential continuity of Western religious thought. In the twentieth century, partly under Kierkegaard's influence, much religious thinking seems to have turned away from the concerns of the earlier rationalist philosophers. Existentialist philosophers and theologians, in particular, with their various phenomenologies of existence and their emphasis on freedom and personal decision, seem to have departed markedly from any identifiable rationalist tradition that precedes them. By observing the rootedness of these views in Kierkegaard, and through him in Kant, we can perceive a flow of intellectual development marked as much by continuity as by change.

ABBREVIATIONS
OF REFERENCES

The following are abbreviations of the major works by Kant and Kierkegaard referred to in the text and notes. Also listed are translations used for longer quotations. References to shorter works by Kant appearing in the *vermischte Schriften* and to translations of these are listed in Appendix B.

A. KANT

Conflict   *The Conflict of the Faculties: Der Streit der Fackultäten.* Trans. Mary J. Gregor. New York: Abaris Books, 1979. This translation also has the German text. All references are to this edition. (*Der Streit der Fackultäten* also appears in GS VII, s. 1–116.)

GR   *Foundations of the Metaphysics of Morals.* Trans. Lewis White Beck. Indianapolis: Bobbs-Merrill, 1959. (*Grundlegung zur Metaphysik der Sitten,* GS IV, s. 385–464.)

GS   *Kants gesammelte Schriften,* herausgegeben von der Königlich preussischen Akademie der Wissenschaften. 28 vols. Berlin: Georg Reimer, 1902.

Judgment   *Critique of Judgment.* Trans. J. H. Bernard. New York: Hafner Press, 1951. (*Kritik der Urteilskraft,* GS V, s. 165–486.)

KPV   *Critique of Practical Reason.* Trans. Lewis White Beck. Indianapolis: Bobbs-Merrill, 1956. (*Kritik der praktischen Vernunft,* GS V, s. 1–164.)

KRV   *Critique of Pure Reason.* Trans. Norman Kemp Smith. New York: St. Martin's Press, 1929. (*Kritik der reinen Vernunft,* 2te. Auflage 1787 GS III, s. 1–552; 1. Auflage 1781 GS IV, S. 1–252.)

KU   *Kritik der Urteilskraft*, GS V, s. 165–486.

LE   *Lectures on Ethics*. Trans. Louis Infield. New York: Harper and Row, 1963. (*Eine Vorlesung Kants über ethik im Auftrage der Kantgesellschaft*. Berlin: Pan Verlag, 1924.)

LPT   *Lectures on Philosophical Theology*. Trans. Allen Wood. Ithaca, N.Y.: Cornell University Press, 1973.

MS   *The Metaphysics of Morals*. Part I translated as *The Metaphysical Elements of Justice*, trans. John Ladd. Indianapolis: Bobbs-Merrill, 1965. Part II translated as *The Metaphysical Principles of Virtue*, trans. James Ellington. Indianapolis: Bobbs-Merrill, 1964. (*Die Metaphysik der Sitten*, GS VI, s. 203–494.)

Religion   *Religion within the Limits of Reason Alone*. Trans. Theodore M. Green and Hoyt H. Hudson. New York: Harper and Row, 1960. (*Die Religion innerhalb der Grenzen der blossen Vernunft*, GS VI, s. 1–202.)

B. KIERKEGAARD

C   *Crisis in the Life of an Actress*. Trans. Stephen Crites. London: Collins, 1967. (*Krisen og en Krise i en Skuespillerindes Liv*, by Inter et Inter. *Fædrelandet* 188–191 July 24–27, 1848.)

CA   *The Concept of Anxiety*. Trans. Reidar Thomte. Princeton: Princeton University Press, 1980. (*Begrebet Angest*, by Vigilius Haufniensis, ed. S. Kierkegaard, 1844.)

CD   *Christian Discourses*, including *The Lilies of the Field and the Birds of the Air* and *Three Discourses at the Communion on Fridays*. Trans. Walter Lowrie. London and New York: Oxford University Press, 1940. (*Christelige Taler*, by S. Kierkegaard, 1848; *Lilien paa Marken og Fuglen under Himlen*, by S. Kierkegaard, 1849; *Tre Taler ved Altergangen om Fredagen*, by S. Kierkegaard, 1849.)

CI   *The Concept of Irony*. Trans. Howard V. Hong and Edna H. Hong. Princeton: Princeton University Press, 1989. (*Om Begrebet Ironi*, by S. Kierkegaard, 1841.)

CUP   *Concluding Unscientific Postscript.* Trans. David F. Swenson and Walter Lowrie. Princeton: Princeton University Press for American-Scandinavian Foundation, 1941. (*Afsluttende uvidenskabelig Efterskrift*, by Johannes Climacus, ed. S. Kierkegaard, 1846.)

ED   *Edifying Discourses*, 1–4. Trans. David F. Swenson and Lillian Marvin Swenson. Minneapolis: Augsburg Publishing House, 1943–1946. (*Opbyggelige Taler*, by S. Kierkegaard, 1843, 1844.)

E/O   *Either/Or.* Trans. Howard V. Hong and Edna H. Hong. 2 vols. Princeton: Princeton University Press, 1987. (*Enten-Eller*, 1–2, ed. Victor Eremita, 1843.)

FT   *Fear and Trembling.* Trans. Howard V. Hong and Edna H. Hong. Princeton: Princeton University Press, 1983. (*Frygt og Bæven*, by Johannes *de silentio*, 1843.) Published with R.

GOS   *The Gospel of Suffering* and *The Lilies of The Field.* Trans. David F. Swenson and Lillian Marvin Swenson. Minneapolis: Augsburg Publishing House, 1948. (*Lidelsernes Evangelium* and *Lilien paa Marken og Fuglen under Himlen.*)

JC-DODE   *Johannes Climacus or De omnibus dubitandum est.* Trans. Howard V. Hong and Edna H. Hong. Princeton: Princeton University Press, 1985. ("Johannes Climacus eller *De omnibus dubitandum est*," written 1842–1843, unpubl., *Papirer* IV B 1; unpubl., 1844.) Published with PF.

JP   *Søren Kierkegaard's Journals and Papers.* Trans. Howard V. Hong and Edna H. Hong, assisted by Gregor Malantschuk. Bloomington and London: Indiana University Press, 1, 1967; 2, 1970; 3–4, 1975; 5–7, 1978. (From *Papirer* I–XI3 and XII–XIII, 2d ed., and *Breve og Akstykker vedrørende Søren Kierkegaard*, ed. Niels Thulstrup, 1–2, 1953–1954.)

KAUC   *Kierkegaard's Attack upon "Christendom," 1854–1855.* Trans. Walter Lowrie. Princeton: Princeton University Press, 1944. (*Bladartikler* I–XXI, by S. Kierkegaard, *Fædrelandet*, 1854–1855; *Dette skal siges; saa være det da sagt*, by S. Kierkegaard, 1855; *Oieblikket*, by S.

Kierkegaard, 1–9, 1855; 10, 1905; *Hvad Christus dommer om officiel Christendom*, by S. Kierkegaard, 1855.)

LD   *Letters and Documents.* Trans. Hendrik Rosenmeier. Princeton: Princeton University Press, 1978.

OAR   *On Authority and Revelation, The Book on Adler.* Trans. Walter Lowrie. Princeton: Princeton University Press, 1955. (*Bogen om Adler*, written 1846–1847, unpubl., *Papirer* VII² B 235; VIII² B 1–27.)

PAP   *Søren Kierkegaards Papirer.* 16 vols. Copenhagen: Gyldendal, 1909–1978.

PF   *Philosophical Fragments.* Trans. Howard V. Hong and Edna H. Hong. Princeton: Princeton University Press, 1985. (*Philosophiske Smuler*, by Johannes Climacus, ed. S. Kierkegaard, 1844.) Published with JC–DODE.

PH   *Purity of Heart.* Trans. Douglas Steere. New York: Harper, 1948. (*Opbyggelige Taler i forskjellig Aand*, by S. Kierkegaard, 1847, Part One, "*En Leiligheds-Tale*".)

PV   *The Point of View etc. Including the Point of View for my Work as an Author, Two Notes about 'The Individual' and On My Work as an Author.* Trans. Walter Lowrie. New York: Oxford University Press, 1939. (*Syndpunktet for min Forfatter-Virksomhed*, posthumously published 1859; *Om min Forfatter-Virksomhed*, 1851.)

R   *Repetition.* Trans. Howard V. Hong and Edna H. Hong. Princeton: Princeton University Press, 1983. (*Gjentagelsen*, by Constantin Constantius, 1843.) Published with FT.

SLW   *Stages on Life's Way.* Trans. Howard V. Hong and Edna H. Hong. Princeton: Princeton University Press, 1988. (*Stadier paa Livets Vej*, ed. Hilarius Bogbinder, 1845.)

SUD   *The Sickness unto Death.* Trans. Howard V. Hong and Edna H. Hong. Princeton: Princeton University Press, 1980. (*Sygdommen til Døden*, by Anti-Climacus, ed. S. Kierkegaard, 1849.)

SV   *Samlede Værker*, 3d Udg. 20 vols. Copenhagen: Gyldendal, 1962.

TA   *Two Ages: The Age of Revolution and the Present Age. A Literary Review.* Trans. Howard V. Hong and Edna H. Hong. Princeton: Princeton University Press, 1978. (*En literair Anmeldelse. To Tidsaldre,* by S. Kierkegaard, 1846.)

TC   *Training in Christianity,* including "The Woman Who Was a Sinner." Trans. Walter Lowrie. London and New York: Oxford University Press, 1941; reprint, Princeton: Princeton University Press, 1944. (*Indøvelse i Christendom,* by Anti-Climacus, ed. S. Kierkegaard, 1850; *En opbyggelig Tale,* by S. Kierkegaard, 1850.)

TD   *Thoughts on Crucial Situations in Human Life (Three Discourses on Imagined Occasions).* Trans. David F. Swenson, ed. Lillian Marvin Swenson. Minneapolis: Augsburg Publishing House, 1941. (*Tre Taler ved tænkte Leiligheder,* by S. Kierkegaard, 1845.)

UD   *Eighteen Upbuilding Discourses.* Trans. Howard V. Hong and Edna H. Hong. Princeton: Princeton University Press, 1990.

WL   *Works of Love.* Trans. Howard V. Hong and Edna H. Hong. New York: Harper and Row, 1962. (*Kjerlighedens Gjerninger,* by S. Kierkegaard, 1947.)

APPENDIX A

There are seventeen references to Kant in Kierkegaard's *Samlede Værker*, as listed in Alastair McKinnon, *The Kierkegaard Indices*, 3 vols., Fundamental Polyglot Konkordans til Kierkegaards Samlede Værker (Leiden: E. J. Brill, 1971). These include the following fourteen references:

CI

3d Udg.		2d Udg.		Engl. trans.	
p. 151	l. 12	p. 210	l. 35	p. 107	l. 32
p. 260	l. 17	p. 342	l. 26	p. 242	l. 20
p. 285	l. 2	p. 372	l. 10	p. 272	l. 1
p. 285	l. 29	p. 373	l. 8	p. 273	l. 1
p. 286	l. 17	p. 373	l. 35	p. 273	l. 27
p. 289	l. 3	p. 377	l. 4	p. 276	l. 25

CA

3d Udg.		2d Udg.		Engl. trans.	
p. 110	l. 37	p. 315	l. 14	p. 11	l. 9
p. 110	l. 38	p. 315	l. 15	p. 11	l. 11
p. 116	l. 45	p. 322	l. 33	p. 18	l. 24

SLW

3d Udg.		2d Udg.		Engl. trans.	
p. 136	l. 29	p. 164	l. 12	p. 152	l. 6

CUP

3d Udg.		2d Udg.		Engl. trans.	
p. 32	l. 27	p. 316	l. 25	p. 292	l. 12
p. 33	l. 1	p. 317	l. 4	p. 292	l. 25
p. 33	l. 5	p. 317	l. 8	p. 292	l. 29
p. 222	l. 2	p. 543	l. 5	p. 491	l. 3

In addition, there is a references to the "Kantianere" ("Kantians") in a small newspaper article from 1834 entitled "Ogsaa et Forsvar for Kvindens høie Anlæg" ("Yet Another Defense of Women's Superior Talents"), SV 1st Udg., p. 13; a reference to "de kantiske 100 Rbd." ("the Kantian 100 thalers") in CI, p. 144; and a reference to the "Kantian" interpretation of the ethical in E/O II, p. 327.

Apart from reading and lecture notes, there are a total of thirty-one references to Kant in Kierkegaard's *Papirer*. These include the following entries: I A 30 *n.d.*, 1834; I A 192 *n.d.*, 1836; I A 328 *n.d.*, 1836–1837; I C 19 *n.d.*, 1834–1835; II A 31 March 19, 1837; II A 47 *n.d.*, 1837; II A 486 July 20, 1839; II A 592 *n.d.*, 1837; II C 48 December 4, 1837; II C 49 December 12, 1837; III A 3 July 5, 1840; IV A 176 *n.d.*, 1844; IV B 18 *n.d.*, 1842–1843; IV C 68 *n.d.*, 1842–1843; IV C 114 *n.d.*, 1842–1843; V B 5:3 *n.d.*, 1844; V C 2 *n.d.*, 1844; VI B 54:16 *n.d.*, 1845; VIII^1 A 11 *n.d.*, 1847; VIII^1 A 358 *n.d.*, 1847; VIII^2 B 81 *n.d.*, 1847; VIII^2 B 176 *n.d.*, 1847; X^1 A 576 *n.d.*, 1849; X^1 A 666 *n.d.*, 1849; X^2 A 328 *n.d.*, 1849–1850; X^2 A 396 *n.d.*, 1850; X^2 A 501 *n.d.*, 1850; X^2 A 517 *n.d.*, 1850; X^2 A 519 *n.d.*, 1850; X^2 A 539 *n.d.*, 1850; XI^1 A 112 *n.d.*, 1854. Of these entries, those translated in JP are the following, as indicated by their entry number: 37 (III A 3), 188 (X^2 A 396), 649 (VIII^2 B 81), 650 (VIII^2 B 82), 1057 (X^2 A 328), 1190 (II A 31), 1191 (II A 592), 1305 (I A 30), 1541 (I A 340), 1600 (IV C 48), 2346 (V C 42), 3089 (VIII^1 A 11), 3093 (X^2 A 501), 3558 (X^1 A 666), 3654 (VI B 54:13, 14, 16), 3875 (X^1 A 112), 4830 (IV C 114), 5181 (1 A 328), 5283 (II C 49), 5702 (IV A 176), 6456 (X^1 A 576). Inexplicably, the Hongs' translation of I A 340 (JP entry 1541) omits Kierkegaard's mention of Kant.

Finally, in the lecture and reading notes published in volumes XII and XIII of the *Papirer*, there are approximately seventy-five references to Kant. These lecture and reading notes include the following. Vol. XII: "Referater af H. N. Clausens Forelæsninger over Dogmatik," I C 19, p. 106; "Excerpter paa Dansk af Fr. Baader, 'Vorlesungen über Speculative Dogmatik,'" 1. Heft, 1828 (Ktl. 396), I C 27, p. 133; "Referat med Citater af Johannes Falk, 'Goethe aus näherm persönlichen Umgange dargestellt,'" 1832 I C 74, p. 215 and I C 76, p. 218; "Referat af Martensens Forelæsninger over den nyere Philosophies Historie fra Kant til Hegel," Vintersemesteret 1838–1839, II C 25, pp. 280–331 (a total of 46 references). Vol. XIII: "Referat af Martensens Forelæsninger over 'Speculativ Dogmatik,'" (Inledning samt SS1–23) II C 26 og 27 (udaterede, fra 1838–1839) (2 references), pp. 1–43; ibid, II C 28 §§ 60–69, pp. 44–116 (8 references); "Referat af Ph. Marheineckes Forelæsninger i Berlin 1841–42 over 'Dogmatisk Theologi med særligt Hensyn til Daubs System,'" III C 26 (Vinteren 1841–1842), pp. 197–252 (2 references); "Referat af Schellings Forelæsninger i Berlin 1841–1842 over 'Philosophie der Offenbarung,'" III C 27 (November 1841–February 1842), pp. 253–329 (11 references).

APPENDIX B
KANT'S
VERMISCHTE SCHRIFTEN
TABLE OF CONTENTS

Imanuel Kants *vermischte Schriften* 3 vols. Halle: in der Rengerschen Buchhandlung, 1799.

(Bracketed items represent the corresponding place of the essay or treatise in GS. Where they exist, English translations are listed.)

Inhalt des Ersten Bandes:

I. Vorbericht des herausgebers, welcher, nebst einigen volläfigen Nachrichten, Bermerkungen zur Geistesgeschichte des V., besonders in Ansehung der Transscendentalphilosophie [sic] desselben, enthalt. i–cxxviii. Signed by Johann Heinrich Tieftrunk.

II. Abhandlungen der Verfassers

1. Gedanken von der wahren Schätzung der lebendigen Kräfte. 1747. s. 1–282.
[GS I, s. 1–182.]
2. Allgemeine Naturgeschichte und Theorie des Himmels. 1755. s. 283–520.
[GS I, s. 214–368. *Universal Natural History and Theory of the Heavens,* trans. Stanley L. Jaki (Edinburgh: Scottish Academic Press, 1981).]
3. Geschichte und Naturbeschribung der merkswürdigsten Vorfälle des Erdbebens, welches am Ende des 1755sten Jahres einen grossen Theil der Erde erschüttert hat. 1756. s. 521–574.
[GS I, s. 429–461.]
4. Die falsche Spitzfindigkeit der vier syllogistischen Figuren erwiesen. 1762. s. 575–610.
[GS II, s. 45–51.]
5. Versuch den Begriff der negativen Grössen in die Weltweisheit einzuführen. 1763. s. 611–676.
[GS II, s. 165–204.]

Inhalt des Zweiten Bandes:

1. Untersuchung über die Deutlichkeit der Grundsätze der natüralichen Theologie und der Moral. Zur Beantwortung der Frage welche die Königl. Akademie der Wissenschaften zu Berlin auf das Jahr 1763 aufgegeben hat. 1763. s. 1–54.
[Untersuchung über die Deutlichkeit der Grundsätze der natüralichen Theologie und der Moral (oder: über die Evidenz in metaphysischen Wissenschaften zur Beantwortung. 1764). GS II, s. 273–301. This appears as "An Inquiry into the Distinctness of the Principles of Natural Theology and Morals," in Immanuel Kant, *Critique of Practical Reason and Other Writings in Moral Philosophy*, trans. and ed. Lewis White Beck (Chicago: University of Chicago Press, 1949), pp. 261–285.]

2. Der einzig mögliche Beweisgrund zu einer Demonstration des Daseins Gottes. 1763. s. 5–246.
[GS II, s. 63–163.]

3. Traüme eines Geistersehers, erläutert durch Traüme der Metaphysik. 1766. s. 247–346.
[GS II, s. 315–373. *Dreams of a Spirit-Seer Illustrated by Dreams of Metaphysics*, trans. Emanuel F. Goerwitz (London: Swan Sonnenschein & Co., 1900).]

4. Beobachtungen über das Gefühl des Schönen und Erhabenen. 1764. s. 347–434.
[GS II, s. 205–256. Immanuel Kant, *Observations on the Feeling of the Beautiful and Sublime*, trans. John T. Goldthwait (Berkeley: University of California Press, 1960).]

5. *De mundi sensibilis atque intelligibilis forma et principiis.* 1770. Nebst einer Verdeutschung dieser Abhandlung. s. 435–566.
[GS II, s. 385–419. *On the Form and Principles of the Sensible and Intelligible Worlds* (Inaugural Dissertation) (1770) in *Kant: Selected Pre-critical Writings and Correspondence with Beck*, trans. G. B. Kerferd and D. E. Walford (Manchester: Manchester University Press, 1968), pp. 454–492.]

6. Kants und Lamberts philosophische Briefe. s. 567–606.
Contains:
13 Nov. 1765 Lambert an Kant, s. 569–574.
31 Dec 1765 Kant an Lambert, s. 575–578.
3 Feb 1766 Lambert an Kant, s. 579–586.
2 Sept 1770 Kant an Lambert, s. 587–591.
13 Oct 1770 Lambert an Kant, s. 592–606.
[Kants Briefwechsel. GS X, s. 48–54, 59–64, 92–95, 98–106. A

translation of the letter of 13 Nov. 1765 appears in *Kant: Selected Precritical Writings and Correspondence with Beck*, pp. 93–102.]
    7. Von den Verschiedenen Racen der Menschen. 1775. s. 607–632.
      [GS II, s. 427–443.]
    8. Bestimmung des Begriffs einer Menschenrace. 1785. s. 633–660.
      [GS VIII, s. 89–106]
    9. Idee zur einer Allgemeinen Geschichte in Welbürgerlicher Absicht. 1784. s. 661–686.
      [GS VIII, s. 15–31. "Idea for a Universal History with a Cosmopolitan Purpose," in *Kant's Political Writings*, ed. Hans Reiss, trans. H. B. Nisbet (Cambridge: Cambridge University Press, 1970), pp. 41–53]
    10. Beantwortung der Frage: Was ist Aufklärung. 1784. s. 687–700.
      [GS VIII, s. 33–42. "An Answer to the Question: 'What Is Enlightenment?'" in *Kant's Political Writings*, pp. 54–60. Also as "What Is Enlightenment," in *Critique of Practical Reason and Other Writings in Moral Philosophy*, trans. and ed. Lewis White Beck (Chicago: University of Chicago Press, 1949), pp. 286–292.]

Inhalt des drittens Bandes:

    1. Ueber die Vulkane im Monde. 1785. s. 1–16.
      [GS VIII, s. 67–76.]
    2. Von der Unrechtmässigkeit des Büchernachdrucks. 1785. s. 17–32.
      [GS VIII, s. 77–87.]
    3. Muthmasslicher Anfang der Menschengeschichte. 1786. s. 33–60.
      [GS VIII, s. 107–123. Translated by Lewis White Beck as "Conjectural Beginning of Human History," in Immanuel Kant, *On History*, ed. Lewis White Beck (Indianapolis: Bobbs-Merrill, 1963), pp. 53–68.]
    4. Was heisst: Sich im Denken Orientiren? 1786. s. 61–88.
      [GS VIII, s. 131–147. Translated as "What is Orientation in Thinking," in Immanuel Kant, *Critique of Practical Reason and other Writings in Moral Philosophy*, pp. 293–305.]
    5. Einige Bemerkungen zu Jakobs Prüfung der Mendelssohnschen Morgenstunden. 1786. s. 89–98.
      [Einige Bemerkungen zu Ludwig Heinrich Jakob's Prüfung der Mendelssohnschen Morgenstunden. GS VIII, s. 149–155.]

6. Ueber den Gebrauch teleologischer Principien in der Philosophie. 1788. s. 99–144.

[GS VIII, s. 157–184.]

7. Ueber das Misslingen aller philosophischen Versuche in der Theodicee. 1791. s. 145–176.

[GS VIII, s. 253–271. "Kant: On the Failure of All Attempted Philosophical Theodicies (1791)," in Michel Despland, *Kant on History and Religion* (Montreal: McGill-Queen's University Press, 1973), pp. 283–297.]

8. Ueber den Gemeinsprach: Das mag in der Theorie richtig sein, taugt aber nicht für die Praxis. 1793. s. 177–248.

[GS VIII, s. 273–313. "On the Common Saying: 'This May be True in Theory, but it does not Apply in Practice,'" in *Kant's Political Writings*, pp. 61–92.]

9. Das Ende aller Dinge. 1795. s. 249–274.

[GS VIII, s. 325–339. "The End of All Things," in Immanuel Kant, *On History*, pp. 69–84.]

10. Etwas über den Einfluss des Mondes auf die Witterung. 1795. s. 275–290.

[GS VIII, s. 315–324.]

11. Zu Sömmering über das Organ der Seele. 1796. s. 291–300.

12. Von einem neuerdings erhobenen vornehmen Ton in der Philosophie. 1796. s. 301–334.

[GS VIII, s. 387–406.]

13. Ausgleichung eines auf Missverstand beruhenden mathematischen Streits. 1796. s. 335–338.

[GS VIII, s. 407–410.]

14. Verkündigung des nahen Abschlusses eines Traktats zum ewigen Frieden in der Philosophie. 1796. s. 339–356.

[GS VIII, s. 411–422.]

15. Ueber ein vermeintes Recht aus Menschenliebe zu lügen. 1797. s. 357–368.

[GS VIII, s. 423–430. As "On a Supposed Right to Lie from Altruistic Motives," in *Critique of Practical Reason and Other Writings in Moral Philosophy*, pp. 346–350.]

16. Erklärung auf herrn Schlettweins hersausforderung in einem Briefe von Greifswalde, den 11 Mai 1797. 1797. s. 369–374.

[GS XII, s. 388–396.]

17. Ueber die Buchmacherei, zwei Briefe an herrn Friedrich Nicolai. 1797. s. 375–388.

[GS VIII, s. 431–438.]

18. Von der Macht des Gemüts, durch dem blossen Vorsatz seiner krankhaften Gefühle Meister zu sein. 1797. s. 389–428.

19. Erneuerte Frage: ob das Menschengeschlecht im beständigen Fortschreiten zum Bessern sei? 1798. s. 429–456.

20. Der Streit der Fakultäten. 1798. s. 457–574. [GS VII, s. 1–116.]

21. Schlettwein an Kant: Eine literarische herausforderung. s. 577–594.

NOTES

INTRODUCTION

1. Ronald M. Green, "The Limits of the Ethical in Kierkegaard's *The Concept of Anxiety* and Kant's *Religion within the Limits of Reason Alone*," in *International Kierkegaard Commentary, The Concept of Anxiety*, ed. Robert L. Perkins (Macon, Ga.: Mercer University Press, 1986), pp. 63–87.

2. Walter Lowrie, *Kierkegaard* (New York: Oxford University Press, 1938).

3. Reidar Thomte, *Kierkegaard's Philosophy of Religion* (Princeton: Princeton University Press, 1948); James Collins, *The Mind of Kierkegaard* (Chicago: Henry Regnery, 1953); Hermann Diem, *Kierkegaard's Dialectic of Existence*, trans. Harold Knight (Edinburgh: Oliver and Boyd, 1959); Gregor Malantschuk, *Kierkegaard's Thought*, ed. and trans. Howard V. Hong and Edna H. Hong (Princeton: Princeton University Press, 1971); Niels Thulstrup, *Kierkegaard's Relation to Hegel*, trans. George L. Stengren (Princeton: Princeton University Press, 1980); Stephen Crites, *In the Twilight of Christendom: Hegel vs. Kierkegaard on Faith and History* (Chambersberg, Pa.: American Academy of Religion, 1972); John W. Elrod, *Being and Existence in Kierkegaard's Pseudonymous Works* (Princeton: Princeton University Press, 1975); and Mark C. Taylor, *Kierkegaard's Pseudonymous Authorship* (Princeton: Princeton University Press, 1975).

4. George Stack, *Kierkegaard's Existential Ethics* (University, Ala.: University of Alabama Press, 1977).

5. "Kierkegaards Kenntnis der philosophischen und theologischen Tradition," *Theologische Zeitung* 35 (November–December 1979), 351–362.

6. Jerry H. Gill, "Kant, Kierkegaard and Religious Knowledge," *Philosophy and Phenomenological Research* 28 (1967–1968), 188–204; also his article "Kant" in *Kierkegaard and Great Tradi-*

tions, Vol. 6 of *Bibliotheca Kierkegaardiana*, ed. Niels Thulstrup
and Maria Mikulová Thulstrup (Copenhagen: C. A. Reitzels
Boghandel, 1981), pp. 223–229; John D. Glenn, Jr., "Kierkegaard's Ethical Philosophy," *Southwestern Journal of Philosophy*
5 (Spring 1974), 121–128; Robert L. Perkins, "For Sanity's Sake:
Kant, Kierkegaard and Father Abraham," in *Kierkegaard's* Fear
and Trembling: *Critical Appraisals*, ed. Robert L. Perkins (University, Ala.: University of Alabama Press, 1981), pp. 43–61; R. Z.
Friedman, "Kierkegaard: First Existentialist or Last Kantian?"
Religious Studies 18:2 (June 1982), 159–170; Peter J. Mehl,
"Kierkegaard and the Relativist Challenge to Practical Philoso-
phy," *Journal of Religious Ethics* 14:2 (1987), 247–278; Jeremy
D. B. Walker, *To Will One Thing: Reflections on Kierkegaard's
'Purity of Heart'* (Montreal and London: McGill-Queen's Univer-
sity Press, 1972); also his *Kierkegaard's Descent into God*
(Kingston and Montreal: McGill-Queen's University Press, 1985);
Alastair Hannay, *Kierkegaard* (London: Routledge and Kegan
Paul, 1982); William D. Peck, "On Autonomy: The Primacy of the
Subject in Kant and Kierkegaard," Ph. D. thesis, Yale University,
1974; C. Stephen Evans, *Subjectivity and Religious Belief* (Wash-
ington, D.C.: University Press of America, 1982). An excellent ear-
lier study in this vein is Geoffrey Clive's "The Connection between
Ethics and Religion in Kant, Kierkegaard and F. H. Bradley," Ph.
D. thesis, Harvard University, 1953. The relationship between
Kierkegaard and Kant is also briefly sketched, but not developed,
by Alasdair MacIntyre in his *After Virtue* (Notre Dame, Indiana:
University of Notre Dame Press, 1981). In his study, *Kierkegaard's
Dialectic of the Imagination* (New York: Peter Lang, 1989), David
J. Gouwens perceives a significant impact of Kant's concept of the
"imagination," as developed in the first *Critique* and *Critique of
Judgment*, on Kierkegaard's thought.

7. See, for example, Emil Brunner, "Das Grundproblem der Philosophie bei Kant und Kierkegaard," *Zwischen den Zeit* 2 (1924),
31–47, and Alfred Baümler, "Kierkegaard und Kant über die Reinheit des Herzen," *Zwischen den Zeit* 3 (1925), 182–187. Also noteworthy in this regard are the frequent observations of ties between
Kierkegaard and Kant made by Theodore W. Adorno in his 1933
study of Kierkegaard's conceptions of the aesthetic. This has recently been translated and edited by Robert Hullot-Kentor as *Kierkegaard: Construction of the Aesthetic* (Minneapolis: University of
Minnesota Press, 1989). More recently, Klaus Schäfer has pointed
out some similarities and contrasts between Kant's and Kierke-

gaard's ontologies in his *Hermeneutische Ontologie in den Clima-cus-Schriften Søren Kierkegaards* (München: Kösel-Verlag, 1968).

8. Peck, "On Autonomy," p. 3.

9. See Appendix A.

10. JP II, pp. 611–612.

11. *Auktionsprotokol over Søren Kierkegaards Bogsamling*, ved H. P. Rohde, English text (København: det Kongelige Bibliotek, 1967). H. P. Rohde discusses Kierkegaard's book purchases, as determinable from booksellers' bills, in the introductory essay to this volume, "Søren Kierkegaard as a Collector of Books," pp. xlvi–lxxviii, and in *Særtryk af Fund og Forskning i Det kongelige Biblioteks Samlinger* (Results of Research in the Collections of the Royal Library) 8 (1961), 79–127. The latter publication also reprints these bills, none of which mentions works by Kant.

12 . The *Auktionsprotokol*, pp. 40 and 95, lists these works by Kant as sold at auction following Kierkegaard's death: Kant's *Kritik der Urteilskraft*, 2te Aufl. (Berlin, 1793), Catalogue No. 594, sold to the bookseller Holm; Kant's *Kritik der reinen Vernunft*, 4te Aufl. (Riga, 1794), Catalogue No. 595, sold to the bookseller Lynge; Kant's *vermischte Schriften*, 3 Bände, 8te [i.e. Aechte] und vollst. Ausg. (Halle, 1799), Ktl. 1731–1733, sold to the bookseller Pio. The table of contents of the *vermischte Schriften* appears in Appendix B. Heinrich Tieftrunk, the editor of this collection, was himself a careful student of Kant's philosophy of religion. This may explain the edition's substantial inclusion of Kant's writings on religion. For a brief discussion of Tieftrunk, see Bernard M. G. Reardon, *Kant as Philosophical Theologian* (Totowa, N.J.: Barnes and Noble, 1988), pp. 179–180.

13. Paul L. Holmer argues for a sharp distinction between scholarship that seeks to locate Kierkegaard historically or intellectually and that which engages his argument philosophically or religiously. See Holmer's "On Understanding Kierkegaard," in *A Kierkegaard Critique,* ed. Howard A. Johnson and Niels Thulstrup (New York: Harper, 1962), pp. 40–53. I might say that I do not accept this rigid distinction. As I show in Chapter 5, understanding Kierkegaard's sources can contribute significantly to our appreciation of the content and nature of his argument.

14. E/O I, p. 9.

CHAPTER 1

1. I A 75 August 1, 1835: JP V–5100.

2. Torsten Bohlin, *Kierkegaard's dogmatische Anschauung*, trans. Ilse Meyer-Lüne (Gütersloh: C. Bertelsmann, 1927), p. 194.

3. Anders Thuborg, *Den Kantiske Periode i Dansk Filosofi 1790–1800* (Copenhagen: Gyldendalske Boghandel Nordisk Forlag, 1951), p. 180.

4. Wolfdietrich v. Kloeden reports that Michael P. Kierkegaard attended the gatherings of the Herrnhutter (Moravian Brethren) community in Copenhagen, and Frithiof Brandt states that he was attracted to the pietistic faith of this group. See Kloeden, "Der Vater M. P. Kierkegaard," in *Kierkegaard as a Person*, Vol. 12 of *Bibliotheca Kierkegaardiana* (1983), p. 18; Frithiof Brandt, *Søren Kierkegaard: His Life—His Works* (Copenhagen: Det Danske Selskab, 1963), p. 8.

5. E/O II, p. 322.

6. Ibid., p. 269.

7. Ibid., pp. 274–275.

8. Ibid., p. 270.

9. Some of this rigorism possibly stems from the influence of the catechism authored by Bishop Balle. This work, *Lærbog i den Evangeliske Christelige Religion*, is mentioned three times by Judge William in E/O II, pp. 267, 270, 323, in connection with his own stern moral upbringing.

10. Bruce H. Kirmmse, *Kierkegaard in Golden Age Denmark* (Bloomington, Ind.: Indiana University Press, 1990), Chapter 10.

11. Ibid., p. 101.

12. Ibid., pp. 103, 101.

13. Ibid., p. 104.

14. Ibid., p. 107.

15. PAP I A 72 June 1, 1835: JP V–5092.

16. Also noteworthy here, but difficult to assess, is the influence on Kierkegaard of two major figures in his personal life and early university career, his teacher and university dean, Frederick Christian

Sibbern (1785–1872), and his close friend and sometimes teacher of ethics, Poul Møller (1794–1838). In the early phases of Sibbern's career, he was attracted to the then more prevalent Kantian philosophy. His early ethical thought evidenced Kantian themes, although he later adopted a speculative approach to religion that was decidedly un-Kantian. Although Sibbern's influence may be a further channel for Kantianism in Kierkegaard's education, there is no evidence in Kierkegaard's writings (where Sibbern is mentioned only a few times in the *Journals and Papers* and not at all in the published works) that Sibbern's thought had a significant impact on the young scholar. Møller's influence is also suggestive but difficult to pin down. His posthumously published writings on moral philosophy (*Efterladte Skrifter* [Kjøbenhavn: C. A. Reiztel, 1843], Tredie Bind, pp. 351–369) evidence several themes that betray Kantian influence, including an emphasis on the role of reason and freedom in moral choice and action. But these writings contain none of the major themes that dominate Kant's treatment of ethics in its relation to religion, themes that Kierkegaard clearly dwells on in his pseudonymous writings. For discussions of both these thinkers, see the articles "Sibbern" by Robert J. Widenmann and "Poul Møller" by H. P. Rohde in *Kierkegaard's Teachers*, Vol. 10 of *Bibliotheca Kierkegaardiana* (1982).

17. "Forelæsninger over Indledning til spekulativ Dogmatik af Marthensen, Vinter Semestret, 37 and 38," PAP 2 C 12–24, Nov. 15–Dec. 23, 1837, pp. 322–340.

18. PAP 2 C 25 *n.d.*, 1838–1839 (XII, pp. 281–331).

19. For a listing of these notes, see Appendix A.

20. Ed. and trans. Howard V. and Edna H. Hong (Princeton: Princeton University Press, 1985). Outlines for this work appear in the *Papirer* at IV B 2:18 *n.d.*, 1842–1843 and at IV B 13:16 *n.d.*, 1842–1843. See JC–DODE, p. 238.

21. See Appendix A. Kant is also frequently mentioned in Kierkegaard's "Notes of Schelling's Berlin Lectures" (reprinted and indexed in CI).

22. PAP 2 A 422 May 13, 1839: JP V–5385.

23. II A 807 *n.d.*, 1838: JP V–5432. For a discussion of the place of this examination in the preparation of a theological candidate of this period, see Skat Arildsen, "His Theological Examination," in *Kierkegaard as a Person*, pp. 63–71.

24. Josiah Thompson, *Kierkegaard* (London: Victor Gollancz, 1974), p. 95.

25. This record is published in *Breve og Aktstykker vedrørende Søren Kierkegaard*, ved Niels Thulstrup (København: Munsgaard, 1953), I, pp. 9–12. A translation of this record, with some minor imprecisions from a moral theorist's point of view, especially the repeated translation of *Princip* as "Precept" instead of "Principle," appears in LD, pp. 10–16. The translation of questions here is my own.

26. In 1840, a first edition of Martensen's book *Cristelige Etik* appeared, some of whose themes, especially the matter of the relationship between Lutheran and philosophical ethics, reappear in the exam questions. The questions on the exam about Kant's ethics are also anticipated in Martensen's lectures.

27. See below, n. 77.

28. The notation system records, in addition to a note on whether the candidate replied, the examiners' corrections or additions to the candidate's response. Apparently, Kierkegaard missed none of the questions on ethics, and the record shows the fewest additions or corrections to his answers in this portion of the exam. See *Breve og Aktstykker*, ed. Thulstup, pp. 10–11 (LD, pp. 13–14). Arildsen concludes ("His Theological Examination," p. 70) that Kierkegaard's best achievements on the exam were in ethics and church history.

29. Arildsen, "His Theological Examination," p. 70. Thompson, *Kierkegaard*, p. 96, states, without any indication of his source, that twenty-seven of sixty-three candidates for the exam, including Kierkegaard, received *laudabilis*.

30. PAP VIII¹ A 23 *n.d.*, 1847: JP V–5978.

31. There is some support for this reading of Kierkegaard's critical comment in an early journal entry from the years 1836–1837. Here he ridicules the contemporary tendency to deify philosophers:

> But in this wild hunt for ideas, it is still very interesting to observe the felicitous moment when one of these new systems achieves supremacy. Now everything is set in motion, and usually this also involves making the system popular— *per systema influxus physici* it lays hold of all men. How Kant was treated in his time is well known, and therefore I

need only mention the infinite mass of lexicons, summaries, popular presentations, and explanations for everyman, etc. And how did Hegel fare later, Hegel, the most modern philosopher, who because of his rigorous form would most likely command silence? (PAP I A 328 *n.d.*, 1836–1837: JP V–5181)

32. H. P. Rohde, "Om Søren Kierkegaard som Bogsamler," *Særtryk af Fund og Forskning i Det kongelige Biblioteks Samlinger* 8 (1961), 79–127.

33. Rohde, "Søren Kierkegaard as a Collector of Books," *Auktionsprotokol*, p. 1.

34. Mary J. Gregor maintains that the section of *The Conflict of the Faculties* dealing with "The Conflict of the Philosophical Faculty with the Theology Faculty" was written between June and October 1794. Hence it follows soon after the writing and publication of the *Religion*. See her "Translator's Introduction," *Conflict*, p. xvi.

35. PAP X² A 539 *n.d.*, 1850: JP II–2239. The editors of the *Papirer* here supply the exact reference to the Tieftrunk edition, III, p. 491.

36. PAP IV A 176 *n.d.*, 1844: JP V–5702.

37. Immanuel Kant, *Dreams of a Spirit-Seer Illustrated by Dreams of Metaphysics*, trans. Emanuel F. Goerwitz (London: Swan Sonnenschein, 1900), p. 42: GS II, s. 317.

38. Ibid., p. 38: GS II, s. 320.

39. The only exception to Kierkegaard's generally very favorable estimate of Kant is a journal entry for 1847 where Kierkegaard mentions somewhat disparagingly an episode of Kant's extreme displeasure over an artisan's effort to sell an unflattering portrait in copper that he had prepared for the philosopher but which Kant had rejected—PAP VIII² B 176, *n.d.*, 1847.

40. PAP X³ A 217 *n.d.*, 1850: JP III–2521.

41. E/O I, p. 35.

42. *Dreams*, p. 84: GS II, s. 348.

43. PAP XI¹ A 61 *n.d.*, 1854: JP III–2546.

44. PAP X² A 517 *n.d.*, 1850: JP II–2237; X² A 519 *n.d.*, 1850: JP II–2238.

45. For the details of these listings, see above, Introduction, pp. xv–xvi.

46. PF, p. 40.

47. CUP, p. 298.

48. "I never reason in conclusion to existence (for in that case I would be mad to want to reason in conclusion to what I know), but I reason in conclusion from existence and am so accommodating to popular opinion as to call it a demonstrative argument. Thus the connection is somewhat different from what Kant meant—that existence is an *accessorium* [addition]—although therein he undeniably has an advantage over Hegel in that he does not confuse" (PAP V B 5:3 *n.d.*, 1844: PF, p. 190).

49. Thulstrup, "Commentary" in *Philosophical Fragments*, trans. David F. Swenson (Princeton: Princeton University Press, 1962), p. 214; A. B. Drachman, SV VI, p. 332.

50. MS, s. 268.

51. *Conflict*, p. 117.

52. CUP, p. 120.

53. KRV A 599 B 627: Norman Kemp Smith, p. 505.

54. PAP VIII² B 81 *n.d.*, 1847: JP I–649; PAP VIII² B 82 *n.d.*, 1847: JP I–650; PAP X¹ A 666 *n.d.*, 1849: JP III–3558.

55. See below, Chapter 4, p. 123.

56. In his *Logic* (*The Logic of Hegel*, trans. William Wallace [Oxford: Clarendon Press, 1892], pp. 107–108), Hegel dismisses as "barbarism in language" Kant's use of a material object like "a hundred sovereigns" to exemplify a concept. Kierkegaard apparently has this discussion in mind when, in the *Postscript* (p. 293), he ironically sides with Hegel against Kant, stating that he is "well aware" of what Hegel had said in reply to "a stupid attack" on the philosophical principle of the identity of thought with being.

57. *The Concept of Irony*, trans. Lee Capel (New York: Harper and Row 1966; Bloomington: Indiana University Press, 1968), p. 123, n. 15 (p. 381): CI, p. 88.

58. PAP IV C 114 *n.d.*, 1842–1843: JP IV–4830. The reference is to the edition of the *Critique* in his possession (2te Aufl., Berlin 1793).

59. Compare the following remark by Kierkegaard in the discourse "Strengthening in the Inner Being" with the second passage from the "Critique of the Teleological Judgment":

> Then everything became confused for him. No longer was there a sovereign in heaven; the wide world was a wild pandemonium of life; there was no ear that brought the confusion together in harmony, no guiding hand that intervened. No matter how a person could find consolation in life, hope was lost, so he thought, and hope remained lost. Then his soul grew concerned. And the more he stared down at the anarchy [jo mere han stirrede ned i den Lovløshed] into which everything seemed to have disintegrated, the more power it gained over him, until it completely bewitched him; his mind reeled, and he himself plunged down into it and lost himself in despair. (UD, p. 94)

> We may then suppose the case of a righteous man [e.g. Spinoza], who holds himself firmly persuaded that there is no God and also (because in respect of the object of morality a similar consequence results) no future life; how is he to judge of his own inner purposive destination, by means of the moral law, which he reveres in practice?. . . Deceit, violence, and envy will always surround him, although he himself be honest, peaceable, and kindly; and the righteous men with whom he meets will, notwithstanding all their worthiness of happiness, be yet subjected by nature, which regards not this, to all the evils of want, disease, and untimely death, just like the beasts of the earth. So it will be until one wide grave engulfs them together (honest or not, it makes no difference) and throws them back—who were able to believe themselves the final purpose of creation—into the abyss of the purposeless chaos of matter [in den Schlund des zwecklosen Chaos der Materie] from which they were drawn. (KU, s. 303)

60. For the references to these notes, see Appendix A.

61. There are nearly eighty references to Kant in these lecture and reading notes. At least seven of them clearly refer to terms or concepts dealt with by Kant only in the *Religion.*

62. CI, pp. 107–108; E/O II, p. 178; PAP 2 A 31 March 19, 1837: JP II–1190; PAP VIII¹ A 11 *n.d.*, 1847: JP III–3089; X² A 501 *n.d.*, 1850: JP III–3093.

63. E/O II, p. 322.

64. E/O II, pp. 271, 274; Cf. Kant, GR 421, 424: Beck, pp. 39, 42.

65. "Kierkegaards Kenntnis der philosophischen und theologischen Tradition," p. 355.

66. Letter of June 1, 1835, I A 72: JP V–5092; cf. PAP IV C 60 *n.d.*, 1842–1843: JP II–1244; SUD, p. 90.

67. GR 405: Beck, p. 21.

68. SUD, p. 94.

69. E/O II, pp. 270, 280.

70. PAP VIII 2 B 89 *n.d.*, 1847: JP I–657.

71. KPV 8n.; Beck, p. 8, n. 5.

72. PAP XI 2 A 8 *n.d.*, 1854; JP III–2450.

73. KPV 120–121: Beck, p. 125.

74. PF, pp. 44–45.

75. See below, Chapter 3, pp. 79–80, 90, 117; Chapter 5, pp. 201–205.

76. An ironic spoof of popular preaching on this topic—admittedly from the skeptical pen of the aesthete "A"—is found in the "Diapsalmata" of E/O I, p. 27.

77. Arildsen lists these questions in his essay, "His Theological Examination," p. 69. The other five questions are as follows:

    1. On what basis does the concept of Jesus' freedom from sin rest, and in what relationship does this stand to the dogma of the God-Man?

    2. [The question about theodicy.]

    3. How have attempts been made to present the duty of truthfulness and its limit, and how must the concept of duty be substantiated in order that the collisions originating in it may be solved?

    4. What were the causes which provoked the transfer of the papal residence to Avignon, and what consequences did the Pope's domicile there have for papal power and the Church?

    5. John 1:6–18.

    6. Ps. 103:1–14, or Joel 4:9–17.

78. "Über das Misslingen aller philosophischen Versuche in der Theodicee," GS VIII, s. 269n. Translated by Michel Despland in his *Kant on History and Religion* (Montreal: McGill-Queen's University Press, 1973), p. 295n.

79. PAP X¹ A 192 *n.d.*, 1854: JP II–1149.

80. Despland, *Kant on History and Religion* (p. 285n.) translates the final sentence here differently. The German reads "Denn in einer göttlichen Regierung kann auch der beste Mensch seiner Wunsch zum Wohlergehen nicht auf die göttliche Gerechtigkeit, sondern muss ihn jederzeit auf seine Güte grunden: weil der, welcher bloss seine Schuldigkeit thut, keinen Rechtsanspruch auf das Wohlthun Gottes haben kann" (GS VIII, s. 258n.).

81. PAP III A 230 *n.d.*, 1842: JP I–890.

82. GS VIII, s. 265. Despland, *Kant on History and Religion* p. 292.

83. Despland, p. 293.

84. Ibid.

85. R, p. 207. For a good discussion of the importance of the concept of freedom in *Repetition,* see M. Jamie Ferreira, "Repetition, Concreteness and Imagination," *International Journal for Philosophy of Religion* 25 (1989), 13–34.

86. Ibid.

87. Ibid., p. 208.

88. PAP III A 126 *n.d.*, 1841: JP III–3386.

89. Immanuel Kant, "The End of All Things," in *Kant on History,* trans. Robert E. Anchor (New York: Macmillan, 1985), p. 78.

90. PAP X³ A 47 *n.d.*, 1850: JP IV–4798.

91. Kant, "The End of All Things," p. 72.

92. CUP, p. 348n. Cf. PAP V A 37 *n.d.*, 1844: JP IV–4536.

93. Kant, "The End of All Things," pp. 72–73.

94. PAP X¹ A 516 *n.d.*, 1849: JP IV–4920.

95. Arildsen, "His Theological Examination," p. 69.

96. PAP IV A 73 *n.d.*, 1843: JP I–897. In SLW, p. 230, Kierkegaard takes a different position and presents Christ as "teleologically"

suspending the ethical to spare his disciples all the truth about his mission.

97. PAP IV A 107, May 17, 1843: JP V–5664.

98. Immanuel Kant, "Conjectural Beginning of Human History," in *On History*, trans. Lewis White Beck (Indianapolis: Bobbs-Merrill, 1963), p. 56. Italics added. The German for this reads as follows:

> Er entdeckte in sich ein Vermögen, sich selbst eine Lebensweise auszuwählen und nicht gleich anderen Thieren an eine einzige gebunden zu sein. Auf das augenblickliche Wohlgefallen, das ihm diese bermerkte Vorzug erwecken mochte, musste doch sofort Angst und Bangigkeit folgen: wie er, der noch kein Ding nach seinen verborgenen Eigenschaften und entfernten Wirkungen kannte, mit seinem neu entdeckte Vermögen zu Werke gehen sollte. Er stand gleichsam am Rande eines Abgrunds; denn aus einzelnen Gegenständen seiner Begierde, die ihm bisher der Instinct angewiesen hatte, war ihm eine Unendlichkeit derselben eröffnet, in deren Wahl er sich noch gar nicht zu finden wusste. (GS VIII, s. 112)

99. *Kierkegaard's Pseudonymous Authorship*, p. 220.

100. Immanuel Kant, *Lectures on Philosophical Theology*, trans. Allen M. Wood and Gertrude M. Clark (Ithaca, N.Y.: Cornell University Press, 1978), p. 161. There is no evidence either for or against Kierkegaard's familiarity with these lectures, and many of the themes in the *Lectures* are also found in Kant's published writings on religion and philosophical theology. Nevertheless, several passages in the *Lectures* more closely approximate remarks Kierkegaard makes about God's nature than do anything in Kant's published writings. For a discussion of these suggestive parallels, see below, Chapter 4, pp. 128–129.

101. James Collins develops this view in *The Mind of Kierkegaard*, p. 148.

102. Rohde, "Søren Kierkegaard as a Collector of Books," *Auktionsprotokol*, p. lxi.

103. Ibid., pp. xlviii–xlix.

104. "At S. K. kan have skilt sig af ned Bøger 'som kunde fortælle eftertiden mere om ham, end den havde godt af vide' er Gatterei

og tillige en Insinuation. Bevis er der ikke Skygge af. Tænker Forf. sig maaske, at S. K. paa sit Natbord havde et slidt og indstreget Exemplar af Sues 'Paris Mysterier', eller fx af Madam Mangors Kogebog, som han smed i Kakkelovnen for at en nysgerrigt snagende Eftertid ikke skuld faa Nys om hans søgelige Tilbøjeligheder?" (Niels Thulstrup, "Om Kierkegaards Bibliotek," *Kierkegaardiana* 4 (1962), 107–108).

105. PAP IV A 85 *n.d.*, 1843: JP V–5645

CHAPTER 2

1. "Words on Words," *The New York Review of Books,* January 18, 1990. Reprinted in *Writings of the East* (New York: The New York Review of Books, 1990), p. 19.

2. KRV B xxx: Norman Kemp Smith, p. 29.

3. KRV A xii, xvii: Norman Kemp Smith, pp. 9, 12.

4. KRV B xxv: Norman Kemp Smith, p. 27.

5. KRV A 51 B 79: Norman Kemp Smith, p. 93.

6. KRV A 156 B 195: Norman Kemp Smith, p.193.

7. Kant offers a complete "table" of the categories at KRV A 80 B 118: Norman Kemp Smith, p. 113.

8. KRV A 91 B 124: Norman Kemp Smith, p. 125.

9. *An Enquiry Concerning Human Understanding,* § 5, Parts 1 and 2.

10. KRV A 93 B 126: Norman Kemp Smith, p. 126.

11. KRV A 146 B 185: Norman Kemp Smith, p. 18.

12. KRV A 322 B 379: Norman Kemp Smith, p. 316.

13. KRV A 598 B 626: Norman Kemp Smith, p. 505.

14. KRV A 598ff. B 626ff.: Norman Kemp Smith, p. 505.

15. KRV B xxv: Norman Kemp Smith, p. 26.

16. KPV 28: Beck, p. 27; LE, p. 122.

17. "Handle nur nach derjenigen Maxime, durch die du zugleich wollen kannst, dass sie ein allgemeines Gesetz werde" (GR 421:

Beck, p. 39). In the *Critique of Practical Reason*, this formulation is slightly altered to read "So act that the maxim of your will could always hold at the same time as a principle establishing universal law" (KPV 30: Beck, p. 30).

18. GR 423: Beck, p. 41.

19. R. M. Hare, *Freedom and Reason* (New York: Oxford University Press, 1965), Ch. 9.

20. KPV 20: Beck, p. 19.

21. KPV 20: Beck, p. 19.

22. GR 429: Beck, p. 47.

23. Kant clearly believed in the legitimacy of punishing criminals, including the use of the death penalty. In the *Foundations* (GR 430n.: Beck, p. 48n.) and elsewhere he views criminal punishment as valid for those who refuse to treat others as ends by violating their person or property, and he does not appear to see this punishment as equivalent to treating the transgressors as "means only."

24. GR 434: Beck, p. 52.

25. There is a substantial influence of Rousseau on Kant's ethics and political philosophy. This is especially evident in his essays "On the Common Saying: 'This May be True in Theory, but it does not Apply in Practice'" and "Perpetual Peace." In his *Theory of Justice* (Cambridge, Mass.: Harvard University Press, 1971), § 40, John Rawls argues that his own contract theory restates major themes in Kant's ethics. For a related statement of this view, see Thomas Hill, "The Kingdom of Ends," *Proceedings of the Third International Kant-Congress* (Dordrecht: D. Reidel, 1972), pp. 307–315.

26. For a fuller discussion of this interpretation of Kant's ethics, see my "The First Formulation of the Categorical Imperative as Literally a 'Legislative' Metaphor," *History of Philosophy Quarterly* 8:2 (April 1991), 163–179.

27. KPV 25: Beck, p. 25.

28. This point is made by William D. Peck in his Yale doctoral dissertation, "On Autonomy: The Primacy of the Subject in Kant and Kierkegaard," pp. 115–116.

29. For example, PAP X² A 396 *n.d.*, 1850: JP I–188.

30. GR 393: Beck, p. 9.

31. LE, pp. 117–118.

32. Ibid., pp. 118–120.

33. There are a number of more or less insightful accounts of Kant's philosophy of religion. These studies include Allen W. Wood, *Kant's Moral Religion* (Ithaca, N.Y.: Cornell University Press, 1970) and *Kant's Rational Theology* (Ithaca, N.Y.: Cornell University Press, 1978); Despland, *Kant on History and Religion*; Reardon, *Kant as Philosophical Theologian*; and Gordon E. Michalson, Jr., *Fallen Freedom: Kant on Radical Evil and Moral Regeneration* (Cambridge: Cambridge University Press, 1990).

34. KPV 110: Beck, pp. 114–115.

35. KPV 122f.: Beck, pp. 126–127.

36. *Judgment,* p. 187. It seems to me that Allen W. Wood partly grasps this issue when, at the conclusion of his discussion of the highest good in his *Kant's Moral Religion*, he locates the driving force behind Kant's argument less in an alleged duty to either seek or attain this end than in human reason's effort to "unify its rules under the idea of a totality" (p. 97). As Wood points out, the attainability of the highest good, for Kant, is an ideal "with which we cannot cease to concern ourselves without forsaking the rationality which is proper to our own nature" (p. 98). It does not seem to me, however, that Wood effectively traces the outlines of the particular rational conflict experienced by a rational individual who acts, whether on prudence or morality, without holding a reasonable belief in the attainability of the highest good in the strict, unexceptional form that Kant gives to it.

37. KPV 115f.: Beck, pp. 119–120.

38. Ibid., 124: Beck, p. 129.

39. Ibid., 116: Beck, p. 120.

40. Ibid., 113: Beck, p. 118.

41. Ibid., 114f.: Beck, p. 119.

42. For a fuller discussion of this, see below, Chapter 4, pp. 147–149.

43. KPV 3–5, 29ff.: Beck, pp. 3–5, 29f.; GR 447–448: Beck, pp. 66–67.

44. Ibid., 121: Beck, p. 125.

45. Ibid., 121: Beck, p. 126.

46. Ibid., 121: Beck, p. 126.

47. In the first *Critique*, Kant appears elliptically to expresses this idea in a passage affirming the "superiority which moral philosophy has over all other occupations of reason" (KRV A840–B868: Norman Kemp Smith, p. 658).

48. Ibid., 146: Beck, p. 151.

49. Ibid., 147: Beck, p. 152. Cf. LPT, p. 123.

50. Ernst Cassirer details the negative reactions to Kant's doctrine of radical evil in his *Kant's Life and Thought*, trans. J. Haden (New Haven and London: Yale University Press, 1981), pp. 391–392. He states, for example, that Goethe remarked bitterly in a letter to Herder that Kant had "slobbered on" his philosopher's cloak "with the blot of radical evil, so that even Christ would be enticed to kiss its hem." A slightly different version of this remark is offered by Karl Barth in his *Protestant Thought from Rousseau to Ritschl* (New York: Harper and Brothers, 1959), p. 176.

51. *Religion*, p. 18.

52. *Judgment*, § 87.

53. KPV 146: Beck, p. 151.

54. *Judgment*, p. 187.

55. Wood, *Kant's Moral Religion*, p. 250.

56. Kant's identification of this element of rational freedom with respect to the moral law is often missed by commentators on Kant's ethics. For example, Nathan Rotenstreich, in his *Practice and Realization: Studies in Kant's Moral Philosophy* (The Hague: Martinus Nijhoff, 1979), pp. 12–13, interprets Kant as standing within the Socratic and Aristotelian traditions for which "freedom is to do what is best" and for which "the choice implied in freedom is detachment from the influence of sensibility to opt for reason." Like other commentators, Rotenstreich misses Kant's discovery that reason has two competing and unadjudicable perspectives.

57. GR 414: Beck, pp. 30–31.

58. *Religion*, p. 17n., p. 38.

59. Ibid., p. 35.

60. Ibid., p. 37. This quotation is from Horace, *Satires*, I, 1.

61. Ibid., p. 38.

62. Ibid., p. 43.

63. Peck, "On Autonomy: The Primacy of the Subject in Kant and Kierkegaard," p. 150.

64. *Religion*, p. 43.

65. Ibid.

66. Ibid., p. 57.

67. Ibid., p. 66.

68. Ibid., p. 69.

69. Ibid., p. 47.

70. Ibid., p. 70.

71. Michalson, *Fallen Freedom*, p. 99.

72. *Religion*, p. 47.

73. Ibid., pp. 68–69.

74. In the same way that moral causality, in Kant's view, can coexist with natural causality.

75. *Religion*, p. 71.

76. Ibid., p. 70.

77. Ibid., p 75.

78. Ibid., p. 70.

79. For a discussion of this controversy, see Mary J. Gregor's "Translator's Introduction," *Conflict*, pp. vii–viii.

80. *Conflict*, pp. 62–63.

81. Ibid., p. 67.

82. Ibid., p. 75.

83. Ibid., p. 77.

84. Ibid., p. 73.

85. Ibid., p. 83.

86. Ibid.

87. Ibid.

88. CUP, p. 491.

CHAPTER 3

1. VIII² B 81 *n.d.*, 1847: JP I–649; Cf. X¹ A 666 *n.d.*, 1849: JP III–3558. The translation here is my own.

2. PAP II C 48 December 4, 1837: JP II–2252.

3. CUP, p. 292.

4. KRV A vii: Norman Kemp Smith, p. 7.

5. PF, p. 37.

6. Kant's *Critique of Practical Reason* is not among the books listed in the *Auktionsprotokol.* Nevertheless, one of the important questions on Kierkegaard's *Attestats,* his degree examination, concerned how Kant made the transition from ethics to religion. (The questions for this examination are found in LD, pp. 10–16.) This transition is rigorously developed only in one place in Kant's writings, the section of the second *Critique* we are now discussing.

7. KPV 120–121: Beck, p. 125.

8. *Conflict,* p. 81.

9. PF, pp. 44–45.

10. KRV A 58 B 82: Norman Kemp Smith, p. 97.

11. KRV A 642 B 670: Norman Kemp Smith, p. 532.

12. CUP, p. 169.

13. *Categoriae,* 14b 15–20.

14. In the first *Critique,* Kant defines practical reason, which is synonymous for him with the faculty of will, as related to its object by *making it actual* (KRV B x: Norman Kemp Smith, p. 18); in the second *Critique* he defines the "faculty of desire," which is

practical reason or will in rational beings, as "the faculty…of causing, through its ideas, the reality of the objects of these ideas" (KPV 9n.: Beck, p. 9, fn. 6).

15. JC–DODE, p. 121.

16. CUP, p. 273.

17. KRV A 203 B 248: Norman Kemp Smith, p. 228.

18. PF, pp. 75f. In their notes to this passage, the Hongs suggest that Kierkegaard's use of the German *Nebeneinander* may be a reference to the romantic philosophy of nature found in Heinrich Steffens or Schelling (PF, p. 303), although the term is also used by Hegel in a different context (*Enzyklopädie* § 254). Since Kant does not use this term in this way, they may be right. Nevertheless, the idea itself is thoroughly Kantian.

19. KRV A 836 B 864: Norman Kemp Smith, pp. 655–656.

20. PF, p. 81. This point is repeated on p. 82.

21. KRV A 293 B 350: Norman Kemp Smith, p. 297. Kant reiterates this point in his *Anthropologie in pragmatischer Hinsicht*, GS VII, s. 146 (*Anthropology from a Pragmatic Point of View*, trans. Mary J. Gregor [The Hague: Martinus Nijhoff, 1974], p. 25).

22. PF, pp. 82–83.

23. Gregor Malantschuk notes this point of relationship between Kant and Kierkegaard when he states the following in *Kierkegaard's Thought*, p. 70: "Kierkegaard denies that the normative can be formed out of experience or the stuff of experience alone. In the following remark he is in line with Kant: 'As soon as I frame a law from experience, I insert something more into it than there is in experience' [IV C 75: JP I–1072]. For K this conception becomes very significant, especially for his view of the historical sciences." See also Robert C. Roberts, *Faith, Reason and History: Rethinking Kierkegaard's* Philosophical Fragments (Macon, Ga.: Mercer University Press, 1987), pp. 126–127.

24 . Many of these references appear in the journals. See, for example, JP I–831 to 847 and JP II–1944 to 1956. Kierkegaard's conception of the afterlife is also closely related to his concept of "blessedness" or "happiness" [*Salighed*]. See Abrahim H. Khan, Salighed *as Happiness? Kierkegaard on the Concept* Salighed (Waterloo, Ontario: Wilfrid Laurier University Press, 1985), pp. 31–39.

25. Kant, "The End of All Things," pp. 69–70.

26. PAP II A 630 *n.d.*, 1837: JP V–5276.

27. PAP X¹ A 48 *n.d.* 1849: JP I–842.

28. Kant, "The End of All Things," pp. 69–70, 73.

29. PH, p. 35.

30. PH, p.186.

31. PH, p. 35.

32. This inscription, a quotation from a hymn written by Hans Adolph Brorson (1694–1764), expresses a fervent anticipation of communication with Jesus at life's end. It is published in LD, pp. 26–27.

33. This seems to be the view of Harrison Hall in his article "Love and Death: Kierkegaard and Heidegger on Authentic and Inauthentic Human Existence," *Inquiry* 27 (1984), 196n. For a rejoinder to Hall, see Gordon D. Marino, "Salvation: A Reply to Harrison Hall's Reading of Kierkegaard," *Inquiry* 28 (1985), 441–453.

34. Studies in the Humanities 16 (University, Ala.: University of Alabama Press, 1977), pp. 169, 174. A similar contrast between Kantian "formalism" and the ethic advanced in E/O is also voiced by David F. Swenson, in his "Translator's Introduction" to the *Philosophical Fragments* (Princeton: Princeton University Press, 1962), p. xxiii; also Walker, *To Will One Thing*, p. 10.

35. FT, p. 54. Hegel's discussion appears on pp. 86–103 of the translation of *The Philosophy of Right* by T. M. Knox (Oxford: Oxford University Press, 1958).

36. *Religion*, p. 175; *Conflict*, p. 115.

37. Immanuel Kant, *Kant's Political Writings*, trans. Hans Reiss (Cambridge: Cambridge University Press, 1970), p. 81.

38. PAP X² A 396 *n.d.*, 1850: JP I–188.

39. CUP, p. 450.

40. E/O II, p. 182.

41. Peck, "On Autonomy," p. 233.

42. Kant, *Kant's Political Writings*, p. 66.

43. PAP VI B 54:3 *n.d.*, 1845: JP I–925.

44. Peck, "On Autonomy," pp. 240–241.

45. Trans. James Ellington (Indianapolis: Bobbs-Merrill, 1964).

46. Despite his emphasis on the sharp differences between Kant and Kierkegaard's ethics, George Stack notes that there are assertions in Kant's *Lectures on Ethics* that "seem to be in the spirit of Kierkegaard's practical ethics" (*Kierkegaard's Existential Ethics*, p. 168).

47. E/O II, p. 239. Cf. Kant's definition of the categorical imperative, GR 421: Beck, p. 39; also KPV 30: Beck, p. 30.

48. Ibid., pp. 91, 260.

49. This point is made by John Rawls in his *Theory of Justice* § 40.

50. E/O II, p. 63.

51. This theme underlies Kierkegaard's theme of the importance and distinctiveness of love for the dead, those who cannot repay our atttention—WL, Chapter 9. For a discussion of this theme, see Theodore W. Adorno, "On Kierkegaard's Doctrine of Love," in *Søren Kierkegaard,* ed. Harold Bloom (New York: Chelsea House Publishers, 1989), pp. 32–34.

52. E/O II, p. 265.

53. PAP III A 202 *n.d.*, 1842: JP I–889.

54. John Ladd, ed., *Ethical Relativism* (Belmont, Calif.: Wadsworth, 1973).

55. GR 428–429: Beck, pp. 46–47.

56. CA, p. 106n; PAP VIII² B 81 *n.d.*, 1847: JP I–649.

57. PAP X¹ A 457 *n.d.*, 1849: JP I–975.

58. E/O II, p. 280.

59. PAP VIII¹ A 60 *n.d.*, 1847; JP I–683. Cf. WL, p. 137.

60. An emphasis on the essential dignity and spiritual equality of persons, despite the unavoidability of worldly distinctions, constitutes a major theme of Kierkegaard's *Works of Love*. See especially Part One, Section II-C, "*You* Shall Love Your Neighbour," WL, pp. 73–98.

61. Part 2 of Kirmmse's *Kierkegaard in Golden Age Denmark* is devoted to developing Kierkegaard's opposition to the religious and social views of Denmark's upper classes as these views took form in the period leading up to and following the constitutional change of 1848. For an insightful review of some of the modern debate occasioned by Kierkegaard's political and social opinions as well as a discussion of the similarities and differences between Kierkegaard's and Marx's thought, see Sylviane Agacinski, *Aparté: Conceptions and Deaths of Søren Kierkegaard*, trans. Kevin Newmark (Tallahassee: Florida State University Press, 1988), pp. 205–212.

62. This theme predominates in his essay "On the Common Saying: 'This May be True in Theory, but it does not Apply in Practice,'"GS VIII, s. 273–313.

63. PH, p. 206.

64. Walker, *To Will One Thing*, p. 115.

65. CUP, p. 125.

66. Ibid., p. 72.

67. Ibid., p. 379.

68. PAP V C 7 *n.d.*, 1844: JP III–2349.

69. In his *Kierkegaard's* Fragments *and* Postscript: *The Religious Philosophy of Johannes Climacus* (Atlantic Highlands, N.J.: Humanities Press, 1983), p. 141, C. Stephen Evans perceives a possible inconsistency in Johannes Climacus's emphasis in the *Postscript* on eternal happiness hand in hand with his belief that "duty must be done for its own sake," but this inconsistency merely expresses Kant's own complex solution to the antinomy of practical reason.

70. CUP, p. 306.

71. GR 417–418: Beck, pp. 81–82.

72. KPV 27: Beck, pp. 27–28. In JC–DODE (p. 146) Kierkegaard seems to apply some of the point and humor of this remark by Kant to a criticism of shared "doubt":

> He was well able to comprehend that an individual could take it into his head to doubt, but he could not understand how it could occur to him to say this to another person, least of all as advice (it would be another matter if it were

said to deter), for if the other person was not too slow, he might very well say, "Thank you, but please forgive me for doubting the correctness of that statement." Now, if the first person in his happiness over the second person's expression of gratitude were to tell a third person that they were in agreement about doubting everything, he actually would be making a fool of the third person, since their agreement was actually nothing more than a wholly abstract expression of their disagreement, unless each was so disrespectful as to consider the other as nothing.

73. PH, p. 56.

74. E/O II, pp. 271–272.

75. Ibid., II, p. 178.

76. Tr. J. H. Bernard, pp. 172–174.

77. E/O I, p. 71.

78. Ibid., p. 135.

79. *Judgment,* pp. 142–145.

80. PAP IV C 114 *n.d.*,1842–1843: JP IV–4830. Cf. PAP X² A 417 *n.d.*,1850: JP IV–3853.

81. E/O II, p. 278.

82. CA, pp. 17–18n.; JC–DODE, p. 170.

83. CUP, p. 277n.

84. JC–DODE, p. 170.

85. In his introduction to Kierkegaard's *Crisis in the Life of an Actress*, Stephen Crites notes Kierkegaard's extension of the concept of the aesthetic to Hegel's entire mode of philosophizing. Crites also suggests Kierkegaard's fundamental alignment with Kant in his perception of the primacy of the ethical–religious over speculative and aesthetic activity. (C, pp. 24–25).

86. E/O II, p. 174.

87. CUP, p. 121.

88. GR 398–399: Beck, pp. 14–15.

89. PH, p. 70.

90. Ibid., p. 149.

91. Peck, "On Autonomy," p. 201.

92. KPR 22: Beck, p. 20, Section 3, Theorem II.

93. X^1 A 635 *n.d.*, 1849: JP III–2425. Also X^5 A 34 *n.d.*, 1852: III–2441; and SUD, p. 45.

94. *Religion*, p. 15.

95. *Judgment*, p. 303.

96. Kant, "The End of All Things," pp. 430–431.

97. PAP X^2 A 57 *n.d.*, 1849: JP I–612.

98. CI, p. 154. Cf. PAP VII^2 B 261:22 *n.d.*, 1846–1847: JP III–2356. For a discussion of Kierkegaard's understanding of the uses of irony and humor see William McDonald, "Translator's Introduction." *Prefaces* by Søren Kierkegaard (Tallahassee: Florida State University Press, 1989).

99. Kant offers a similar definition of irony in his *Anthropology from a Pragmatic Point of View*: "*Ironic* wit issues from a mind disposed to *paradox*: from behind the candid tone of innocence the (artful) scamp peeks out to ridicule someone (or his opinion) by exalting with intended eulogy (persiflage), the opposite of what deserves approval" (*Anthropologie in pragmatischer Hinsicht*, GS VII, 221–222. [*Anthropology from a Pragmatic Point of View*, trans. Mary J. Gregor, pp. 90–91]).

100. *Dreams*, p. 83: GS II, s. 348.

101. M. Kronenberg, *Kant; Sein Leben und Seine Lehre* (München: Beck, 1897), VII, pp. 161, 163. Quoted in Kant, *Dreams of a Spirit-Seer Illustrated by Dreams of Metaphysics*, p. vii.

102. OAR, pp. 92–139.

103. *Conflict*, pp. 37, 39, 45. In the essay "An Answer to the Question 'What is Enlightenment,'" in *Kant's Political Writings*, p. 289, Kant remarks: "[A clergyman] if he believed he had found [something contrary to inner religion] in [church statutes], he could not conscientiously discharge the duties of his office; he would have to give it up."

104. There may be an oblique and Kant-inspired reference to Adler in the *Postscript* (p. 219), in a passage where Kierkegaard/Climacus

describes paganism as consisting in the fact that "God is related to man directly, as the obviously extraordinary to the astonished observer." He offers the example of God appearing to someone in "the figure of a very rare and tremendously large green bird, with a red beak, sitting in a tree on the mound, and perhaps even whistling in an unheard of manner." This description brings to mind Adler's own "revelations" delivered in a scratchy, whistling voice (OAR, p. xi), and it recalls Kierkegaard's repeated description of him in *The Book on Adler* as an *extraordinarius*. In the passages surrounding this one, Kierkegaard/Climacus makes the point that (for Christianity) God does not reveal himself this way but only in a "prior irruption of inwardness, which corresponds to the divine elusiveness that God has nothing obvious about Him, that God is so far from being obvious that He is invisible." This criticism of spurious, phenomenal revelations suggests that Kant's epistemologically grounded critique of Swedenborg's metaphysical illuminism in *Dreams of a Spirit-Seer* may have been on Kierkegaard's mind as he prepared his attack against Adler.

105. PAP VII² B 261:22 *n.d.*, 1846–1847: JP III–2356.

106. Wilhelm Gottlieb Tennemann, *Geschichte der Philosophie,* 11 vols. (Leipzig, 1798–1819). This edition appears in the *Auktionsprotokol* as Ktl. 815–826.

107. PF, p. 44.

108. Although Kant usually refers to this as the "physico-theological" proof, he also repeatedly describes this position as physical-teleology (*Judgment,* pp. 291–292).

109. CA, p. 3.

110. KRV B xxxi: Norman Kemp Smith, p. 30.

111. PAP II C 23. Dec. 23, 1837.

112. GR 463: Beck, p. 83.

113. PF, p. 9.

114. Ibid., p. 11. Cf. p. 14—"If the teacher is to be the occasion that reminds the learner, he cannot assist him to recollect that he actually does know the truth, for the learner is indeed untruth. That for which the teacher can become the occasion of his recollecting is that he is untruth."

The Danish text for both these passages is as follows:

Socratisk seet, er ethvert Udgangspunkt i Tiden *eo ipso* et Tilfældigt, et Forsvindende, en Anledning; Læreren er ei heller mere...

Skal Læreren være Anledningen, der minder den Lærende, da kan han jo ikke bidrage til at han erinder, at han egentligen veed Sanheden, thi den Lærende er jo Unsandheden. Det Læreren da kan vorde ham Anledning til at han erindrer, er, at han er Unsandheden. (SV, 3d Udg., Vol. 6, pp. 16, 19)

115. H. A. Nielsen, *Where the Passion Is: A Reading of Kierkegaard's Philosophical Fragments* (Tallahassee: University Presses of Florida, 1983), p. 175.

116. X^2 A 539 *n.d.*, 1850: JP II–2239.

117. *Conflict*, p. 63. The italics in the translated passage are my own. The German for the latter part of this passage reads as follows: "...weil die dazu erforderlichen Begriffe und Gründsatze eigentlich nicht von irgend einem andern gelernt, sondern nur bei Veranlassung eines Vortrages aus der eigenen Vernunft des Lehrers entwickelt werden müssen" (*Conflict*, p. 62).

118. Stephen N. Dunning, *Kierkegaard's Dialectic of Inwardness* (Princeton: Princeton University Press, 1985), p. 13. These titles are "The Conception Made Possible," "The Conception Made Actual," and "The Conception Made Necessary."

CHAPTER 4

1. CUP, p. 438.

2. PF, pp. 40, 42. The Kantian influence on these statements in the *Fragments* is noted by Louis Pojman in *The Logic of Subjectivity: Kierkegaard's Philosophy of Religion* (University, Ala.: University of Alabama Press, 1984), p. 29.

3. Ibid., pp. 39–41.

4. CUP, pp. 297–298; PAP X^2 A 328 *n.d.* 1849–1850: JP I–1057.

5. PF, p. 41n.

6. KRV A 600 B 628; Norman Kemp Smith, p. 505.

7. PAP X^2 A 328 *n.d.*, 1849–1850: JP I–1057.

8. CUP, p. 293.

9. *The Logic of Hegel*, trans. William Wallace (Oxford: Clarendon Press, 1892), pp. 107–108.

10. KRV A 615 B 643: Norman Kemp Smith, p. 515.

11. KRV A 617 B 645: Norman Kemp Smith, p. 516.

12. PF, p. 74.

13. E.g., PF, p. 81, lines 29–30; 83, line 18; 86, lines 4–6.

14. CUP, p. 90.

15. PF, p. 86.

16. PAP XI² A 54 *n.d.*, 1854: JP III–2570.

17. CUP, p. 178.

18. KRV A 642 B 670: Norman Kemp Smith, p. 531.

19. LPT, p. 161.

20. PF, p. 63.

21. Gordon Michalson, Jr., *Lessing's "Ugly Ditch": A Study of Theology and History* (University Park: Pennsylvania State University Press, 1985), p. 17.

22. *Conflict,* p. 115.

23. *Religion,* p. 175. A second reference on pp. 81–82 is more critical of the kind of conduct in which Abraham engaged but does not mention Abraham by name.

24. See above, Chapter 1, pp. 14–16.

25. *Conflict,* p. 121n.

26. CUP, p. 296.

27. KRV B 71: Norman Kemp Smith, p. 90.

28. All of God's knowledge is grounded on his being an *ens entium*, an independent original being. For if God were not the cause of things, then either he would not know them at all (because there would be nothing in his nature which could acquaint him with things external to him); or else things would have to have some influence on him in order to give him a characteristic of their existence. But in that case, God would have to have sensible knowl-

edge of things. Consequently, he would have to be *passibilis,* which contradicts his independence as an *entis originarii.* If God is thus able to know things apart from sensibility, he cannot know them except by being conscious of himself as the cause of everything. Thus the divine knowledge of all things is nothing but the knowledge God has of himself as an effective power. (LPT, p. 89)

29. Ibid.

30. JC-DODE, p. 141.

31. Kant deals explicitly with the changelessness of God in LPT, pp. 71–72.

32. UD, pp. 25, 31. Also, PAP VII¹ A 143 *n.d.,* 1846: JP II–1348; PAP IX A 374 *n.d.,* 1848: JP II–1379.

33. PAP VII¹ A 143 *n.d.,* 1846: JP II–1348. Kierkegaard here calls the idea of God's changeability an *anthropopathetic conception,* a term reminiscent of Kant's criticisms of religious anthropomorphism and "pathological" determining grounds in ethics.

34. *Religion,* pp. 183–185 and 183n.

35. PH, p. 51.

36. PAP X⁵ A 73 *n.d.,* 1853: JP III–2823.

37. Kierkegaard makes reference to the distinction between theoretical and practical reason, although he attributes this to Pascal rather than Kant. See, for example, PAP X³ A 609 *n.d.,* 1850: JP III–3109; cf. *The Concept of Irony,* p. 202.

38. CUP, p. 347; PAP X¹ A 360 *n.d.,* 1849: JP I–972; PAP X³ A 609 *n.d.,* 1850: JP III–3109; X⁵ A 73 *n.d.,* 1853: JP III–2823. In CUP, p. 205, he condemns as "gnosticism" the giving of thought primacy over the individual's ethical reality.

39. CUP, p. 178.

40. KPV A 822 B 859: Norman Kemp Smith, p. 646.

41. KPV 146: Beck, p. 151.

42. GR 97: Beck, p. 13.

43. KPV 147: Beck, p. 152. See also LPT, p. 123.

44. PF, p. 62.

45. UD, pp. 136.

46. PF, p. 83; cf. CUP, p. 91; PAP I A 36 November 25, 1834: JP II–1094.

47. PAP IX A 32 *n.d.*, 1848: JP I–255.

48. PF, p. 105.

49. Ibid.

50. CUP, p. 182.

51. Ibid.

52. Ibid, pp. 30–31.

53. A similar point is made by R. Z. Friedman. Speaking of Kierkegaard's understanding of the transition from morality to religion, he observes, "Kierkegaard's repudiation of Kant's position is extensive but not as extreme as Kierkegaard's polemical language would have it. In an important sense Kierkegaard's labours are simply criticisms of Kant within a framework which is essentially Kantian." See his "Kierkegaard: First Existentialist or Last Kantian?" 164–165.

54. CUP, p. 188.

55. Kant's own stated objections to this idea are not epistemological but moral. In the *Religion* (p. 57) he concedes the possibility of a "supernaturally begotten" individual who is the example of a man well pleasing to God, but he adds that if we regard this individual as fundamentally different from us, he loses his value as an example of what human beings can become.

56. In an application of this general point, Allen Wood, in his *Kant's Rational Theology* (p. 59), observes that "Kant adopts a strictly agnostic position on the question of whether *realitates noumena*, the pure realities which might constitute the divine nature," can conflict with one another in the way that phenomenal realities can be said to conflict.

57. PF, p. 62.

58. Ibid., p. 87.

59. PAP VI B 45 *n.d.*, 1845: JP III–3085. PF, p. 222.

60. CUP, p. 179.

61. Ibid., p. 86.

62. *Gotthold Ephraim Lessings Sämtliche Werke*, ed. Karl Lachmann and Franz Muncker, 23 vols. (Leipzig: G. J. Göschen'sche Verlagshandlung, 1886–1924), B. 13, s. 7; *Lessing's Theological Writings*, ed. and trans. Henry Chadwick (Stanford: Stanford University Press, 1957), pp. 53–55.

63. CUP, p. 90.

64. *Religion*, p. 111.

65. "Von einem neuerdings erhobenen vornehmen Ton in der Philosophie," 1796, GS VIII, s. 387–406; "On the Common Saying: 'This May be True in Theory, but it does not Apply in Practice,'" in *Kant's Political Writings*, p. 86; "An Answer to the Question: 'What is Enlightenment?,'" in *Kant's Political Writings*, p. 55.

66. KRV A 209, 228 B 254, 281: Norman Kemp Smith, pp. 231–232, 248–249.

67. KRV A 457–459 B 485–487: Norman Kemp Smith, pp. 418–420.

68. Book 1: Chapter 7.

69. Niels Thulstrup, *Commentary on Kierkegaard's Concluding Unscientific Postscript*, trans. Robert J. Widenmann (Princeton: Princeton University Press, 1984).

70. Ibid., p. 215.

71. PAP V B 1:3 *n.d.*, 1844: JP III–2342. Kierkegaard adds here that "whether it is an expression or a thought is a matter of indifference." For a discussion of these nuances, see Claus V. Bormann, "Lessing," in *Kierkegaard's Teachers*, Vol. 10 of *Bibliotheca Kierkgaardiana* (1982), pp. 135–157.

72. CUP, p. 89.

73. See above, Chapter 3, pp. 117–118.

74. CUP, p. 96.

75. Ibid, p. 97.

76. See above, Chapter 3, p. 106.

77. See above, p. 125—KRV A 617–618 B 645–646: Norman Kemp Smith, p. 516.

78. Apart from the use in the *Postscript* we are discussing, Kierkegaard uses this phrase again at p. 121. This utilization, quoted

above, Chapter 3, p. 106, is noteworthy because here it refers to the Kantian point that there is a qualitative transition from prudence to duty. Kierkegaard also employs this phrase twice in the draft of *The Book on Adler* that appears in the *Papirer* at VII² B 235, pp. 7 and 81. Lowrie employs only the latter in his translation (OAR, p. 61). Finally, this phrase is used independently in the *Papirer* at X¹ A 361 *n.d.*, 1849 and X² A 537 *n.d.*, 1850.

79. PAP VII² B 235, p. 81. Cf. VII² B 235, p. 7.

80. *Religion*, p. 54.

81. *Die Religion innerhalb der Grenzen der blossen Vernunft*, GS VI, s. 65n. The translation here is my own, since Greene and Hudson's translation (*Religion*, p. 59n.) misses the explicit use of the noun *leap* (*Sprung*).

82. "An Answer to the Question: 'What is Enlightenment?,'" p. 55.

83. PAP I A 72 June 1, 1835: V–5092.

84. SUD, pp. 13ff. For a discussion of Kierkegaard's understanding of human beings' bondage to sin, see Eugene Webb, *Philosophers of Consciousness* (Seattle: University of Washington Press, 1988), pp. 261–269.

85. GR 448: Beck, pp. 66–67.

86. KPV 29, 4: Beck, pp. 29, 4.

87. KPV 30: Beck, p. 30. In a footnote in the *Religion* (p. 45), Kant states that "we are certainly and immediately conscious of a power to overcome, by a firm resolve, every incentive, however great, to transgression." He supports this view with a quote from Juvenal (*Satires* VIII, 81–82): "Though Phalaris himself should command you to be false and bring up his bull and dictate perjuries." A reference to Phalaris's bull also appears at the beginning of E/O (I, p. 19). This episode was probably well known to a Latin scholar like Kierkegaard, and we need not suppose any debt to Kant.

88. KPV, p. 3–4: Beck, p. 3.

89. E/O II, p. 250.

90. Ibid. II, p. 216.

91. CUP, p. 124.

92. PF, p. 17. PAP X³ A 467 *n.d.,* 1850: JP IV–4033. For a discussion of the role freedom plays in human self-definition in SUD, see John D. Glenn, Jr., "The Definition of the Self and the Structure of Kierkegaard's Work," in *International Kierkegaard Commentary: Sickness unto Death,* ed. Robert L. Perkins (Macon, Ga.: Mercer University Press, 1987), pp. 5–21.

93. PAP XI² A 439 September 25, 1855: JP VI–6969.

94. CUP, pp. 347, 261.

95. PAP V A 10 *n.d.,* 1844: JP I–452.

96. PAP X⁵ A 64 *n.d.,* 1853: JP II–1492.

97. PAP X⁴ A 362 *n.d.,* 1851: JP I–998.

98. PAP X³ A 734 *n.d.,* 1851: JP I–993.

99. CA, pp. 16–17.

100. Interestingly, this conception of rational personality as involving the choice of a rule of choice, rather than remaining subject to inconstant whims and desires, seems very similar to the basic preethical move from the aesthetic to the ethical so central to Judge William's position in *Either/Or.* If so, this suggests another possible link between the Judge's ethics and Kant's. See above, pp. 92–95.

101. *Religion,* pp. 17–20.

102. PAP XI¹ A 112 *n.d.* 1854: JP IV–3875.

103. PH, pp. 74–75.

104. CUP, pp. 376–377.

105. For a discussion of Hegel's position here, see Niels Thulstrup, *Commentary on Kierkegaard's Concluding Unscientific Postscript,* p. 345.

106. *Religion,* p. 46.

107. Ibid., p. 51.

108. Ibid., pp. 17–18.

109. In the *Religion* (p. 46) Kant explicitly uses the term *postulate* to describe the cognitive status of required belief about our inner moral character. This suggests that the belief in "innate" or "rad-

ical evil" functions as a negative analog to and epistemological equivalent of the postulates of God, immortality, and freedom.

110. Ibid, p. 66. See below, pp. 163–164.

111. Ibid., p. 35.

112. Ibid, p. 37.

113. References include CI, pp. 107–108; E/O II, pp. 174, 175. References in the *Papirer* include the following: 2 A 31 March 19, 1837: II–1190; VIII¹ A 11 *n.d.*, 1847: JP III–3089. Explicit references to this idea or clear references to these passages in the *Religion* are found in the lecture notes in the *Papirer*, including Vol. II, "Forelæsninger over Indledning til spekulativ Dogmatik af Marthensen, Vinter Semestret. 37 and 38," II C 12–24, p. 338; Vol. XIII, "Referat af Martensens Forelæsninger over 'Speculativ Dogmatik' (Indledning samt §§ 60–99), II C 28, p. 54; "Referat af Ph. Marheineckes Forelæsninger i Berlin 1841–42 over 'Dogmatiksk Theologi med særligt Hensyn til Daubs System,'" III C26 (Vinteren 1841–1842), p. 213. Mention of Kant's concept of evil is also made in a reading note on Fr. Baader's "Vorlesungen über Speculative Dogmatik," PAP (Vol. XII I C 27, p. 133).

114. PAP III A 118 *n.d.*, 1841: JP IV–4004.

115. CA, p. 21.

116. Ibid, p. 50.

117. Ibid., p. 30.

118. Ibid, p. 112.

119. CI, pp. 107–108.

120. PAP VIII¹ A 11 *n.d.*, 1847: JP III–3089.

121. PAP II C 23 December 21, 1837; 2 C 48 December 4, 1837: JP II–2252.

122. Kierkegaard seems to have been greatly interested in the topic of categories. As Stephen N. Dunning points out, as early as *The Concept of Irony* Kierkegaard displays a solid familiarity with Kant's thinking on this subject—see his *Kierkegaard's Dialectic of Inwardness*, p. 13. This same interest in the idea of a category seems to have motivated Kierkegaard's study of Trendelenberg. In the last analysis, however, it must be said that Kierkegaard never provides a clear definition of what he means by a category, and

he employs the term in various ways, often merely to designate a mode of thinking. See, for example, PAP IV C 63–66 *n.d.*, 1842–1843: JP II–1595–1598; PAP X⁴ A 369 *n.d.*, 1851: JP II–1906; PAP VIII¹ A 286 *n.d.*, 1847: JP II–2002; PAP VIII¹ A 11 *n.d.*, 1847: JP III–3089.

123. Breslau: Josef Mar und Comp., 1844.

124. PAP X² A 501 *n.d.*, 1851: III–3093.

125. TD, p. 33.

126. SUD, pp. 106–107.

127. Ibid., p. 107.

128. CUP, p. 475. Cf. PF, p. 16. In the *Fragments*, pp. 16–17, Kierkegaard attributes this view of the irreversibility of sin to Aristotle. Aristotle's position with regard to the habitual nature of vice and virtue, of course, is very different from the view espoused by Kierkegaard—or Kant.

129. Diese ursprüngliche, oder überhaupt vor jedem Guten, was er immer tun mag, vorhergehende Schuld, die auch dasjenige ist, was, und nichts mehr, wir unter dem radicalen Bösen verstanden (S. das erste Stück), kann aber auch, so viel wir nach unserem Vernunftrecht einsehen, nicht von einem anderen getilgt werden...—Da nun das Sittliche-Böse (Übertretung des moralischen Gesetz als göttlichen Gebotes, SÜNDE genannt) nicht sowohl wegen der Unendlichkeit des höchsten Gesetzgebers, dessen Autorität dadurch verletzt worden...sondern als ein Böses in der Gesinnung und den Maximen überhaupt (wie allgemeine Grundsätze vergleichungsweise gegen einzelne Übertretung) eine Unendlichkeit von Verletzung des Gesetz, mithin der Schuld bei sich führt (welches vor einem menschlichen Gerichtshofe, der nur das einzelne Verbrechen, mithin nur die Tat und darauf bezogene, nicht aber die allgemeine Gesinnung in Betracht zieht, anders ist), so würde jeder Mensch sich einer unendlichen Strafe und Verstossung aus dem Reiche Gottes zu gewärtigen haben. (*Die Religion innerhalb der Grenzen der blossen Vernunft*, GS VI, s. 72)

130. "Den, der blot ved Endeligheden lærer sin Skyldighed at kjende, han er fortabt i Endeligheden, og endeligt lader det Spørgsmaal sig ikke afgjøre, om et Menneske er skyldigt, uden paa en udvortes, juridisk, høist ufuldkommen Maade. Den, der derfor kun skal lære sin Skyld at kjende ved Analogier til Politie- og

Høiesteretsdomme, han fatter egentlig aldrig, at han er skyldig; thi er et Menneske skyldig, da er han uendelig Skyldig" (SV 3d Udg., VI, pp. 239: CA, p. 161). I have amended the Hongs' translation here slightly, changing "endlessly" (*uendelig*) in the last sentence to "infinitely" in order to highlight the exact terminological parallel to Kant's use of the cognate term *unendlich*.

131. CA, pp. 26–28.

132. *Religion*, p. 36.

133. CA, p. 30.

134. Ibid., p. 30.

135. Ibid., p. 31. The close parallelism between Kierkegaard and Kant on this matter is noted by Allen Wood in his *Kant's Moral Religion*, p. 224.

136. See above, p. 64

137. "If you know one, you know all" (CA, p. 79). The draft of the manuscript shows that Kierkegaard meant to use this phrase early in his discussion, in connection with the issue of the ideality of ethics. See PAP V B 49:15 *n.d.*, 1844.

138. PAP III C26 (Vol. XIII, p. 213).

139. Immanuel Kant, *The Metaphysical Principles of Virtue*, trans. James Ellington (Indianapolis: Bobbs-Merrill, 1964), pp. 85–88.

140. See above, p. 28.

141. *Conflict*, p. 67.

142. *Religion*, p. 62.

143. CUP, p. 471.

144. *Religion*, p. 66.

145. Ibid., p. 66.

146. Ibid., pp. 68–69.

147. PAP X³ A 437 *n.d.*, 1850: JP III–3318.

148. CA, p. 115.

149. E/O II, pp. 175, 237–238.

150. FT, p. 98n.

151. CA, p. 117.

152. Ibid.

153. Ibid., p. 118. Kierkegaard expresses a similar criticism of repentance as interfering with ethical conduct in PAP IV A 112 *n.d.*, 1843: JP I–902, and PH, p. 40.

154. CA, p. 118.

155. *Religion*, p. 66.

156. PAP III A 202 *n. d.*, 1842: JP I–649. Cf. PAP IV A 112 *n.d.*, 1843: JP I–902.

157. The most relevant remark appears in Johann Gottlieb Fichte's answer to an open letter from F. H. Jacobi in *Nachgelassene Werke*, ed. I. H. Fichte (Bonn, 1834–1835), III, s. 349. This is quoted and translated in CA, p. 249, n. 12:

> To be occupied with incessant self-examination of one's own character in general and by way of preparation for a general confession is quite useless, just as if the world were not replete with other tasks and actions. Instead, a person should permit his weak side to be forcefully touched and uncovered by life; but the hidden corner of life that is yet untouched and stirred up by his reflection is partly sin, for it is idleness, and partly through an excessive humility does he bring along all manner of impurities when he definitely and conscientiously searches himself. Let us be content with a simple fidelity to the divine within us and follow where it leads us, and not cultivate by one's own piety an artificial self-remorse that is not of oneself.

A similar criticism of mordant self-preoccupation is expressed in *Die Anweisung zum seligen Leben* and in *Die Grundzüge des gegenwärtigen Zeitalters, Johann Gottlieb Fichte's* [sic] *sämmtliche Werke,* ed. I. H. Fichte (Berlin, 1845–1846), V, s. 565; VIII, s. 14.

158. *Die Bestimmung des Menschen*, in *Johann Gottlieb Fichte's* [sic] *sämmtliche Werke*, II, s. 188: "The Vocation of Man," in *The Popular Works of Johann Gottlieb Fichte*, trans. William Smith (London: John Chapman, 1858), pp. 394–395.

159. See above, p. 164.

160. CA, pp. 115–116.

161. CUP, p. 482.

162. *Religion*, pp. 68–70; *Conflict*, p. 75.

163. PAP IV A 116 *n.d.*, 1843: JP III–3078.

164. PAP X⁴ A 491 *n.d.*, 1852: JP II–1909.

165. PF, p. 15.

166. *Fallen Freedom*, pp. 129–130.

167. GR 408: Beck, p. 25.

168. See above, Chapter 3, pp. 117–118.

169. *Conflict*, p. 119.

170. PF, pp. 15–18.

171. Ibid., p. 61.

172. *Kierkegaard*, p. 200.

173. CUP, Chapter 1.

174. *Conflict*, p. 83.

175. Michalson traces Kierkegaard's tendency to religiously invalidate historical experience back to Lessing. Michalson observes that "even though his position appears to require the endorsement of a certain historical event as the very center of faith, Kierkegaard has no more desire than does Lessing to make assent to matters of historical detail a prerequisite for discipleship" (*Lessing's "Ugly Ditch": A Study of Theology and History*, p. 17).

176. *Conflict*, p. 75; *Religion*, p. 70.

177. *Religion*, p. 108.

178. PAP X⁴ A 545 *n.d.*, 1852: JP VI–6801.

179. PAP X³ A 411 *n.d.*, 1850: JP II–1878.

180. Kant, "The End of All Things," p. 72.

181. *Religion*, pp. 111–112n.

182. *Conflict*, p. 71.

183. CUP, p. 516.

184. OAR, p. 130.

185. Early entries appear to favor the concept of divine foreknowledge—PAP I A 20 December 6, 1834: JP III–3544, and PAP I A
43 *n.d.*, 1834: JP III–3546.

186. PAP XI² A 439 September 25, 1855: JP VI–6969.

187. PAP X⁴ A 180 *n.d.*, 1851: JP III–3550.

CHAPTER 5

1. P. 115. There is a small typographical error in Gregor's translation I have corrected.

2. An important recent exception to this is Edward F. Mooney's
Knights of Faith and Resignation: Reading Kierkegaard's Fear
and Trembling (Albany: State University of New York Press,
1991). Focusing primarily on the ethical as opposed to the theological dimensions of *Fear and Trembling*, Mooney defends the
view that Kierkegaard's "much advertised 'irrationalism' is less a
critique of reason or deliberation than an exasperated reaction to
the bloated intellectualism, hyperrationalism, and antiindividual-
ism of his time" (p. 7). Important discussions of *Fear and Trembling* that treat it primarily as dealing with normative ethical
questions include essays by John Donnelly and C. Stephen Evans
in *Kierkegaard's* Fear and Trembling: *Critical Appraisals,* ed.
Robert L. Perkins (University, Ala.: University of Alabama Press,
1981); Gene Outka, "Religion and Moral Duty: Notes on *Fear
and Trembling." Religion and Morality,* ed. Gene Outka and
John P. Reeder, Jr. (Garden City, N.Y.: Anchor Books, 1973), pp.
204–254; and Philip L. Quinn "Agamenmon and Abraham: The
Tragic Dilemma of Kierkegaard's Knight of Faith." *Journal of
Literature & Theology* 4 (1990), 191–192.

3. FT, p. 3.

4. This epigraph had previously been used by Hamann for his own
conveyance of a secret message. See Niels Thulstrup, "His
Library," in *Kierkegaard as a Person*, pp. 95–96.

5. Howard and Edna Hong, in their "Historical Introduction" to
the new Princeton edition of *Fear and Trembling* and *Repetition*
(Princeton: Princeton University Press, 1883), pp. xi and xiv,
regard Regine as the "secret reader" of the book. A similar reading is offered by Gregor Malantschuk in *The Controversial*

Kierkegaard, trans. Howard V. Hong and Edna H. Hong (Atlantic Highlands, N.J.: Humanities Press, 1980), p. 19.

6. Ibid., pp. 41–47, 94–99. Additional romantic references include the tale of secret love that cannot be realized because of its damage to a family, pp. 85–87; Aristotle's story of a marriage prevented by auguries of impending calamity for the bridegroom, pp. 89–94; the story of Tobias and Sarah from the Book of Tobit, pp. 102–104; and a brief mention of Faust and Margaret, pp. 109–110.

7. Kierkegaard introduces the first of these ideas in Problema I and II; he deals with what he terms the "two movements" of resignation and faith (ibid., p. 115) throughout the volume in connection with the idea of the "knight of faith."

8. Ibid., p. 59.

9. Ibid., p. 57.

10. Ibid., p.81.

11. Ibid., p. 28.

12. In different ways, the four "Exordia" that begin the book illustrate these faithless or doubting responses.

13. PAP IV A 107 May 17, 1843: JP V–5664.

14. For a discussion of alternative ways in which Kierkegaard might have conceived a faithful response as possible in his own romantic circumstance, see Sylvia Fleming Crocker, "Sacrifice in Kierkegaard's *Fear and Trembling,*" *Harvard Theological Review* 68 (April 1975), 125–139.

15. It appears that Regine saw the message of *Fear and Trembling* this way. Many years after the event, her friend Hanne Mourier, writing a memoir to Regine recording what the latter had told her, states that "Kierkegaard's motive for this parting was his conception of his religious task; he dared not bind himself to anyone on this earth, so that he might not be checked in his calling; he had to sacrifice his dearest possession in order to labour as demanded of him by God; he therefore sacrificed his love for you in favour of his literary activities." Quoted in Thulstrup, *Kierkegaard as a Person,* p. 38.

16. FT, pp. 56, 81, 120.

17. Ibid., pp. 56, 81.

18. Ibid., pp. xii–xiii.

19. X¹ A 485 n.d., 1849: JP III–2607. Kierkegaard explains his conduct in these terms several times in his journals and papers. In a letter of 1842, for example, he states, "It was a godsend that I did not break the engagement for my own sake; then it would have overwhelmed me...I broke it for her sake" (JP V–5551).

20. FT, p. 62.

21. Ibid., pp. 98–99. The initial italics here are my own.

22. Ibid., p. 99. Interestingly, at one point in his papers of 1843–1844, Kierkegaard speculates on the possibility of presenting Abraham within the context of sin: "One could also have Abraham's previous life be not devoid of guilt and have him secretly ruminate on the thought that this was God's punishment, perhaps even have him get the melancholy thought that he must ask God to help make the punishment as severe as possible" (PAP IV A 77 n.d., 1843: JP V–5641).

23. FT, p. 98.

24. The importance of the themes of sin and redemption in *Fear and Trembling* has previously been noted by Louis Mackey, Gregor Malantschuk, and John H. Whittaker. See Mackey's "The View from Pisgah: A Reading of *Fear and Trembling*," in Josiah Thompson, ed., *Kierkegaard: A Collection of Critical Essays* (Garden City, N.Y.: Anchor Books, 1972), pp. 420–426, and his *Kierkegaard: A Kind of Poet* (Philadelphia: University of Pennsylvania Press, 1971), pp. 206–220; Whittaker "The Suspension of the Ethical in *Fear and Trembling*," *Kierkegaardiana* 14 (1988), 101–113; Malantschuk's, *Kierkegaard's Thought*, pp. 236–241.

25. Hegel deals with the issues of sin and repentance in the section entitled "Absolute Spirit" in his *Encyclopedia of Philosophy*, trans. Gustav Emil Mueller (New York: Philosophical Library, 1959), p. 228. The issue of original sin is dealt with by him in his *Logic* (*Hegel's Logic*, trans. William Wallace [Oxford: Clarendon Press, 1892], pp. 54–55) and in his early *Lectures on the Philosophy of Religion*, trans. E. B. Speirs and J. B. Sanderson (London: Kegan Paul, Trench, Trübner, 1895), I, pp. 275–279; II, pp. 202–204.

26. PAP X² A 401 n.d., 1850: JP IV–4555,

27. CA, pp. 113–118.

28. SUD, pp. 130–131.

29. In a journal entry critical of Schopenhauer's effort to water down the ethical demand, Kierkegaard shows that Kant is on his mind in this discussion of the comediac results of carrying ethics to its logical conclusion:

> *Is Not Moral Philosophy Like Astrology, Alchemy—a Science that Concerns Itself with Something That Does Not Exist?*
>
> Schopenhauer vigorously attacks treating moral philosophy as Kant did—presenting this ideal *you shall*, ideal virtues and obligations, without regard to anyone's doing it. No, says Schopenhauer. Moral philosophy, like any other science, must stick to actual life. But—he goes on to say— then one could raise the objection: does not moral philosophy then becomes a science *a la* astrology and alchemy, a science which concerns itself with something that does not exist.
>
> Schopenhauer himself does not really seem to perceive how extremely funny he is here, for he raises this objection earnestly, rejects it earnestly, and then proceeds to write his moral philosophy. (PAP XI¹ A 112: JP IV–3875)

30. CUP, p. 234.

31. Ibid.

32. Ibid., p. 238.

33. A journal entry (PAP VII¹ A 5 *n.d.*, 1846: JP V–5874) reveals that Kierkegaard knew of this event.

34. For a brief treatment of the father-son relationship and a bibliography of works treating this topic, see Wolfdietrich v. Kloeden, "Der Vater M. P. Kierkegaard," in *Kierkegaard as a Person*, pp. 14–25.

35. Kierkegaard repeatedly alludes to this tradition of familial sin. It is suggested, for example, in the treatment of Antigone in E/O I, pp. 155–156, and in the various narratives of SLW, including those of Solomon's dream (pp. 250–52) and "A Leper's Self-Contemplation"(pp. 232–234). A sketch for the latter appears in PAP IV A 111 *n.d.*, 1843: JP V–5667. Brandt points out that Kierkegaard's experience gave some support to this belief: of seven children, only

he and an elder brother survived the father (*Søren Kierkegaard*, p. 10). Sylviane Agacinski, argues—on the basis, I think, of very slender evidence—that the special sin which haunted the Kierkegaard family might have been Michael Pedersen Kierkegaard's rape of Kierkegaard's mother. See Agacinski's *Aparté: Conceptions and Deaths of Søren Kierkegaard*, pp. 244–253.

36. "The Consequence of the Fact of Generation," CA, pp. 56–66.

37. Kierkegaard's journals contain repeated allusions to his youthful sexual misconduct—e.g., PAP II A 520 July 28, 1839: JP V–5403. Some commentators have also seen biographical content in the narrative sketched in the journal (PAP IV A 65 *n.d.*, 1843: JP V–5622) and developed in SLW (pp. 283–284) concerning an individual tormented by the fact that he might have sired a child following an evening spent with a prostitute.

38. PAP IV A 107 May 17, 1843: JP V–5664. Similarly: "The next day I saw that I had made a mistake. Penitent that I was, my *vita ante acta*, my melancholy—that was sufficient...But there was a divine protest, so it seemed to me. Marriage. I would have had to keep too much from her, base the whole marriage on a lie" (PAP X⁵ A 149 *n.d.* 1849: JP VI–6472). See also PAP IV A 133 *n.d.*, 1843: JP V–5680; PAP X⁵ A 158 *n.d.*, 1849: JP VI–6306. In a recent study, Louis Mackey goes beyond this explanation by Kierkegaard of the break to offer a quasi-Freudian interpretation: "It was necessary to make reparation for the father's crimes: because the mother had been violated, women (read: Regine) must be left intact, and because his father had defied God, the son must practice a perfect submission" (*Points of View: Readings of Kierkegaard* [Tallahassee: University Presses of Florida, 1986], p. 169).

39. PAP IV A 76 *n.d.*, 1843: JP V– 5640.

40. *Kierkegaard's Thought*, pp. 236–243.

41. Brandt, *Søren Kierkegaard*, p. 8.

42. CUP, p. 234.

43. It is worth noting here that there may be another, quite different familial metaphor in *Fear and Trembling* linking its argument to the problem of sin. In his *Knights of Faith and Resignation* (pp. 30–31), Edward F. Mooney develops at length Kierkegaard/Silentio's presentation of the Abraham story in terms of a mother's "blackening her breast" at the time she weans her child (FT, pp.

11–14). Mooney observes that, among other things, this enigmatic series of references to maternal nurturance and distancing may be understood in terms of God's own "weaning" of Abraham as part of the patriarch's process of spiritual development. Mooney adds that in the *Postscript* (p. 232) Kierkegaard-Climacus presents God's creation of free human beings as a similar distancing act of this sort, needed in order to give them "independence over against himself." If we keep in mind that this discussion of the problem of God and human freedom in the *Postscript* serves to introduce Kierkegaard-Climacus's treatment there of *Fear and Trembling*, Mooney's provocative interpretation of the weaning motif in *Fear and Trembling* provides another hint of *Fear and Trembling*'s concern with themes of human freedom, sin, and forgiveness.

44. Kierkegaard makes one brief reference to the narratives dealing with Hagar and Ishmael. Here he links the expulsion of Hagar to Sarah's vacillation and lack of faith—FT, p. 13. I am indebted to my former student Richard Hoch for drawing my attention to this link between the Genesis narratives and Kierkegaard's biography.

The elder Kierkegaard's poor treatment of his second wife—he initially saw to it that Ane was not to be given a wife's usual inheritance rights, but only household effects and 200 rd. a year if he should die or end the marriage—is an additional interesting parallel to the Hagar narrative. That this episode was on Kierkegaard's mind as he prepared the early pseudonymous works is suggested by a remark by Judge William in E/O. Defending his own highly ethicalized view of marriage (and of marriage untouched by sin), he states, "My wife is not the slave woman in Abraham's house, whom I banish with the child" (E/O II, p. 81).

45. The suggestion that FT is directed to Kierkegaard's father is independently supported by several other comments in Kierkegaard's writings. One is this remark (appended to the previously quoted statement from his journals, "He who has explained this riddle has explained my life"): "But who of my contemporaries has understood this?" (IV A 77 *n.d.*, 1843: JP V–5640). In an entry for 1843 apparently intended for the title page material for the book but later deleted from the manuscript, Kierkegaard also records the following remarks:

> "Write."—"For whom?"—"Write for the dead, for those in the past whom you love."—"Will they read me?"—"Yes, for they come back as posterity."
>
> An old saying.

"Write."—"For whom?"—Write for the dead, for those
in the past whom you love."—"Will they read me?"—"No!"
An old saying slightly altered.
(PAP IV B 96 1a, 1b, 1c *n.d.*, 1843: JP II–1550)

46. *Philosophical Fragments* has the figure of Jesus Christ at its center; *The Concept of Anxiety* is subtitled "A Simple Psychological
Deliberation Oriented in the Direction of the Dogmatic Problem
of Original Sin," and *The Sickness unto Death* is a psychological
exploration of selfhood and sin. Additionally, two of the *Three
Upbuilding Discourses* (1843), both entitled "Love Will Hide a
Multitude of Sins," deal with the issue of personal discovery and
response to one's sins (UD, pp. 55–78).

47. It is interesting that Kant in the *Religion* (p. 62) approvingly
quotes Philippians 2:12 ("work out our own salvation *with fear
and trembling*"). This remark, says Kant, expresses the importance of recognizing our own moral frailty, since "man is never
more easily deceived than in what promotes his good opinion of
himself." Nevertheless, he adds, the teaching of this text is "a
hard saying which, if misunderstood, is capable of driving a man
to the blackest fanaticism."

48. *Religion*, p. 175.

49. Ibid., pp. 81–82.

50. Hegel's treatment of Abraham, an antisemitic characterization of
the patriarch as "the true progenitor of the Jews," has little bearing, one way or the other, on Kierkegaard's discussion. For
Hegel, Abraham is "a stranger on earth, a stranger to the soil and
men alike." The episode of Genesis 22 shows that "love alone is
beyond his powers; even the one love he had, his love for his
son..." (*Early Theological Writings*, trans. T. M. Knox [Chicago:
Chicago University Press, 1948], pp. 182–188)

51. For a discussion of this tradition, see David Lerch, *Isaaks Opferung christlich gedeutet* (Tübingen: J. C. B. Mohr, 1950). Kierkegaard's familiarity with this tradition before writing *Fear and
Trembling* is evidenced by a journal entry for 1839. (PAP II A
569 September 13, 1839: JP I–298)

52. P. 121n.

53. "The View from Pisgah: A Reading of *Fear and Trembling*," pp.
420–426. *Kierkegaard: A Kind of Poet*, pp. 222–223.

CONCLUSION

1. Harold Bloom, *The Anxiety of Influence* (New York: Oxford University Press, 1973), p. 64.

2. The first (p. 292) is a criticism of Hegel's response to Kant's scepticism. "A scepticism which attacks thought itself cannot be vanquished by thinking it through, since the very instrument by which this would have to be done is in revolt," says Kierkegaard. "There is only one thing to do with such a scepticism, and that is to break with it. To answer Kant within the fantastic shadow-play of pure thought is precisely not to answer him. The only thing-in-itself which cannot be thought is existence, and this does not come within the province of thought to think."
   In the second reference (p. 491), Kierkegaard uses Kant in a flattering way to poke fun at other philosophers: "If a man like Kant who stands at the pinnacle of scientific culture were to say regarding the proofs of God's existence, 'Well, I know nothing more about it except that my father told me it was so,' this would be humorous."

3. SUD, p. 5.

4. PAP X^1 A 571 *n.d.* 1849: JP VI–6456. Cf. LD, no. 240 (December, 1849), p. 337; PAP X^6 B 128 *n.d.*, 1849–50: JP VI–6596.

5. See, for example, his treatment of the "public" in his essay "The Present Age," in TA, pp. 90–96.

6. CA, p. 7.

7. For a discussion of this, see H. P. Rohde's article "Poul Møller," in *Kierkegaard's Teachers*, pp. 89–109.

8. Ibid., pp. 30, 39, 59, 147–148.

9. Ibid. p. 11.

10. XI^2 A 59 *n.d.*, 1854: JP IV–3886.

11. PAP V B 24 *n.d.*, 1844; FT, p. 184.

12. PF, p. 73.

13. Kierkegaard mentions Kant twice early in *The Concept of Anxiety* (pp. 11, 18). Both references deal with epistemological matters. The first touches on Kant's skepticism and questions whether Hegel has really grasped Kant's points. The second

brings a remark by Constantin Constantius in *Repetition* concerning metaphysics' "interest" into connection with Kant's defense—in the *Critique of Judgment*—of esthetics' disinterestedness. Kant is not mentioned at all when Kierkegaard undertakes his treatment of sin.

14. PF, p. 17n. The reference is to the *Nicomachean Ethics* III, 5, 1114a.

15. *Kierkegaard's Existential Ethics*, p. 46. It is noteworthy, however, that in a journal entry for 1844, Kierkegaard admits he had not read a word of Aristotle until a year and a half before (PAP V A 98 *n.d.*, 1844: JP III–3300).

16. Heinrich Heine, *Religion und Philosophie in Deutschland*, *Gesammelte Werke*, ed. Gustav Karpeles (Berlin, 1887), V, s. 98.

17. Collins, *The Mind of Kierkegaard*, p. ix.

18. Kierkegaard accuses Martensen of having "gone beyond" Hegel "without first having got to him" (quoted in J. H. Schjørring, "Martensen," in *Kierkegaard's Teachers*, p. 200).

19. PAP I A 87 October 7, 1835: JP III–3244.

20. Fenger, *Kierkegaard, The Myths and Their Origins*, trans. George C. Schoolfield (New Haven: Yale University Press, 1980), Chapter 4.

21. New York: Oxford University Press, 1973, p. 64.

22. Kierkegaard is a haunting presence in Bloom's study. See, for example, pp. 26, 32, 56, 72–73, 76, 82 and 116.

23. Christoph Schrempf, *Søren Kierkegaard: Eine Biographie*, Vol. 1 (Jena, 1927), pp. 40–43. Cf. Ibid., vol 2 (Jena, 1928), pp. 100–102.

24. Bloom, *The Anxiety of Influence*, pp. 26, 56, 73. This statement is drawn from FT, p. 27.

25. See his opening essay "Starting from Scratch" in *Points of View*.

26. PAP III B 2 *n.d.*, 1840–41: JP V–5484.

27. Ibid, p. 97.

28. PF, pp. 21, 35, 53, 68, 105, 109.

29. PF, p. 105. For a discussion of this see above, p. 134.

30. "What matters is to find a purpose, to see what it really is that God wills that *I* shall do; the crucial thing is to find a truth which is a truth *for me*, to find *the idea for which I am willing to live and die.*" (PAP I A 75 August 1, 1835: JP V–5100). In *To Be One Thing: Personal Unity in Kierkegaard's Thought* (Macon, Ga.: Mercer University Press, 1985), pp. 10–11, George Connell makes the point that Kant's insistence on the formal unity of thought may have helped shape Kierkegaard's youthful wish to organize his life around a system of ideas.

31. PAP I A 340 *n.d.:* JP II–1541.

32. CUP, p. 450n.

33. E/O II, pp. 174, 175.

34. For a critical analysis of Kierkegaard's alleged irrationalism, see Alastair McKinnon, "Kierkegaard," in *Nineteenth Century Religious Thought in the West,* ed. Ninian Smart et al. (Cambridge: Cambridge University Press, 1985), Vol. 1, pp. 191–213.

35. CUP, p. 438; PAP IV A 191 *n.d.:* JP II–1110; PAP September 12, 1836: JP II–1540.

WORKS CITED

Adorno, Theodore W. *Kierkegaard: Construction of the Aesthetic.* Ed. Robert Hullot-Kentor. Minneapolis: University of Minnesota Press, 1933, 1989.

———. "On Kierkegaard's Doctrine of Love." *Søren Kierkegaard.* Ed. Harold Bloom. New York: Chelsea House Publishers, 1989.

Agacinski, Sylviane. *Aparté: Conceptions and Deaths of Søren Kierkegaard.* Trans. Kevin Newmark. Tallahassee: Florida State University Press, 1988.

Barth, Karl. *Protestant Thought from Rousseau to Ritschl.* New York: Harper & Brothers, 1959.

Baümler, Alfred. "Kierkegaard und Kant über die Reinheit des Herzen." *Zwischen den Zeit* 3 (1925).

Bloom, Harold. *The Anxiety of Influence.* New York: Oxford University Press, 1973.

Bohlin, Torsten. *Kierkegaard's dogmatische Anschauung.* Trans. Ilse Meyer-Lüne. Gütersloh: C. Bertelsmann, 1927.

Brandt, Frithiof. *Søren Kierkegaard: His Life—His Works.* Copenhagen: Det Danske Selskab, 1963.

Brunner, Emil. "Das Grundproblem der Philosophie bei Kant und Kierkegaard." *Zwischen den Zeit* 2 (1924).

Cassirer, Ernst. *Kant's Life and Thought.* Trans. J. Haden. New Haven and London: Yale University Press, 1981.

Clive, Geoffrey. "The Connection between Ethics and Religion in Kant, Kierkegaard and F. H. Bradley." Ph. D. Thesis, Harvard University, 1953.

Collins, James. *The Mind of Kierkegaard.* Chicago: Henry Regnery Company, 1953.

Connell, George. *To Be One Thing: Personal Unity in Kierkegaard's Thought.* Macon Ga.: Mercer University Press, 1985.

Crites, Stephen. *In the Twilight of Christendom: Hegel vs. Kierkegaard on Faith and History.* Chambersberg, Pa.: American Academy of Religion, 1972.

Crocker, Sylvia Fleming. "Sacrifice in Kierkegaard's *Fear and Trembling.*" *Harvard Theological Review* 68 (April 1975), 125–139.

Despland, Michael. *Kant on History and Religion*. Montreal: McGill-Queen's University Press, 1973.

Diem, Hermann. *Kierkegaard's Dialectic of Existence*. Trans. Harold Knight. Edinburgh: Oliver and Boyd, 1959.

Donnelly, John. "Kierkegaard's Problema I and Problema II: An Analytic Perspective." *Kierkegaard's* Fear and Trembling: *Critical Appraisals*. Ed. Robert L. Perkins. University, Alabama: University of Alabama Press, 1981.

Dunning, Stephen N. *Kierkegaard's Dialectic of Inwardness*. Princeton: Princeton University Press, 1985.

Elrod, John W. *Being and Existence in Kierkegaard's Pseudonymous Works*. Princeton: Princeton University Press, 1975.

Evans, C. Stephen. *Kierkegaard's* Fragments *and* Postscript: *The Religious Philosophy of Johannes Climacus*. Atlantic Highlands, N.J.: Humanities Press, 1983.

———. *Subjectivity and Religious Belief*. Washington, D.C.: University Press of America, 1982.

Fenger, Henning. *Kierkegaard, The Myths and Their Origins*. Trans. George C. Schoolfield. New Haven: Yale University Press, 1980.

Ferreira, M. Jamie. "Repetition, Concreteness and Imagination." *International Journal for Philosophy of Religion* 25 (1989).

Fichte, Johann Gottlieb. *Johann Gottlieb Fichte's sämmtliche Werke*, 8 vols. Ed. I. H. Fichte. Berlin: 1845–46.

———. *The Popular Works of Johann Gottlieb Fichte*. Trans. William Smith. London: John Chapman, 1858.

Friedman, R. Z. "Kierkegaard: First Existentialist or Last Kantian?" *Religious Studies* 18:2 (June 1982).

Gill, Jerry H. "Kant, Kierkegaard and Religious Knowledge." *Philosophy and Phenomenological Research* 28 (1967–68).

———. "Kant." *Kierkegaard and Great Traditions*, vol. 6 in *Bibliotheca Kierkegaardiana*. Eds. Niels Thulstrup and Maria Mikulová Thulstrup. Copenhagen: C. A. Reitzels Boghandel, 1981.

Glenn, John D., Jr. "Kierkegaard's Ethical Philosophy." *Southwestern Journal of Philosophy* 5 (Spring 1974).

———. "The Definition of the Self and the Structure of Kierkegaard's Work" *International Kierkegaard Commentary:* Sickness unto Death. Ed. Robert L. Perkins. Macon, Ga.: Mercer University Press, 1987.

Gouwens, David J. *Kierkegaard's Dialectic of the Imagination*. New York: Peter Lang, 1989.

Green, Ronald M. "The Limits of the Ethical in Kierkegaard's *The Concept of Anxiety* and Kant's *Religion within the Limits of Reason*

Alone." *International Kierkegaard Commentary,* The Concept of Anxiety. Ed. Robert L. Perkins. Macon, Georgia: Mercer University Press, 1986.

———. *Religion and Moral Reason.* New York: Oxford University Press, 1988.

———. "The First Formulation of the Categorical Imperative as Literally a 'Legislative' Metaphor." *History of Philosophy Quarterly* 8:2 (April 1991).

Hall, Harrison. "Love and Death: Kierkegaard and Heidegger on Authentic and Inauthentic Human Existence." *Inquiry* 27 (1984).

Hannay, Alastair. *Kierkegaard.* London: Routledge and Kegan Paul, 1982.

Hare, R. M. *Freedom and Reason.* New York: Oxford University Press, 1965.

Hegel, Georg Wilhelm Friedrich. *The Logic of Hegel.* Trans. William Wallace. Oxford: The Clarendon Press, 1892.

———. *Lectures on the Philosophy of Religion.* Trans. E.B. Speirs and J. B. Sanderson. London: Kegan Paul, Trench, Trübner, 1895.

———. *Early Theological Writings.* Trans. T. M. Knox. Chicago: Chicago University Press, 1948.

———. *Encyclopedia of Philosophy.* Trans. Gustav Emil Mueller. New York: Philosophical Library, 1959.

Heine, Heinrich. *Gesammelte Werke.* Ed. Gustav Karpeles. 9 vols. Berlin, 1887.

Hill, Thomas. "The Kingdom of Ends." *Proceedings of the Third International Kant-Congress.* Dordrecht: D. Reidel, 1972.

Holmer, Paul L. "On Understanding Kierkegaard." *A Kierkegaard Critique.* Eds. Howard A. Johnson and Niels Thulstrup. New York: Harper & Brothers, 1962.

Jacobi, F. H. *Nachgelassene Werke.* 3 vols. Ed. I. H. Fichte. Bonn: 1834–35.

Khan, Abrahim H. Salighed *as Happiness?: Kierkegaard on the Concept* Salighed. Waterloo, Ont.: Wilfrid Laurier University Press, 1985.

Kirmmse, Bruce H. *Kierkegaard in Golden Age Denmark.* Bloomington, Indiana: Indiana University Press, 1990.

Ladd, John, ed. *Ethical Relativism.* Belmont, Ca.: Wadsworth, 1973.

Lerch, David. *Isaaks Opferung christlich gedeutet.* Tübingen: J. C. B. Mohr, 1950.

Lessing, Gotthold Ephraim. *Gotthold Ephraim Lessings Sämtliche Werke.* Ed. Karl Lachmann and Franz Muncker. 23 vols. Leipzig: G. J. Göschen'sche Verlagshandlung, 1886–1924.

Lowrie, Walter. *Kierkegaard*. New York: Oxford University Press, 1938.

MacIntyre, Alasdair. *After Virtue*. Notre Dame, Indiana: University of Notre Dame Press, 1981.

Mackey, Louis. *Kierkegaard: A Kind of Poet*. Philadelphia: University of Pennsylvania Press, 1971.

———. "The View from Pisgah: A Reading of *Fear and Trembling*." *Kierkegaard: A Collection of Critical Essays*. Ed. Josiah Thompson. Garden City, New York: Anchor Books, 1972.

———. *Points of View: Readings of Kierkegaard*. Tallahassee: University Presses of Florida, 1986.

Malantschuk, Gregor. *Kierkegaard's Thought*. Ed. and Trans. Howard V. Hong and Edna H. Hong. Princeton: Princeton University Press, 1971.

———. *The Controversial Kierkegaard*. Ed. Alastair McKinnon, Trans. Howard V. Hong and Edna H. Hong. Atlantic Highlands, N.J.: Humanities Press, 1980.

Marino, Gordon D. "Salvation: A Reply to Harrison Hall's Reading of Kierkegaard." *Inquiry* 28 (1985).

McDonald, William. "Translator's Introduction." *Prefaces* by Søren Kierkegaard. Tallahassee: Florida State University Press, 1989.

McKinnon, Alastair. "Kierkegaard." *Nineteenth Century Religious Thought in the West*. Vol. 1. Ed. Ninian Smart et al. Cambridge: Cambridge University Press, 1985.

Mehl, Peter J. "Kierkegaard and the Relativist Challenge to Practical Philosophy." *Journal of Religious Ethics* 14 (1987).

Michalson, Gordon E., Jr. *Lessing's "Ugly Ditch": A Study of Theology and History*. University Park, Pennsylvania: The Pennsylvania State University Press, 1985.

———. *Fallen Freedom: Kant on Radical Evil and Moral Regeneration*. Cambridge: Cambridge University Press, 1990.

Mooney, Edward F. *Knights of Faith and Resignation: Reading Kierkegaard's* Fear and Trembling. Albany: State University of New York Press, 1991.

Møller, Poul. *Efterladte Skrifter*. Kjøbenhavn: C. A. Reiztel, 1843.

Nielsen, H. A. *Where the Passion Is: A Reading of Kierkegaard's Philosophical Fragments*. Tallahassee, Florida: University Presses of Florida, 1983.

Outka, Gene. "Religion and Moral Duty: Notes on *Fear and Trembling*." *Religion and Morality*. Ed. Gene Outka and John P. Reeder, Jr. Garden City, N.Y.: Anchor Books, 1973.

Peck, William D. *On Autonomy: The Primacy of the Subject in Kant and Kierkegaard.* Ph. D. Dissertation, Yale University. New Haven, Connecticut, 1974.

Perkins, Robert L. "For Sanity's Sake: Kant, Kierkegaard and Father Abraham." *Kierkegaard's* Fear and Trembling: *Critical Appraisals.* Ed. Robert L. Perkins. University, Alabama: University of Alabama Press, 1981.

————. Ed. *Kierkegaard's* Fear and Trembling: *Critical Appraisals.* University, Alabama: University of Alabama Press, 1981

————. *International Kierkegaard Commentary:* Sickness unto Death. Macon, Ga.: Mercer University Press, 1987.

————. *International Kierkegaard Commentary:* Fear and Trembling *and* Repetition. Macon, Ga.: Mercer University Press, 1991.

Pojman, Louis P. *The Logic of Subjectivity: Kierkegaard's Philosophy of Religion.* University, Alabama: University of Alabama Press, 1984.

Quinn, Philip L. "Agamemnon and Abraham: The Tragic Dilemma of Kierkegaard's Knight of Faith." *Journal of Literature & Theology* 4 (1990).

Rawls, John. *A Theory of Justice.* Cambridge, Mass.: Harvard University Press, 1971.

Reardon, Bernard M. G. *Kant as Philosophical Theologian.* Totowa, N.J.: Barnes & Noble Books, 1988.

Roberts, Robert C. *Faith, Reason and History: Rethinking Kierkegaard's* Philosophical Fragments. Macon, Ga.: Mercer University Press, 1987.

Rohde, H. P. "Søren Kierkegaard as a Collector of Books." pp. xlvi–lxxviii, in *Særtryk af Fund og Forskning i Det kongelige Biblioteks Samlinger* [Results of Research in the Collections of the Royal Library] 8, (1961).

————. Ed. *Auktionsprotokol over Søren Kierkegaards Bogsamling,* English text. København: det Kongelige Bibliotek, 1967.

Rotenstreich, Nathan. *Practice and Realization: Studies in Kant's Moral Philosophy.* The Hague: Martinus Nijhoff, 1979.

Santurri, Edmund N. "Kierkegaard's *Fear and Trembling* in a Logical Perspective." *Journal of Religious Ethics* 5 (1977).

Schäfer, Klaus. *Hermeneutische Ontologie in den Climacus-Schriften Søren Kierkegaards.* München: Kösel-Verlag, 1968.

Schrempf, Christoph. *Søren Kierkegaard: Eine Biographie.* 2 vols. Jena, 1927–1928.

Stack, George. *Kierkegaard's Existential Ethics.* University, Alabama: University of Alabama Press, 1977.

Taylor, Mark C. *Kierkegaard's Pseudonymous Authorship.* Princeton: Princeton University Press, 1975.

Taylor, Mark L. *God is Love.* Atlanta, Ga. : Scholars Press, 1986.

Tennemann, Wilhelm Gottlieb. *Geschichte der Philosophie.* 11 vols. Leipzig, 1798–1819.

Thompson, Josiah. *Kierkegaard.* London: Victor Gollancz, 1974.

Thomte, Reidar. *Kierkegaard's Philosophy of Religion.* Princeton: Princeton University Press, 1948.

Thuborg, Anders, *Den Kantiske Periode i Dansk Filosofi 1790–1800.* Copenhagen: Gyldendalske Boghandel Nordisk Forlag, 1951.

Thulstrup, Niels. "Om Kierkegaards Bibliotek." *Kierkegaardiana* 4 (1962).

———. "Kierkegaards Kenntnis der philosophischen und theologischen Tradition." *Theologische Zeitung* 35 (Nov.–Dec. 1979).

———. *Kierkegaard's Relation to Hegel.* Trans. George L. Stengren. Princeton: Princeton University Press, 1980.

———. *Commentary on Kierkegaard's Concluding Unscientific Postscript.* Trans. Robert J. Widenmann. Princeton: Princeton University Press, 1984.

———. Ed. *Breve og Aktstykker vedrørende Søren Kierkegaard.* København: Munsgaard, 1953.

Thulstrup, Niels, and Marie Mikulová Thulstrup, eds. *Kierkegaard's Teachers.* Vol. 10 of *Bibliotheca Kierkegaardiana.* Copenhagen: C. A. Reitzels Forlag, 1982.

———. *Kierkegaard as a Person.* Vol. 12 of *Bibliotheca Kierkegaardiana.* Copenhagen: C. A. Reitzels Forlag, 1983.

Walker, Jeremy D. B. *To Will One Thing: Reflections on Kierkegaard's 'Purity of Heart'.* Montreal and London: McGill-Queen's University Press, 1972.

———. *Kierkegaard's Descent into God.* Kingston and Montreal: McGill-Queen's University Press, 1985.

Webb, Eugene. *Philosophers of Consciousness.* Seattle: University of Washington Press, 1988.

Whittaker, John H. "The Suspension of the Ethical in *Fear and Trembling.*" *Kierkegaardiana* 14 (1988).

Wood, Allen W. *Kant's Moral Religion.* Ithaca, N.Y.: Cornell University Press, 1970.

———. *Kant's Rational Theology.* Ithaca, N.Y.: Cornell University Press, 1978.

INDEX

A priori knowledge, 35–39, 42, 43, 56, 80–81, 96, 124, 148

Abraham, xviii, 11, 15, 87–90, 128, 129, 184–92, 196, 199, 201–7, 211, 267 n.23, 280 n.22, 282 n.43, 284 n.50

"Accessorium," 14, 15, 129, 144, 208, 248 n.48

Adler, Magister A. P., 112, 113, 145, 264 n.104

Adorno, Theodore W., 242 n.7, 261 n.51

Agacinski, Sylviane, 262 n.61, 282 n.35

Agamemnon, 186

Agnes and the Merman, Story of, in *Fear and Trembling*, 185, 190–92, 197, 199

Aid, mutual, 44, 45, 94, 95

Anti-Climacus, 208

Anxiety, 23, 28, 126, 166, 174, 193

Arildsen, Skat, 245 n.23, 246 n.28, 250 n.77

Aristotle, 3, 80, 83, 142, 143, 151, 213, 214, 256 n.56, 274 n.128, 279 n.6, 286 n.15; *Ethica Nicomachea*, 151, 213; *Posterior Analytics*, 142

Atheism, philosophical, 49

Atonement, 15, 130, 170, 171, 174, 180, 181, 204

Augustine, 99, 193

Auktionsprotokol (Auctioneer's Sales Record), xv, 9, 10, 14, 18, 30, 243 n.12

Autonomy, moral, xi, xiii, 18, 46, 49, 90, 91, 98, 149, 174, 183; versus religious ethics, 88, 202–4

Baader, Franz, 6, 17, 209, 273 n. 113

Balle, Bishop, 244 n.9

Barrabas, 108

Barth, Karl, 256 n.50

Berger, Johan Erik, 2

Bible/Scriptures, xii, 7, 15, 27, 67, 70–72, 79, 106, 117, 164, 165, 167, 170, 176, 177, 200, 215, 219, 220, 222

Bloom, Harold, 207, 216, 217, 286 n.22; *The Anxiety of Influence*, 207, 216

Bohlin, D. Torsten, 1

Bormann, Claus V., 270 n.71

Brandt, Frithiof, 244 n.4, 281 n.35

Brorson, Hans Adolph, 260 n.32

Brutus, 186

Capel, Lee, 16

Cassirer, Ernst, 256 n.50

Categorical imperative, 7, 8, 18, 20, 43–50, 52, 53, 55, 60, 89, 92–100, 107, 116, 152

Causality, 37–40, 54, 55, 64, 69, 81, 82, 124, 125, 136, 141, 142, 147, 149, 158, 160, 178, 257 n.74

Christ, 4, 27, 67, 68, 112, 113, 117, 118, 129, 136, 146, 168, 170, 178, 250 n.77, 251 n.96, 256 n.50, 260 n.32, 284 n.46; Historicity of, 83, 117, 128, 136, 137, 145, 146, 174, 176, 177, 204

Christian Church, 7, 69, 112

Christianity, 20, 74, 83, 109, 112, 113, 138, 150, 161, 164, 166, 167, 173, 175, 176, 179, 181,

295